JUSTICE

JUSTICE
A Global Adventure

Walter J. Burghardt, S.J.

ORBIS BOOKS

Maryknoll, New York 10545

Founded in 1970, Orbis Books endeavors to publish works that enlighten the mind, nourish the spirit, and challenge the conscience. The publishing arm of the Maryknoll Fathers and Brothers, Orbis seeks to explore the global dimensions of the Christian faith and mission, to invite dialogue with diverse cultures and religious traditions, and to serve the cause of reconciliation and peace. The books published reflect the opinions of their authors and are not meant to represent the official position of the Maryknoll Society. To obtain more information about Maryknoll and Orbis Books, please visit our website at www.maryknoll.org.

Library of Congress Cataloging in Publication Data

Burghardt, Walter J.
   Justice : a global adventure / Walter J. Burghardt.
      p. cm.
   Includes bibliographical references and index.
      ISBN 1-57075-519-1 (pbk.)
      1. Christianity and justice. 2. Church and social problems. 3. Church work. 4. Vatican Council (2nd : 1962-1965) 5. Catholic Church—Doctrines. I. Title.
   BR115.J8 B86 2004
   261.8—dc22

                                        2003019932

DEDICATED

with grateful affection

to

Raymond Baker Kemp,

priest of the Archdiocese of Washington, D.C.,

for revealing by expression and example

that God delights in every human color;

and to Marian Wright Edelman

and her colleagues at the Children's Defense Fund

for ceaselessly striving

to uproot and banish the tragedy

of every sixth child growing up hungry and hopeless

in the richest country on earth.

Contents

Preface

Justice. A rich and raw reality. And yet, in my first three decades (1941-70) as a priest/theologian, justice was not a significant word in my vocabulary. Strange indeed, since the earliest Christian theologians, the Fathers of the Church on whom I lectured at Woodstock College, had developed a quite impressive social doctrine.

In 1970, when Woodstock College moved from its 650 rural acres 18 miles outside of Baltimore and relocated in the concrete and asphalt, the hustle and bustle, the poverty and affluence of New York City, my theology and life changed dramatically. Here I list only three of the most powerful influences on my thinking and writing, on my teaching and preaching.

First, largely through Jesuit Scripture scholar John R. Donahue, I discovered biblical justice, God's justice. I mean fidelity to relationships that stem from a covenant with God. Relationships to God, to people, and to the earth. Love God above all human idols. Love every human person, enemy as well as friend, as a child of God, fashioned in God's image. Touch "things," God's material creation, with respect and reverence, gifts to be shared generously, not clutched possessively. A justice that does not exclude the ethical and the legal, but rises above them.

Second, largely through Marian Wright Edelman and the Children's Defense Fund, I discovered the tragedy of America's "sixth child." In the richest country on earth, one of every six children is born into poverty. Not the genteel poverty of Jesus in Nazareth. A poverty that includes hunger and homelessness, a poverty that stunts mind and body, a poverty that kills.

Third, largely through the program Preaching the Just Word, I have discovered the indispensable relationship between justice and the liturgy. Liturgy, specifically the Eucharist, is the most powerful means the Church and the Christian have at our disposal for bringing about a just family, a just city, a just country, a just world. Why? Because the Eucharist is the living presence of "the Just One"—in the people gathered, in the Word proclaimed, in the body and blood received.

In this connection, I cannot fail to acknowledge the ceaseless inspiration of Fr. Raymond B. Kemp, whose dynamic vision of the just city, struggle for justice, and powerful preaching have energized more than a hundred Preaching the Just Word retreats/workshops and almost four thousand participants. Without such inspiration and that of untold others, this book would never have seen the light. I cannot, however, fail to express profound gratitude to one person who merits explicit mention for his years of contributions: Gerard P. Walker, Project Manager of Preaching the Just Word, whose expertise with the computer compensated for my own inadequacies with this new medium.

When my eyesight began to falter and I wondered whether this project could be completed, a dear friend of three decades and more stepped in with a practical solution: If she, Katharyn L. Waldron, contributed the final section not yet written, proofread again and again an expanding manuscript, and worked with me on revisions, this book would be published.

The result? My own growing vision of justice is being brought to light despite the darkening of my world.

Walter J. Burghardt, S.J.
September 2003

I

JUSTICE ANALYZED

The 1971 Synod of Bishops of the Roman Catholic Church introduced its reflections on the meaning of justice in world society with a statement that has stimulated animated discussion, provoked heated argument, and led to significant results: "Action on behalf of justice and participation in the transformation of the world fully appear to us as a constitutive dimension of the preaching of the gospel, or, in other words, of the Church's mission for the redemption of the human race and its liberation from every oppressive situation."[1]

What is the justice in question here, and in what sense is action on behalf of such justice "constitutive" in the preaching of the gospel?

Justice

Before Vatican II and the 1971 synod, justice would have been interpreted, in its most general sense—as a pithy Latin phrase had it— *suum cuique*: to each his/her due. From Aristotle and Plato, through Locke and Marx, down to John Rawls, that lapidary phrase has been understood in different ways.[2] The Catholic understanding can only be grasped if we see the synod's statement in the context of a century of social-ethical discussion beginning with Pope Leo XIII.

Leo's 1891 encyclical *Rerum novarum* (On the Condition of Labor) has for its purpose to specify the "principles which truth and justice dictate" for dealing with the "misery and wretchedness" in the major social changes caused by the process of industrialization, and to do this by defining "the relative rights and the mutual duties of the rich and the poor, of capital and labor."[3] As in the entire modern Catholic tradition, Leo stresses rights and duties; rights are always relational, "can be neither specified nor understood apart from the web of social interdependence which entails mutual obligation and duty."[4]

Modern Catholic teaching stresses the essentially social nature of persons so prominent in the Aristotelian and Thomistic traditions. And even though the major encyclicals are philosophical and empirical in nature, they often appeal to a bond of love at the root of the obligations of justice. A passage from *Quadragesimo anno* is pertinent here.

> Justice alone can, if faithfully observed, remove the causes of social conflict but can never bring about union of minds and hearts. Indeed all the institutions for the establishment of peace and the promotion of mutual help among men, however perfect these may seem, have the principal foundation of their stability in the mutual bond of minds and hearts whereby the members are united with one another. . . . And so, only then will true cooperation be possible for a single common good when the constituent parts of society deeply feel themselves members of one great family and children of the same heavenly Father; nay, that they are one body in Christ, but severally members one of another.[5]

Clearly, the encyclical tradition from Leo XIII to Paul VI distinguished justice from love. Justice needs love to achieve peace, to solidify cooperation for the common good; but "justice alone" does not include love. In this connection I recall, with some amusement, that in the late 1930s at the Jesuit school of theology in Woodstock, Maryland, the treatise on justice (in Latin) in the moral-theology course dealt only with contracts: *Do ut des* (literally, "I give [to you] that you may give [to me]"). Mutual agreement, clearly stated. Love was left to a course in spiritual theology.

Legal Justice
"To each his/her due." A significant area here is legal justice, what is due because it has been written into human law. The legal profession sees to it that just laws foster the common good, that human rights written into law are protected, that the scales of Lady Justice are not weighted in favor of the rich and powerful, that men and women remain innocent until proven guilty, that the punishment fits the proven crime. The burden of law is precisely to give others what is their due, what they deserve, not to be swayed from justice by love or sentiment, by anything less than the law on the books or the need to correct injustice. The law's goddess is the Roman *Justitia*, the lady

with scales and a sword, her eyes blindfolded or closed in token of impartiality. A proud profession indeed, for without it "America the beautiful" would be a nation in anarchy, a country uncommonly unfree. "Equal before the law" is still an ideal; but largely because of the legal profession, because of judges and lawyers, schools of law and legal scholars, we are moving slowly, and I hope relentlessly, toward the ideal, toward increasing impartiality.

True, our legal hands are not lily-white. We look back with shame on a Dred Scott decision that declared slaves to be property. We blush that in this "land of the free" women have been second-class citizens without the right to vote, that it is taking us longer to free women than it did to free the slaves. We weep because justice is often so slow, weep when human beings rot in jail for months before they can come to trial, weep when the men and women we imprison return to society more brutal than before. We grow cynical when the powerful can delay or gerrymander justice. We mourn those in the profession for whom the law is a game whose name is victory or wealth, where the prize goes to the brilliant and the prestigious, to the crafty and the manipulator. And untold millions of us still regard the Supreme Court's decisions on abortion (*Roe* v. *Wade*, *Doe* v. *Bolton*) as unsound from logical, biomedical, moral, and legal perspectives, defective in their anthropology, and appalling in their pretensions to historical scholarship.[6]

The law is a powerful profession—powerful for a paradoxical reason. Powerful because its representatives are servants. And service has an honorable history. It goes back to ancient Athens, where the Greek word we translate as "liturgy" (*leitourgia*) meant a burdensome public office or duty which the richer citizens discharged at their own expense—a service for the polis, for the commonwealth, for the people or the state. Service goes back to an Abraham who at God's command left country and kindred, "not knowing where he was to go" (Heb 11:8), knowing only that he was called to shape "a great nation" (Gen 12:2). Service goes back to a Jesus who told us he "came not to be served but to serve"—in fact, "to give his life" for others (Mt 20:28). Service goes back to lawyers like St. Thomas More, who died merrily on the scaffold declaring himself "the king's good servant, but God's first."

Bench and bar, schools of law and centers of research, here servants rule. And they serve not an abstract quality called justice but their own flesh and blood. It can be a strange, unsettling service. For some serve by prosecuting the "inside trader" and the murdering mafioso, the Weavers and the Wacos; others, by defending them. Sometimes they serve by shackling a sister or brother for months or years, sometimes by lifting the shackles that imprison them. Some hassle us for the IRS (what a friend amusingly called the "eternal revenue service"); others keep corporations from being taxed to death. Constantly they confront one another; ceaselessly they bedazzle juries and bewilder Jesuits with their rhetoric; now they may even compete for bodies on TV and the Internet. And every so often they prove to 12 good folk and true that one of their own flesh and blood deserves to die.

All this they do for one overriding purpose: the common good. Not that the individual is unimportant, slavish subject of the state, imprisoned to the whim or will of a majority. Not that the common good is a reality easily grasped. For even if we say, in broad terms, that the common good is the sum total of those conditions of social living whereby men and women are enabled to achieve their own perfection more fully and more readily,[7] even if we say more simply that the purpose of human law is "the well-being of the people and the public welfare of the political community,"[8] the common good is not static; it grows, it changes with changes in social conditions. But rather than detour in that direction, I prefer to close this segment on legal justice with a passage from a remarkable thinker dead almost four decades, a passage that makes me think of men and women of the law, of justice, of legal argument. Within a thoughtful book entitled *We Hold These Truths: Catholic Reflections on the American Proposition*,[9] in a chapter entitled "The Civilization of the Pluralist Society," Jesuit theologian John Courtney Murray wrote in characteristically distinguished rhetoric:

. . . the distinctive bond of the civil multitude is reason, or more exactly, that exercise of reason which is argument.

Hence the climate of the City is likewise distinctive. It is not feral or familial but forensic. It is not hot and humid, like the climate of the animal kingdom. It lacks the cordial warmth of love and unreasoning loyalty that pervades the family. It is cool and dry, with the coolness and dryness that characterize good argument among informed and responsible men [and women]. Civic amity gives to this climate its vital quality. This form of friendship is a special kind of moral virtue, a thing of reason and intelligence, laboriously cultivated by the discipline of passion, prejudice, and narrow self-interest. It is the sentiment proper to the City. It has nothing to do with the cleavage of a David to a

Jonathan, or with the kinship of the clan, or with the charity, *fortis ut mors*, that makes the solidarity of the Church. It is in distinct contrast with the passionate fanaticism of the Jacobin: "Be my brother or I'll kill you!" Ideally, I suppose, there should be only one passion in the City—the passion for justice. But the will to justice, though it engages the heart, finds its measure as it finds its origin in intelligence, in a clear understanding of what is due to the equal citizen from the City and to the City from the citizenry according to the mode of their equality. This commonly shared will to justice is the ground of civic amity as it is also the ground of that unity which is called peace. This unity, qualified by amity, is the highest good of the civil multitude and the perfection of its civility.[10]

For the meditation of the legal community, from a master of what he called "civilized conversation": a passion for justice, rooted in a clear understanding of what is due to the City and the citizen. Such is the high vocation of the law. Indispensable for human living, for civilized existence, if life on earth is not to become unrelenting warfare.

Ethical Justice

Turn now to ethical justice. In its concern for the mutual claims of concrete persons, the Catholic social tradition distinguishes three modes or types of justice: commutative, distributive, and social. What distinguishes these three modes of justice is the specific type of human relationship and interdependence to which each refers.

Commutative justice concerns the claims which exist in relations between individual and individual or between groups which are essentially private and non-political, such as voluntary associations. Commutative justice is the form of justice which demands fidelity to agreements, contracts, or promises made between persons or groups outside the political or public process. The obligation of commutative justice is one of fidelity to freely formed mutual bonds and of fairness in exchange. It is rooted in the fundamental equality of persons, an equality which implies that no one may ever presume an arbitrary sovereignty over another by setting aside contracts or promises which have bound two free beings into a relation of mutual interdependence. It implies further that if contracts or agreements are to be just, they must be genuinely free. This latter condition of commutative justice is used extensively throughout the tradition to argue that wage agreements cannot be in accord with commutative justice when a worker is compelled to accept an insufficient wage simply because the only alternative is no wage at all.[11]

Distributive justice and social justice concern the relative rights and mutual duties that obtain between persons and public societies, especially the state and civil society as a whole. Distributive justice specifies the claim all persons have to share in some fashion in goods that are essentially public or social: for example, the earth's fertility, an economy's productivity, healthcare, social insurance. Even those who have only helped minimally or not at all to create these public goods —the aged, the infirm, children—have a right, created by their membership in the human community, to share in the public good to a degree compatible with human dignity.

Social justice, in the Roman Catholic ethical tradition, differs from distributive justice in that it

> refers to the obligations of all citizens to aid in the creation of patterns of societal organization and activity which are essential both for the protection of minimal human rights and for the creation of mutuality and participation by all in social life. In other words, social justice is a political virtue. It is distinguished from the other forms of justice because it is based on that form of human interdependence which occurs through the state. Citizens have a personal obligation, mediated through political obligation, to those activities necessary for the creation of a society in which the concerns of agape can be made effective, namely concern for concrete needs of all persons and for the creation of reciprocal interdependence.[12]

So much for what is often called "the encyclical tradition"—a substantive, impressive, compelling argument from reason for human justice. I mean the Catholic insistence that there are claims every man, woman, and child may make on others not because they are wellborn or highly intelligent or otherwise gifted, but because they are human, are children of the same God. Without such justice—a wedding of the ethical and the legal—life on earth ceases to be civilized, becomes a jungle, survival of the fittest, where the prize is to the shrewd, the swift, and the savage, and the devil take the hindmost. A justice that is indispensable for human living, but insufficient for Christian living. What, then, is lacking?

Biblical Justice

After Vatican II, and especially after the 1971 synodal document *Justice in the World*, "justice became a call to the Christian from the God of the two Testaments."[13] Not sheer reason but Sacred Scripture took center stage. What is crucially new here? When the prophet Micah declared to Israel, "What does the Lord require of you but to act justly?" (Mic 6:8), he was not imposing on God's people simply or primarily an ethical or a legal construct. What, then, was the justice God wanted to "roll down like waters" (Amos 5:24)? In point of fact, the biblical concept of justice is too rich, too opulent, too complex to be imprisoned in a definition. Still, back in 1977 biblical scholar John R. Donahue shaped a working definition with admirable succinctness:

In general terms the biblical idea of justice can be described as *fidelity to the demands of a relationship*. In contrast to modern individualism the Israelite is in a world where "to live" is to be united with others in a social context either by bonds of family or by covenant relationships. This web of relationships—king with people, judge with complaints, family with tribe and kinfolk, the community with the resident alien and [with the] suffering in their midst and all with the covenant God—constitutes the world in which life is played out.[14]

In the same essay Donahue tried to describe the elusive concept of the Hebrew *ṣĕdāqāh/ṣedeq* (with some allusion to its related concept *mišpāṭ*) by stating that *ṣĕdāqāh* is used for a wide variety of things: for example,

"God who has led me by the right way" (Gen 24:48), "just" weights (Lev 19:36), "You shall have honest balances, honest weights, an honest ephah" (Deut 25:15), "You shall have only a full and honest measure" (see Ezek 45:10), "just" sacrifices (Deut 33:19; Pss 4:5, 51:19). Scales are "just" when they give fair measure; paths are "just" when they get you where you should be going. "Justice" is also used in the sense of "victory" or saving act: "They repeat the triumphs (*sidqôth*) of the Lord" (Judg 5:11) and "all the saving seed of the Lord" (1 Sam 12:7).

Later research persuaded Donahue to supplement these reflections with the insights of J. P. M. Walsh:

[In his book *The Mighty from Their Thrones*] Walsh underscores the social dimension of *ṣedeq* by describing it as "consensus" about what is right. People in all societies have some innate sense of this, even though it differs in concrete situations. Biblical revelation of *ṣedeq* involves the consensus that is to shape God's people. More carefully than I, Walsh relates *ṣedeq* to *mišpāt*, the implementation of justice (*ṣedeq*) by action (juridical or otherwise). Finally, he treats *nāqām* (literally, vengeance) as the process by which "consensus" or sense of rightness is restored. The thrust of Walsh's whole work is that the biblical tradition gives a different vision of these seminal concepts than does the modern liberal tradition. In the biblical tradition these terms define a consensus against the misuse of power and disclose a God who is on the side of the marginal.[15]

Right relationships, covenant relationships, here is the heart of the biblical message. The Hebrew Scriptures apply the concept to both God and Israel. God is just because God always acts as God should, is invariably faithful to God's promises. Justice is an intrinsic quality manifest in relation to human beings; God's justice is revealed in saving deeds. The texts are many, especially in the Psalms.

> In you, Lord, I take refuge;
> let me never be put to shame;
> In your justice deliver me.
> (Ps 31:2)

And at fair length in Ps 71:

> In you, Lord, I take refuge;
> let me never be put to shame.
> In your justice rescue and deliver me;
> listen to me and save me!
> My mouth shall proclaim your just deeds,
> day after day your acts of deliverance,
> though I cannot number them all.
> I will speak of the mighty works of the Lord;
> O God, I will tell of your singular justice.

God, you have taught me from my youth;
  to this day I proclaim your wondrous deeds.
Now that I am old and gray,
  do not forsake me, God,
That I may proclaim your might
  to all generations yet to come,
Your power and justice, God,
  to the highest heaven.
Restore my honor;
  turn and comfort me,
That I may praise you with the lyre
  for your faithfulness, my God,
And sing to you with the harp,
  O Holy One of Israel!
My lips will shout for joy as I sing your praise;
  my soul, too, which you have redeemed.
Yes, my tongue shall recount
  your justice day by day.
                    (Ps 71:1-2, 15-19, 21-24a)

Defend the lowly and fatherless;
  render justice to the afflicted and needy.
Rescue the lowly and poor;
  deliver them from the hand of the wicked.
                    (Ps 82:3-4)

The Lord has made His victory known;
  has revealed His triumph for the nations to see,
Has remembered faithful love
  toward the house of Israel.
                    (Ps 98:2-3)

Justice and judgment are the foundation of your throne;
  love and loyalty march before you.
                    (Ps 89:14)

And very trenchantly:

Happy those whose help is Jacob's,
  whose hope is in the Lord, their God,
The maker of heaven and earth,

the seas and all that is in them,
Who keeps faith for ever;
    secures justice for the oppressed;
    gives food to the hungry.
The Lord sets prisoners free;
    the Lord gives sight to the blind.
The Lord raises up those who are bowed down;
    the Lord loves the righteous.
The Lord protects the stranger,
    sustains the orphan and the widow,
    but thwarts the way of the wicked.
                    (Ps 146:5-9)

Such is God's covenant fidelity. I find it movingly declared when Moses addressed the Israelites about to enter the Promised Land (Deut 7:7-10a):

It was not because you are the largest of all nations that the Lord set His heart on you and chose you, for you are really the smallest of all nations. It was because the Lord loved you and because of His fidelity to the oath He had sworn to your fathers, that He brought you out with His strong hand from the place of slavery, and ransomed you from the hand of Pharaoh king of Egypt. Understand, then, that the Lord, your God, is God indeed, the faithful God who keeps His merciful covenant down to the thousandth generation toward those who love Him and keep His commandments, but who repays with destruction the person who hates Him.

When are people just? Once again it is a question of right relationships. Right relationship to God, to their sisters and brothers, to the whole of created reality. Each relationship merits consideration.

Right relationship to God? It is summarized in what Jesus called "the greatest and first commandment" of the law (Mt 22:38). Moses had revealed it to all Israel: "The Lord is our God, the Lord alone! Therefore you shall love the Lord your God with all your heart, and with all your soul, and with all your strength" (Deut 6:4-5). It is God's stern prohibition: "I, the Lord, am your God, who brought you out of the land of Egypt, that place of slavery. You shall not have other gods besides me" (Deut 5:6-7). Not an idle command. Not when we recall the golden calf in Exodus (32:1ff.). Not when we read Hosea and discover how Israel had forsaken Yahweh to worship the fertility gods of Canaan, the Baals. Or Jeremiah denouncing the idolatry of the people and the superficiality of the covenantal observances. Or Ezekiel's Yahweh: "Because you have defiled my sanctuary with all your detestable abominations, I swear to cut you down" (Ezek 5:11).

Right relationship to sisters and brothers? For an Israelite, to be just was to be properly postured not only toward God but also toward all men and women within the community. The profound basis of this relationship was Israel's covenant with God. The Israelites were to father the fatherless and mother the motherless, were to welcome the stranger, feed the sojourner, show hospitality to the resident alien, not because the orphan and the outsider deserved it, but because this was the way God had acted toward Israel. A passage in Deuteronomy is telling: "You too must befriend the alien, for you were once aliens yourselves in the land of Egypt" (Deut 10:19). In freeing the oppressed, they were mirroring the loving God who had delivered *them* from oppression, had freed them from Pharaoh.

Another way of phrasing it: Justice, for the Jew, was not a question simply, or primarily, of human deserving, of human law. The Jews were to give to others what they themselves had been given by God, were to act toward one another and toward the stranger as God had acted toward Israel—and *precisely because* God had acted this way. Their justice was to image not the justice of woman and man but the justice of Yahweh. For Israel, the practice of justice thus understood was an expression of steadfast love—God's love and their own. Not to execute justice was not to worship God.

Right relationship to the earth? It is not exploitation that the Hebrew word for "have dominion" (Gen 1:26) mandates but reverential care for God's creation. The very context "suggests that this human dominion is to be carried out 'in the image of God,' an image that suggests nurture, blessing, and care rather than exploitation, abuse, and subjugation."[16]

Social Focus of Scripture

At this point an even broader context is imperative. For a perilous proposition pervades a large segment of our American Christian culture. It asserts that Christianity, by its very nature, is concerned exclusively with the relation of the soul to eternity, that the essential realization religion should provide is the worthlessness of human expectations of a better life on earth. It insists that the Son of God took our flesh not to relieve our sufferings but to forgive our sins, and so the Church's function is to focus not on violations of social justice but on the undying hardness of human hearts.

The thesis does violence to Scripture. Those who read in the biblical text a sheerly personal, individualistic morality have not understood the Torah, have not sung the Psalms, have not been burned by the prophets, have not perceived the implications and the very burden of Jesus' message, and must inevitably play fast and loose with St. Paul.

The social focus of God's Book is evident on the first page; the song of creation is its overture. Our incredibly imaginative God did not have in mind isolated units, autonomous entities, scattered disparately around a globe, basically independent each of every other—entities that might one day decide through a social contract to join together for self-aggrandizement, huddle together for self-protection. God had in mind a people, a human family, a community of persons, a body genuinely one. A people who would see and touch God's material creation, earth and sea and sky, with reverence. John R. Donahue has summed up the significance of the creation stories in two powerful sentences: "Men and women are God's representatives and conversation partners in the world, with a fundamental dignity that must be respected and fostered. They are to exist in interdependence and mutual support and are to care for the world with respect, as for a gift received from God."[17]

Here the "image of God" is a theme of high significance. Donahue has noted that in its original significance it did

> not mean some human quality (intellect or free will) or the possession of "sanctifying grace." Two interpretations enjoy some exegetical support today. One view is that, just as ancient Near Eastern kings erected "images" of themselves in subject territory, so humans are God's representatives, to be given the same honor due God. Claus Westermann argues that the phrase means that humans were created to be God's counterpart, creatures analogous to God with whom God can speak and who will hear God's word. . . . In either of these interpretations, all men and women prior to identification by race, social status, religion, or sex are worthy of respect and reverence.[18]

This divine idea began to take concrete shape when God, bringing an oppressed mass out of Egypt, created a *people* which was to gather in prayer and thanksgiving (cult) and to live according to God's constitution (*torah*). Why this particular body of men and women? Not because they deserved it; simply God's mysterious love. Those who were no people God made into a people. The Exodus, therefore, was not simply a liberation from slavery; it was the formation of a new social order, in sharp contrast to the Egypt of their experience. *Freedom from*, yes; but equally or more important, *freedom for* the formation of a community that would live under a covenant with God. Moses assured the people that if they diligently observed God's commandments, they would "be in the right" (Deut 6:25).

In the right. This covenant between God and God's people was a symbol of proper relationships. It is a reminder of the moment when God declared all of creation "very good" (Gen 1:31), because simply everything was in right order, in proper relation: humanity (*adam*) to God, humans among themselves, humans and nonhuman reality toward one another.

In one of our Preaching the Just Word retreat/workshops, Scripture scholar Carolyn Osiek explained concretely how the Israelite relationships that flowed from common identity as members of the covenant community can be seen through four concerns.

1. *Trustworthiness.* What Yahweh desires is "steadfast love" rather than sheer sacrifice (Hos 6:6). What does the Lord require of Israel? "Do justice (*mišpāṭ*), love goodness (*ḥesed*), and walk humbly with your God" (Mic 6:8). Particularly prohibited is partiality in lawsuits, even partiality toward the poor (Exod 23:3; Lev 19:15). This does not contradict the special consideration that the powerful are to provide the poor and defenseless.

2. *Relationships between rich and poor.* Save in legal contexts, justice is not *equal* treatment; justice is *appropriate* treatment that will equalize the relationship and provide access to resources. Examples are vivid. When grain, grapes, or olives are harvested, the reaper is not to return to pick up what was missed the first time. These "leftovers" must go to the poor, to the widow and the orphan, to the resident alien (Lev 19:9-10; Deut 24:19-22). Interest must not be taken, save from an alien (Exod 22:21; Lev 25:35-37; Deut 23:20-21). A cloak taken in pledge from a poor person must be returned before nightfall, "for this is his only covering, it is his mantle for his body; in what else shall he sleep?" (Exod 22:26-27). Abuses of such sensitive relationships provoke outraged outcries from the prophets:

The Lord enters into judgment
with the elders and princes of His people:
"It is you who have devoured the vineyard,
the spoil of the poor is in your houses.
What do you mean by crushing my people,
by grinding the face of the poor?"
(Isa 3:14-15)

3. *Relationships between male and female.* In the patriarchal society that was Israel, women ranked among the defenseless who had to
be protected, first by the powerful males of their own family, but also
by the powerful of the society. In consequence, we find legislation for
the rights of a girl sold into slavery by her parents—protective indeed,
but hardly consonant with the dignity today's Jew or Christian would
demand for a daughter of God (Exod 21:7-11). There is legislation for
the rights of a widow (Exod 22:21-23). New in Deuteronomy is protection of a wife's reputation against slander (22:13-19) and the rights
of a female captive (21:10-14).

4. *Relationships between citizen and stranger, or resident alien.*
Here it is not a question of hospitality, which is directed by different
rules; here it is treatment of non-Israelites living in Israelite territory:
"You shall not oppress a resident alien; you know the heart of an alien
[you know how an alien feels], for you were aliens in the land of
Egypt" (Exod 23:9; see 22:21). More than not oppressing, "you shall
also love the stranger, for you were strangers in the land of Egypt"
(Deut 10:19; see 24:17). What lies behind such ordinances? The land
actually is God's; all humans, even Israelites, are aliens. "The land is
mine; with me you are but aliens and tenants" (Deut 25:23).

Even though all this is guaranteed by law, behind the law lies the
covenant, "the great God, mighty and awesome, who is not partial
and takes no bribe, who executes justice for the orphan and the
widow, and who loves the strangers, providing them food and clothing" (Deut 10:17-18). Behind the law is the Lord who dealt thus with
Israel when the people were aliens, strangers, in Egypt (v. 19). The
rights do not stem primarily from the law; for the law itself is an effort
to express what the covenant demands in actual living.

The covenant relationship explains why concern for the poor and
the marginal is pervasive in the Hebrew Bible. Take the male prophets. Through Isaiah and Hosea, through Amos and Micah and Jeremiah, Yahweh ceaselessly proclaims to Israel that the Lord rejects
precisely those things the Israelites think will make God happy.

Yahweh is weary of burnt offerings, delights not in the blood of bulls or lambs, finds incense an abomination, hates their appointed feasts, will not listen to their prayers and to the melody of their harps, does not want rivers of oil, thousands of rams, even their firstborn. Not because these are unacceptable in themselves; rather because two essential ingredients are missing: steadfast love and justice (see Isa 1:11-18; 42:1-4; Hos 2:18-20; 6:6; Amos 5:18-25; Mic 6:6-8; Jer 7:5-7). One passage from Isaiah says it all in powerful rhetoric:

> Is not this the fast that I choose:
>   to loose the bonds of injustice,
>   to undo the thongs of the yoke,
> to let the oppressed go free,
>   and to break every yoke?
> Is it not to share your bread with the hungry,
>   and bring the homeless poor into your house;
> when you see the naked, to cover them,
>   and not to hide yourself from your own flesh?
> Then your light shall break forth like the dawn,
>   and your healing shall spring up quickly;
> your vindication shall go before you,
>   the glory of the Lord shall be your rear guard.
> Then you shall call, and the Lord will answer;
>   you shall cry for help, and He will say: Here I am.
>   (Isa 58:6-9a)

It is precisely this fashioning of a people, this call to community, that gives sin its most significant characteristic. In Scripture, sin involves not only our traditional "offense against God" (see Psalm 51) but also the sundering of community. The whole of Scripture from Genesis to Revelation is the story of struggle for community, of lapses into disintegration, division, enmity. Think of Eden, of the first sin: the man's excuse, "The woman you gave me"; the fig leaves that symbolize their separation (Gen 3:7, 12). Think of the first murder, of Cain's cynical "Am I my brother's keeper?" (Gen 4:9). Think of the Tower of Babel: a community "with one language" agreeing to "build a tower with its top in the heavens—let us make a name for ourselves," then "scattered abroad over the face of all the earth" (Gen 11:1-9). Think of David, God's specially chosen, taking Bathsheba out of lust, sending her husband Uriah to be killed in battle. The list is endless. If biblical justice is fidelity to the demands of a relationship, then sin is a refusal of responsibility; sin creates division, alienation, dissension, marginalization, rejection. Sin dis-members the body.

Justice and God's Earth

God's good earth, material creation, merits special consideration, specifically for its place in Scripture. Some critics blame our ecological crisis on the Christian understanding of the Hebrew Testament. As they see it, the scientific and the popular stance of the Western world toward material creation can be traced back to the first chapter of the Bible: "God created humankind in His image, in the image of God He created them; male and female He created them. God blessed them, and God said to them, 'Be fruitful and multiply, and fill the earth and subdue it; and have dominion over the fish of the sea and over the birds of the air and over every living thing that moves upon the earth'" (Gen 1:27-28).[19]

Subdue . . . have dominion. In consequence (so the charge runs), Christianity sees in humankind the one center of the universe. All else—soil and sea and sky, blue marlin or bird of paradise, oil or coal or natural gas—all that is not man or woman has for purpose, for destiny, to serve humans, to serve their purpose, to serve their pleasure. In laboratory and forest, in factory and refectory, we pillage and we rape, we devour and we waste. And why not? It is I who am God's image, master actually or potentially of all I survey—king of the earth (said some early Christian writers) as God is King of the universe. We humans will be utterly one with nature only when "things" no longer resist our will, no longer struggle against us.

I shall reserve for the next main section the practical applications of this conviction. In this biblical section I wish simply to state that the despotism drawn by Christians and others from the Genesis passage is not warranted by the text and context.

> The Hebrew term [for "have dominion"] is used in other places to describe the royal care that characterizes a king as God's vice-regent (Pss 72:8; 110:2; see also Ps 8:5-9). Like ancient kings, men and women are to be the mediators of prosperity and well-being. . . . Reverential care for God's creation rather than exploitation is the mandate given humanity in this section of Genesis.[20]

This interpretation is supported by the context; I mean the formation of man and woman in the image of God. The kind of dominion man and woman are enjoined to exercise should reflect in its own way the care for material creation characteristic of its Creator. As God's vice-regents, we humans are not despots but stewards; and a steward is one who manages what is someone else's. A steward cares, is concerned, at times agonizes. Stewards may not plunder or waste; they are responsible, can be called to account for their stewardship. Yes indeed, "The earth is the Lord's, and all that is in it" (Ps 24:1).

Before leaving Genesis, I believe it is only fair to mention an approach to material creation that contrasts the Priestly "steward" and the Yahwist's "service" of nature. It has been expressed succinctly by Theodore Hiebert:

Two distinct postures within creation are assumed by the human being in Priestly and Yahwistic perspectives. The Priestly human occupies a superior position within the created order. Created in God's image, humans are distinguished from the rest of creation and granted unique authority over it. They are to exercise this authority by populating the earth, ruling its animals, and subduing its land. . . . The human of Genesis 1 shares many of the characteristics of the priestly role itself. This was the role of a distinct, elite party in Israelite society, closely allied to royalty, that regarded itself as the mediator of divine rule to Israel and to creation itself. . . .

By contrast, the human being in the Yahwist's epic occupies a subordinate role within the created order. Created out of arable soil, the Yahwist's human is united with the rest of creation and placed in a subservient relationship to it. This subservience is expressed in the image of the soil as the beginning and end of human life and in the depiction of the cultivation of the soil as "serving" rather than "subduing." . . . Basic to this image of the human is the ancient farmer's sense of dependence upon the soil, of the necessity of meeting its demands and cooperating with its processes, and of the ultimate lack of control over nature's own orders and powers.[21]

Justice and Jesus

It is the Israelite tradition on justice that sparked the ministry of Jesus. It was summed up in the synagogue of his hometown Nazareth, in what Luke presents as Jesus' program on earth: "The Spirit of the Lord is upon me, for [the Lord] has anointed me, has sent me to preach good news to the poor, to proclaim release for prisoners and sight for the blind, to send the downtrodden away relieved" (Lk 4:18). Matthew had already grasped this, for he applied to Jesus the prophecy in Isaiah: "I will put my Spirit upon him, and he will proclaim justice to the Gentiles. . . . He will not break a bruised reed or quench a smoldering wick until he brings justice to victory" (Mt 12:18-20; cf. Isa 42:1-4). In harmony with Hosea (6:6), Jesus wants not sacrifice but compassion, mercy (Mt 12:7; 23:23).

Jesus is "the Righteous One," "the Just One" (*ho dikaios:* Lk 23:47; Acts 3:14; 7:52; 22:14). One of his beatitudes declares, "Blessed are they who hunger and thirst for justice (righteousness, holiness)" (Mt 5:6); another pronounces, "Blessed are those who are persecuted for justice' sake" (Mt 5:6, 10). In the Parable of the Good Samaritan (Lk 10:29-37) Jesus intimates who the "neighbor" is: not just the person next door, not only someone with whom we are on good terms, but "anyone in need with whom one comes into contact and to whom one can show pity and kindness, even beyond the bounds of one's own ethnic or religious group."[22] The Parable of the Rich Man and Lazarus (Lk 16:19-31) "further illustrates the teaching of the Lucan Jesus about the prudent use of material possessions and gives new meaning to the 'dwellings that are everlasting' (v. 9). It is a vivid restatement of the beatitude and the woe of 6:20, 24 and illustrates the proverb at the end of 16:15, 'What is of highest human value is an abomination in God's sight.'"[23]

For Jesus, faithful to the tradition, the just man or woman is not simply someone who gives to another what that other *deserves.* Jesus inaugurates a new covenant, in which the most significant relationship is the monosyllable that says it all: love. The Hebrew Testament had already commanded it: "You shall love your neighbor as yourself" (Lev 19:18). What, then, is "new" in Jesus' commandment? He told us with admirable brevity: "I give you a new commandment, that you love one another. Just as I have loved you, you also should love one another" (Jn 13:34; see 15:12). The first newness? Love as he loved: with no distinction of persons, without reservation, even unto crucifixion. A second newness? The second commandment of the law and the gospel "is like" the first. Loving another is like loving God (Mt 22:39). "The combination of these two commands is not clearly attested before Jesus and marks an important moral advance."[24] Admittedly, "Love your neighbor as yourself" is not a psychological balancing act: As much or as little as you love yourself, that much love or that little love shower or trickle on your neighbor. Therefore

the command "includes a right form of self-love."[25] I wonder, however, if the command does not at least suggest that I am to love my
neighbor as if he or she were another "I," as if I were standing in his
or her shoes, especially the paper-thin shoes of the poor, the downtrodden, the despised.

New Testament justice? Love as Jesus loved. The kind of love that
impelled God's unique Son to wear our flesh; to be born of a woman
as we are born; to thirst and tire as we do; to respond with compassion to a hungry crowd, the bereavement of a mother, the sorrow of
a sinful woman; to weep over a dead friend and a hostile city; to
spend himself especially for the bedeviled and the bewildered, the
poverty-stricken and the marginalized; to die in exquisite agony so
that others might come to life.

In Preaching the Just Word retreat/workshops, Scripture scholar
Sarah Ann Sharkey, O.P., has suggested that, to appreciate justice in
Jesus, we should read Mark's Gospel in its entirety, carefully watch-
ing Jesus, his disciples, and other characters, particularly the "little"
people. Without speaking specifically of justice, Jesus is constantly
dealing with the reality: making all relationships right. Among the
instances: Peter's fevered mother-in-law and the woman hemorrhaging for 12 years; the ostracized leper and Levi the tax collector; the
convulsed boy foaming at the mouth and the man emerging from the
tombs with an unclean spirit; the living child Jesus took into his arms
and the dead 12-year-old daughter of a synagogue leader he said was
only sleeping; the blind beggar Bartimaeus and the thousands who sat
close to Jesus for three days with nothing to eat; the man who yearned
for eternal life but was terribly attached to his own possessions and
the poor widow compelled by an unjust religious situation to put her
last penny in the treasury. And there are those grouped together simply as "sinners." All these, and others, Jesus moved in different ways
to right relationships.

The four community relationships highlighted in Carolyn Osiek's
treatment of the Israelite tradition are paralleled in Jesus' own
approach to justice as a son of the covenant. (1) Jesus demanded that
his disciples be *trustworthy*, that is, reliable servants waiting for their
master's return (Mt 24:42-45; Lk 12:35-48), even if they had to confess themselves "unprofitable, worthless, useless" (Lk 17:10).
(2) Jesus came from the peasant class and represented a *peasant perspective* in an agrarian society. While exposing the wealthy and the
powerful, he also pointed an accusatory finger at the underclass: for
example, the unjust slave forgiven a huge debt by his master yet refus-

ing to have patience with a fellow slave's much smaller debt. Moreover, Jesus' harsh critique of wealth raises the question whether in his mind wealth is compatible with Christianity (e.g., Lk 6:24). (3) Always respectful of *women*, Jesus related to them at times in ways unacceptable to the culture and prejudicial to his reputation: healing a bent woman on the Sabbath (Lk 13:10-17); permitting a "sinner" (Lk 7:36-50) and an unclean (hemorrhaging) woman to touch him (Mt 9:20-22; Mk 5:25-34; Lk 8:43-48); attending a private dinner with two women friends, Martha and Mary (Lk 10:38-42); speaking to a female stranger in public, and she a Samaritan (Jn 4:1-42). (4) As for the *stranger*, the outsider, Jesus was uncommonly open to Gentiles, even felt comfortable in their territory, on their turf (especially in Mark). And there are the striking Matthean "book ends": the astrologers from the East (2:1-12) and the commissioning of the Eleven to "make disciples of all nations" (28:16-20).

Such was, in large measure, the profound approach of the early Church, envisioning itself as the covenant community of the baptized—the Body of Christ, branches abiding in the vine (Jn 15:5), disciples committed to loving all others "as I have loved you" (Jn 15:12).

1. To be trustworthy was essential to Christian living; for "as surely as God is faithful," as surely as in Jesus "every one of God's promises is a yes," so through Jesus the disciple is always ready to respond with a yes, an amen "to the glory of God" (2 Cor 1:18-20). In fact, Ananias and Sapphira lost their lives not because they kept from the community some of the proceeds from the sale of their property, but because they had lied to the Holy Spirit and to the community (Acts 5:1-11).

2. The Letter of James (2:1-9) protests "partiality," "favoritism" shown to the rich when Christians assemble: for example, priority seating. It contradicts genuine belief in the Lord Jesus; it is failing to love our neighbors as other selves; it is sinful. Nor can faith save if it is divorced from deeds, specifically failure to "supply the bodily needs of the hungry and the naked" (2:14-17).

3. As for male–female relationships, we have what Osiek calls "ambiguous new beginnings in a patriarchal society in which male and female were not understood to be equal." The holiness of baptized women, specifically the sanctifying influence of a believing wife, is recognized by Paul (1 Cor 7:12-16). Women such as Phoebe and Prisca (Priscilla) play an active role in Christian ministry (Rom 16:1-5). For Mark, Luke, and John, women are the first to witness and proclaim Jesus' resurrection (Mk 16:9-10; Lk 24:1-12; Jn 20:17-18)—so

prominently that in one striking tradition Mary Magdalene has been termed "apostle to the apostles."[26] A Samaritan woman of dubious reputation "has a real missionary function," "has sown the seed and thus prepared for the apostolic harvest" (Jn 4).[27] Still, as Osiek has pointed out, the traditional restrictions on women in the assembly, marriage, and public life remain (1 Cor 14:34-35; 1 Tim 2:11-15; 1 Pet 3:1-7).

4. As for the stranger, the alien, the unbeliever, the immoral, there is a recurrent tension between the holy community and openness to "the world." Examples abound. Certain evildoers are to be avoided, but to avoid all "you would then need to go out of the world" (1 Cor 5:9-13). It would seem that Christian prayer services were open to outsiders (1 Cor 14:16) but not the Lord's Supper. An unbeliever's invitation to a meal need not be refused, unless scandal is involved—for example, food "offered in sacrifice" (1 Cor 10:23-30). The once alien Gentiles are now "citizens with the saints and also members of the household of God" (Eph 2:11-22), while Christians are actually "aliens and exiles" in the world, with their citizenship in heaven (1 Pet 1:17; 2:11).

The response of the early Christian communities to the "new commandment" of Jesus finds something of a summary in Matthew's presentation of the Last Judgment (25:31-46). If *anyone* is hungry or thirsty, naked or a stranger, sick or in prison, it is always Christ who clamors for bread or water, Christ who cries to be clothed or welcomed, Christ whom you visit on a bed of pain or behind bars.[28] And the First Letter of John is terribly uncompromising: "If anyone has the world's goods and sees his brother in need, yet closes his heart against him, how does God's love abide in him?" (1 Jn 3:17). Here is a vision of community where, as Paul puts it, no one, absolutely no one, can say to any other, "I have no need of you" (1 Cor 12:12ff.). Not the rich to the poor, not the powerful to the powerless, not the bold and beautiful to the timid and repulsive. For we are to be one as Jesus and his Father are one (Jn 17:20-23).

In summary, salvation as divinely designed takes place within a single, all-embracing community. A shivering, exhilarating awakening. My salvation depends on fidelity to three relationships: Do I love God above all else, above all created idols? Do I love each sister and brother as Jesus has loved and loves me? Do I touch each "thing" (that ice-cold word) with the reverence, the respect, the restraint God asked of humankind at its birthing?

The Common Good

In this context I believe it important to add a word on an aspect of justice that is central to Christian living, indeed to all human living, and yet is in serious trouble today. I mean the common good.[29]

> Over two millennia ago, Aristotle argued that the good of the community should set the direction for the lives of individuals, for it is a higher or more "divine" good than the particular goods of private individuals. This theme has echoed and re-echoed throughout much of the later history of Christian reflection. For example, St. Thomas argued that God's own self is the highest good we can attain, and that a right relation to God requires a commitment to the common good of our neighbors and of all creation. For Christians, the pursuit of the common good follows from the double commandment to love God from all one's heart and to love one's neighbor as one's self.[30]

This vision of the common good, John Rawls asserts, "is no longer a political possibility for those who accept the constraints of liberty and toleration of democratic institutions."[31] Our fundamental divergences in culture, tradition, and way of life make interaction, neighborliness, common sharing appear as threats rather than a desirable good. The American memory of slavery, lynchings, ethnic exclusion, and discrimination has convinced certain minority groups that traditional ways and institutions do not guarantee the good life. There is a widespread contention that the United States is not only pluralistic but culturally at war with itself over a broad range of moral values. Sociologist Alan Wolfe has suggested that conflict is being avoided precisely by abandoning the pursuit of the common good. His *One Nation after All*[32] found that what the middle class in the United States values most highly is tolerance: Whether it is religion, the structure of family life, gender roles, immigration, or race, "Thou shalt not judge thy neighbor." Given the dangers in a culture war, Wolfe concluded that a "morality writ small," aspiring to "modest virtues" and "ordinary duties" such as kindness and honesty, was preferable to larger goals such as social justice and social equality.

> But shortly after the appearance of his book, Wolfe confessed that his research left him somewhat depressed. For morality writ small lacks "a shared sense of national purpose." Americans

have a distinct lack of enthusiasm for meeting the responsibilities of national citizenship. "They seemed to want the benefits of being American without the obligations of paying taxes or paying attention." They are also distinctly unenthusiastic about the international responsibilities that go along with being American in the emerging global context. Wolfe conjectures that this narrowness of vision is a by-product of the prosperity of the middle-class. In the comfortable world of the middle-class, morality writ small translates into "couch-potato politics," an unwillingness or inability to articulate common purposes and act to secure them. In other words, middle-class Americans lack a vision of the common good, both in their approach to national life and in their understanding of the role of the United States internationally. Avoidance of conflict has its virtues to be sure, but there are major social and political questions today that call for more vision than tolerance can generate on its own.[33]

In what ways is Catholic social thought able to foster recognition of the significance of the common good? Several areas.[34] It bases its understanding of the common good on the recognition that the dignity of human persons can be achieved only in community. This understanding has its roots not only in the Aristotelian notion of the human person as a social or political animal, but in the biblical notion of covenant: God called Israel not as a multitude of individuals but precisely as a people. Such an understanding is critical for an integral sense of freedom. Freedom is not primarily negative, freedom from bondage, from constraint, uninvaded privacy. "For the ancient Greeks, privacy was a state of deprivation, a fact echoed in the etymological link of privacy and privation."[35] And in the Hebrew Scriptures, as indicated earlier, the Exodus was not simply a liberation *from slavery;* perhaps even more importantly, it was *freedom for* the formation of a community living under a covenant.

This social dimension of freedom is highlighted time and again by John Paul II. It is evident in his insistence that genuine democracy, its success over the long haul, depends in large measure on the link between the life of virtue and commitment to the common good. It is striking in his stress not only on a solidarity of private, like-minded enclaves, but, more universal in scope, positive engagement with those who are different.

When interdependence becomes recognized [as a system determining relationships in the contemporary world, in its economic, cultural, political, and religious dimensions] and accepted as a moral category, the correlative response as a moral and social attitude, as a "virtue," is solidarity. This . . . is a firm and persevering determination to commit oneself to the common good; that is to say, to the good of all and of each individual, because we are all really responsible for all. . . .[36]

This solidarity in commitment to the common good has, as David Hollenbach insists, social dimensions; it influences how we understand and live justice in the social-economic order. Rosemary Haughton expressed it powerfully two decades ago in *The Passionate God*, where she submits that the model of life is an exchange of love.

If we say that oppression is evil, in its effects on the oppressed but also on the oppressor, we have to remember what kind of thing evil is—not a thing-in-itself but basically a distortion of things inherently good. Evil is a lying use of good. Injustice is not an alternative to justice, it is a refusal to recognize the nature of justice. The facts about human beings are those of exchange; people are people in the network of exchange, which is love. "Justice" is the clear recognition of this and is therefore concerned with the kinds of actions which result from seeing human society in those terms. Injustice is simply a view of, and resulting decisions about, human society which are false, and this is so even when those who hold and practice injustice are sincere and highly motivated. It is important to hold on to the fact that injustice in the political sphere means an unreal vision of things, resulting from a failure to perceive the proper relationships in the organic body, in just the same way that sexual sin is the result of failure (culpable or not) to perceive the inherent meaning of being bodily. . . . Social and sexual sin are both, at bottom, the result of false statements about the nature of reality.[37]

At this point it might be helpful to state clearly and swiftly the difference between biblical justice and other forms of justice rooted in the philosophical tradition: commutative justice, distributive justice, social justice. Here John Donahue has been instructive.

1. Biblical justice does not permit a strict philosophical definition; in the texts it is often linked with qualities such as mercy, steadfast love, and fidelity. "The traditional contrast between obligations in charity and obligations in justice is foreign to the Bible."[38]

2. Fundamentally, biblical justice is *making things right*, not simply recognizing or defining *individual rights*. Its concern is the right relation of human beings to God and to one another. "There is no conflict between the 'vertical dimension,' that is, the proper relationship to God and God's commands and the 'horizontal dimension,' the need to structure social life in a way that respects human dignity and is concerned for the vulnerable in the community."[39]

3. Biblical justice is neither "blind" nor totally impartial. "It is partial to those most affected by evil and oppression," symbolized in the Old Testament by widows, orphans, the poor, and strangers. It is "embodied in the NT by Jesus' mission to those on the social and religious margin of society."[40]

I am delighted with Donahue's summation:

> There are "two women of justice," one with a scale and her eyes blinded, and the other, who proclaims: "He has shown might with his arm, dispersed the arrogant of mind and heart. He has thrown down rulers from their thrones, but lifted up the lowly. The hungry he has filled with good things, the rich he has sent away empty" (Luke 1:51-53).[41]

Catholic Social Tradition[42]

Biblical justice, fidelity to relationships and responsibilities that stem from a covenant with God, is not something static. It is not frozen in any one era (B.C.E., for example), any one culture (say, Western), any one people (e.g., Roman Catholics). It develops, undergoes modification, as it touches new ages, new peoples, new problems. Within Catholicism we call it tradition. But not tradition as some musty museum piece, beyond alteration and improvement. Rather tradition in its most pregnant sense: the best of our past, infused with the insights of the present, with a view to a richer, more catholic future. At this moment in the tradition, one way of expressing whereto we have come is to outline six fundamental facets of Catholic social teaching.

First, the center of that teaching is the *dignity of the human person*, a dignity rooted in the image and reflection of God in each human person, an imaging of God that can be defaced but never obliterated. From that unique dignity flow significant rights. Not only the right to life but related rights necessary for each one's integral development as a person: for example, the right to a job, to a living wage, to decent housing, to education, to healthcare, to respect.

Second, God's human images have *not only rights but responsibilities*. In our time, an understandable clamor for human rights threatens to drown out the less attractive warning about responsibilities. Catholic social teaching insistently pairs rights and responsibilities. If biblical justice is fidelity to relationships, then each of us has responsibilities: to love God above all else; to love our sisters and brothers as other selves; to reverence and cherish every facet of God's creation, from rich earth to giant redwood to shooting star, as a precious gift.

Third, the heart and soul of community is the *family*. Catholicism has never wavered in visualizing the family as the building block of civilizations and cultures, as the primordial natural community, as the Church in miniature. In consequence, the family deserves special protection, particularly in a culture where the traditional family structure is threatened; in an America where half the marriages break up and single-parent families are mushrooming; in a climate where increasingly people are questioning whether anyone can realistically say "for ever." Protective measures must include (but often do not) the rights of the unborn, of children, of the aging, of workers to a family wage.

Fourth, a *preferential option for the poor*, the disadvantaged, the forgotten. Not because they are necessarily holier; only because they stand in greater need. This is what the God of Israel demanded of kings (see Ps 72); what Jesus persistently preached in his preference for the sinner and the sufferer, the outcast and the oppressed; what Fathers of the Church like Basil and Chrysostom proclaimed to powerful princes and powerless people. The expression may be recent; the reality is as ancient as the Exodus.

Fifth, *solidarity*. For, as Edward Arroyo has succinctly phrased it echoing John Paul II, "if interdependence is an accurate description of our modern world, then solidarity is the appropriate Christian response to this reality."[43] In harmony with God's creative intent, we humans are called to overcome barriers of race and religion, of ethnicity and gender, of economic status and nationality. Extraordinarily difficult, as millennia of "civilized" existence have tragically shown.

The sixth principle, *care for nonhuman creation*, is something of a newcomer on the justice scene. Why such a lengthy lag, in the Catholic magisterium as well as among theologians of all Christian persuasions? For more than three decades I have been intrigued, in fact influenced, by the insight of Lutheran theologian Joseph Sittler.

He insisted that our basic ecological error is that we Christians have separated creation and redemption. The reason why we can worship nature in Vermont and at the same time manipulate nature in New York is because, in our view, the redemption wrought by Christ leaves untouched the creation wrought by God. And once we wrench creation from redemption, once we put nature out there and grace in here, as long as we omit from our theology of grace humans' transaction with nature, it is irrelevant to Christians whether we reverence the earth or ravish it.[44]

Happily, recent decades have witnessed an ecological awakening within Catholicism. There are the feminist theologians who have been emphasizing, on the one hand, the connection between patriarchal culture, the technological dream of progress, and the environmental crisis, and, on the other hand, an idolatrously one-sided masculine idea of God, women who see "no liberation for them and no solution to the ecological crisis within a society whose fundamental model of relationships continues to be one of domination."[45] There are Catholic ecologists like Thomas Berry, who has argued that if we lose the environment, we lose God.[46] Three of his 12 principles for understanding the universe and the role of the human in the universe process merit reproduction here.

> 2. The universe is a unity, an interacting and genetically related community of beings bound together in an inseparable relationship in space and time. The unity of the planet earth is especially clear; each being of the planet is profoundly implicated in the existence and functioning of every other being of the planet.
>
> 7. The earth, within the solar system, is a self-emergent, self-propagating, self-nourishing, self-educating, self-governing, self-healing, self-fulfilling community. All particular life systems in their being, their sexuality, their nourishment, their education, their governing, their healing, their fulfillment, must integrate their functioning within this larger complex of mutually dependent earth systems.
>
> 12. The main human task of the immediate future is to assist in activating the inter-communion of all the living and non-living components of the earth community in what can be considered the emerging ecological period of earth development.[47]

I have been impressed by theologian John Haught's conviction that process theology comes closer than any other theological alternative to "giving us a framework within which to pull together the insights of science and religion into a cosmology that encourages in us an evolutionary adventurousness as well as a preservative care that might inspire ethical attitudes toward nature."[48] With the help of science we can see religious searching as "expressive of the adventurous nature of the universe itself," need not "feel 'lost in the cosmos' in order to embrace the homelessness that religion requires."[49] Religion's essential role in the earth's ecology will take shape primarily in our "unembarrassed cultivation of its inherent sacramentalism and the genuine reverence toward nature that this implies"—a sacramentalism that needs to be nourished by mysticism, silence, and action.[50] Haught has compelled me to probe ever more deeply into the person (the human as well as the divine) not primarily as an independently conscious subject but as essentially *relational*. "Personality means the capacity for continually intensifying the depth and breadth of relationship to other persons, nature and God,"[51] even less restricted beyond the grave.

Summary

If this section were summed up in a single word, I suggest that the word has to be "relationships." Most—I am tempted to say all—of human living takes place in relationships, in imitation (not usually acknowledged) of the triune God, where the essence of each Person is (in a venerable Latin theological expression) *esse ad*—literally, "being toward," that is, in relation to the others. Similarly, our earthly existence makes sense only in relation to God, to other humans, and to the earth (nonhuman creation). Here is that threefold relationship again, in somewhat different language.

Even on the legendary desert isle, I do not exist in solitary splendor. Know it or not, like it or not, God and I are in relationship. As long as I live, God and I are related as Creator to creature, the Maker to the made, the Artist and the work of art. It is simply God's presence. Not a static presence; God active, at work like a laborer, Ignatius Loyola said, in all that exists. Scholastic philosophy called it God's continuing creation. Besides God's ceaseless activity in all that exists, there is the kinship between God and those who love His Son: "Whoever loves me will keep my word, and my Father will love him, and we will come to him and make our dwelling with him" (Jn 14:23).

There is the relationship of Christ the Head to the members of his Body, the Church. For many, there is the presence of Christ within the believer in Communion: "This is my body, which will be given for you. This cup is the new covenant in my blood, which will be shed for you" (Lk 22:19-20). What the Pauline Second Letter to Timothy says of Jesus is true of God: "If we are unfaithful, he remains faithful, for he cannot deny himself" (2 Tim 2:13).

Second, know it or not, like it or not, we humans exist in a basic relationship with one another that cannot be broken. We are children of God, images of God no matter how flawed, sisters and brothers by creation and redemption. In the context of Leviticus, "You shall love your neighbor as yourself" (Lev 19:18) is restricted to fellow countrymen; but Jesus extended the meaning of Leviticus, not only through the Parable of the Good Samaritan but explicitly in the Sermon on the Mount. "You have heard that it was said, 'You shall love your neighbor and hate your enemy.' But I say to you, love your enemies, and pray for those who persecute you, that you may be children of your heavenly Father; for He makes His sun rise on the bad and the good, and causes rain to fall on the just and the unjust" (Mt 5:43-45). And the Christian approach is for ever enshrined in the lapidary injunction of Jesus, "This I command you: Love one another" (Jn 15:17). And not in some vague fashion. "As I have loved you, so you also shall love one another" (Jn 13:34). Love as Jesus loved.

Third, whatever we touch on God's earth, in God's nonhuman creation, we are to handle it with reverence. We are not despots, do not have unlimited power over created reality; we are God's representatives. And for a Catholic Christian, our responsibility for the earth and all it holds is an essential part of our faith.

The principles are reasonably clear; the problems surge up when the principles confront earthly reality. I mean the real God of everyday existence, often hidden, always mysterious; real people of flesh and blood, of different colors; different presuppositions and prejudices; the air we breathe and the soil we sow, the roads we walk and the trees we grow, the water we drink and the food we eat. To all this I shall address myself in the second section, aware of my own inadequacy, yet hoping to cast some rays of light on relationships as they are and as they ought to be.

I I

JUSTICE APPLIED

Back in September of 1999, during a telephone conversation with good friend Presbyterian William Johnston Wiseman of Tulsa, Oklahoma, he recalled a remarkable quotation from Emil Brunner, "Love is justice passed around." Instantly I felt that those five words could serve as a preliminary summary of this section, "Justice Applied." Specifically because biblical justice is fidelity to three relationships of love: for God, for God's people, for God's good earth.

From a Judeo-Christian perspective, it is hardly possible to transcend the human relationship to God expressed in "the greatest and first commandment" of the law and the gospel, "You shall love the Lord your God with all your heart, and with all your soul, and with all your mind, and with all your strength" (Deut 6:5; Mt 22:37-38).

Praise and thanks—such is an expression of love that echoes and re-echoes through the Prior Testament and the New. Again and again the Psalmist commands God's people, "Praise the Lord!"

> I will bless the Lord at all times;
>   praise shall be always in my mouth.
> My soul will glory in the Lord
>   that the poor may hear and be glad.
> Magnify the Lord with me;
>   let us exalt His name together.
>   (Ps 34:2-4)

Gratitude as well:

> You changed my mourning into dancing;
>   you took off my sackcloth.
>   and clothed me with gladness.
> With my whole being I sing

endless praise to you.
O Lord, my God,
forever will I give you thanks.
(Ps 30:12-13)

Such is the love newly pregnant Mary of Nazareth declared in her Magnificat, the outburst "My soul proclaims the greatness of the Lord" (Lk 1:46)—the same prayer of praise that reveals the justice of God, who is merciful to those who fear him and disperses the arrogant, brings down the powerful and lifts up the lowly, fills the hungry with good things and sends the rich away empty.

Such is the just love the Eucharist re-enacts and commends: the love that brought God's unique Son to wear our flesh and walk our earth. The love that he expressed so simply and so profoundly, "I do not seek my own will but the will of the One who sent me" (Jn 5:30). The love that prostrated him in a garden begging his Father not to let him die: "My Father, if it is possible, let this cup pass from me; yet not as I will, but as you will" (Mt 26:39). The love that transformed a shameful cross into a mute cry for forgiveness. Here, in our flesh and blood, is God's fidelity to God's promises, God's own Justice, the Suffering Servant to whom the Church applies God's words to Israel:

Here is my servant whom I uphold,
    my chosen one with whom I am pleased,
Upon whom I have put my spirit;
    he shall bring forth justice to the nations,
Not crying out, not shouting,
    Not making his voice heard in the street.
A bruised reed he shall not break,
    and a smoldering wick he shall not quench;
Until he establishes justice on the earth;
    the coastlands will wait for his teaching.
(Isa 42:1-4)

All well and good. Still, biblical justice is not exhausted in the first commandment of the law and the gospel. A second commandment, Jesus insisted, "is like" the first: "You shall love your neighbor as yourself" (Mt 22:39). The "neighbor"? Not simply the man or woman next door, not only someone I like. Jesus' story of the wounded Jew and the schismatic Samaritan who had compassion on him (Lk 10:29-37) is pertinent here. On the one hand, the parable answers by implication the lawyer's question, "Who is my neighbor?" Your neighbor is anyone in need with whom you come in contact. On the other hand, Jesus takes the lawyer's question and turns it on its head: "Which of these three [priest, Levite, Samaritan], do you think, was a neighbor to the man who fell into the hands of the robbers?" Jesus says in effect: "Don't ask about who belongs to God's people and thus is the object of my neighborly affection, but rather ask about the conduct incumbent upon a member of God's chosen people. . . . Because he did the law, the outcast Samaritan shows that he is a neighbor, a member of God's people, one who inherits eternal life."[1]

In a Christian perspective, the neighbor is my "fellow man," every man and woman and child, each human, each brother and sister—yes, enemy as well as friend. Especially the human in need. Here we confront the so-called "preferential option for the poor." The formula did indeed originate within Latin American liberation theology, but it has put its stamp on various levels of the Catholic magisterium. Suggested at the second meeting of the Latin American episcopate at Medellín, Colombia, in 1968, and explicitly adopted during its third meeting in Puebla, Mexico, in 1979, it has been solidly endorsed by John Paul II. It does not glorify poverty, does not canonize the poor. It does involve a new way of viewing the reality wherein we live, seeing it not from the standpoint of the powerful and the comfortable but from the perspective of the powerless and the pressured; a new way of reading Scripture, with a preference for those whom Jesus himself favored.

And who were they? One unexpectedly enchanted evening I discovered them in very human terms; I read Mark's Gospel from beginning to end. There were the varied afflictions Jesus healed: the unclean spirits and the fever; the leprosy and the paralysis; the withered hand and the sightless eyes, the ears that could not hear and the tongue that would not speak; the hemorrhage of 12 long years. There were the powerless and the marginalized, the downtrodden and the forgotten: the tax collectors and sinners with whom he ate; the crowds of ordinary folk he called his brothers, his sisters, his mother; the hungry thousands he fed with word and bread in a deserted place; the poor widow who put into the treasury all she had to live on; the woman who poured a costly ointment on his head, to the scandal of the diners. Yes, the lovable but mixed-up disciples who could not understand why he had to make his way to hostile Jerusalem, could not watch one hour with him in his agony, abandoned him almost without exception when he needed them most.

All these I presume to list under "the poor," whatever their economic condition.[2] The poor are all those on whose behalf the Lord God castigated His chosen people through the prophets:

> Put away your misdeeds from before my eyes;
>   cease doing evil; learn to do good.
> Make justice your aim; redress the wronged,
>   hear the orphan's plea, defend the widow.
>   (Isa 1:16-17)

Who are the similarly poor in our time, the oppressed, those who cry aloud or mutely for justice human and/or divine? What are some of the categories I see as highly critical areas of injustice as we move into the third millennium?

Children

As I write, the most vulnerable in our country are the children. In the United States the younger you are, the poorer you are. With apologies to the Children's Defense Fund, I am transferring the vivid imagery it used of America's "fifth child" in *The State of America's Children Yearbook 2000* to the current problem of America's "sixth child"—one of every six children grows up poor.

I am asking you to imagine a wealthy family with six children. Five of the six are fed three times a day with nourishing food, sleep in warm, comfortable rooms; the sixth is sent to school hungry, sleeps in a cold room or on the streets or in a temporary shelter. Five get regular medical checkups, all the customary shots, immediate attention when illness strikes; the sixth is plagued by chronic infections and respiratory diseases. Five are read to at night by father or mother; the sixth watches TV. Five go to good, safe schools, with books, computers, laboratories, science equipment, and well-trained teachers; the sixth is sent to crumbling school buildings, with ceilings peeling, asbestos in the paint, few books, teachers inadequate in number and training. Five engage in sports, music, and arts enrichment after school hours, attend summer camps; the sixth hangs out with his friends on the street or returns to an empty home.

All would agree that such a family is dysfunctional. Should not the same word characterize the United States where its children are concerned?

A number of other sobering facts. Among industrialized countries
the United States ranks number one in military technology, military
exports, Gross Domestic Product, the number of millionaires and bil-
lionaires, health technology, and defense expenditures; ranks sixteenth in living standards among our poorest one-fifth of children,
sixteenth in efforts to lift children out of poverty, eighteenth in the gap
between rich and poor children, twenty-second in infant mortality,
ranks last in protecting our children against gun violence. I am no
longer surprised that, as children's expert Sylvia Hewlett remarked in
an interview with *Time* magazine some years ago, in the United States
there are greater tax benefits for breeding horses than for producing
children.

To invest statistics with flesh and blood, to picture what poverty
does to the mind of a child, let me introduce you to little Peter. His
iron is low, and that slows his ability to solve problems, distracts his
attention, keeps him from concentrating. His growth has been
stunted, and so he scores lower than others on several tests of academic ability. His family has had to move again and again, and this has
disrupted his schooling, even made him drop out for a while. Cold,
dampness, mold, allergies cause all sorts of respiratory diseases such
as asthma, even take him from school. Crowding at home and accompanying stress interfere with his homework. In his home water is leak-
ing, paint is peeling, plaster is falling, lead is poisoning. He attends
one of the poorest inner-city schools, and so his level of achievement
is lower than that of a friend in a suburban school with the latest in
machines and the best in teachers. His parents cannot afford to buy
him exciting books and magazines, maps and encyclopedias, a computer. He has several responsibilities at home: younger siblings to care
for, a job 20 hours a week to help the family eat. When college beck-
ons, he simply will not be able to pay for it, even with financial assistance from the institution.[3]

Not irrelevant to the United States is Malachy McCourt's powerful
recollection of growing up in poverty in Limerick:

> I did not like being damp all the time. I did not like being cold
> and wet in the winter. I did not like looking in windows of shops
> filled with meats sweets biscuits breads, and my eyes bulging, the
> mouth aching for the chance to chew on something substantial.
> I did not like being eaten by fleas, gorging themselves on my bit-
> ter blood. I did not like having lice and nits in my hair my arse
> my armpits my eyebrows and every seam of the trousers and

gansey I wore. I didn't like the boils and pimples on my small epidermis, not to mention the shame of scabies and ringworm. I didn't like having badly patched clothes and broken boots that Van Gogh would have sneered at. I didn't like having caked shit in my trousers because they couldn't be washed for the want of a replacement to wear while they were drying. I didn't like being made fun of and sneered at by the upper classes, who had tea and buns in the afternoon and electric light in every room.

I have never liked the smell of the newly made, newly varnished coffins that were brought in to take away our dead forever.[4]

Pertinent to the problem is a political reality: The children have no lobby of any consequence, no influence with Congress. Guns have a powerful lobby; so too capital gains; so too tobacco; but not our children. How different things would be if each of 16 million poor children had a vote!

Preaching on poverty, I have often expressed a dream of mine. Imagine every family with a fair share of this world's goods adopting one poor child. Not legal adoption. Rather a consistent effort to ensure that one specific child personally known will have one need supplied. It might be one nutritious meal each week; or a warm jacket; or a pair of Nike shoes; or a set of the *World Book Encyclopedia;* or a space heater; or a paint job on peeling walls; or a dinner for the family in your home; information on Head Start, on insurance, on available funds; or simply a shoulder on which to rest. I admit, it takes not only imagination but courage. To lessen the peril of aloneness, of singularity, it would help if a whole parish were to organize so precious a project. You know, were a dream like this to catch fire, it could transform this country now sixteenth among industrialized nations in its efforts to lift children out of poverty. Small beginnings, like Habitat for Humanity, can grow like the Gospel's mustard seed.

Another remarkable defender of the poor was Brazilian Archbishop Helder Pessoa Camera of Olinda and Recife, who died of cancer August 7, 1999, at the age of ninety. His passionate advocacy of land reform and human rights in the impoverished northeastern Brazil archdiocese from 1964 to 1985 earned him death threats and the lasting enmity of the military then in power. "When I feed the poor," he once said, "I'm called a saint. When I ask why the poor have no food, I'm called a communist."

Dom Helder lived the life of the poor he loved. For 35 years before his death he lived in a single back room of the Church of the Frontiers in Olinda. It had for furnishings a sink, a little stove, a table, and for his bed a hammock hung from the ceiling. More than any other Latin American Church figure of his time, he symbolized the fight for human rights and the effort to get the Church in the political, economic, and social struggles of the poor. Nonviolent social change was his dream—that and the participation of the poor in the decision making of Brazil.

Nor is Brazil unique. In an address at Saint Joseph's University, Philadelphia (probably early in 1997), Xavier Gorstiage, S.J., rector of the Central American University of Managua, Nicaragua, claimed that in both Central America and Africa people today experience quality-of-life levels that are lower than those 500 years ago in the same areas. The greatest scandal of our age, he said, is that more than 70 percent of the women, men, and children in Central America live in poverty and 50 percent in economic misery, and these percentages rise yearly. This scandal, he said, shouts out to us that something is "profoundly wrong and sinful in our civilization."[5]

The Elderly

As one who has surpassed the Psalmist's prediction, "Seventy is the sum of our years, or eighty, if we are strong" (Ps 90:10), I am increasingly concerned about justice as it touches the elderly. Here a question of attitude is all-important. I mean the way our American culture looks at aging and the aged, in contrast to other cultures.

What we Americans stress is youth, strength, beauty. It reveals itself in most of our advertising and commercials; in the space and time allotted to sports; in the "Style" section of newspapers. The wrinkled, the weak, the unattractive claim our attention ordinarily in obits, crises, accidents, December/June nuptials. Some of the aging are indeed celebrities—Paul Newman and Sophia Loren, Pope John Paul II and Maya Angelou, Nelson Mandela and Sargent Shriver—but in some measure because they do not *seem* to age.

Where lies the injustice? First, in an American attitude. Growing old is synonymous with retiring. And to retire is to be literally useless. The elderly rarely "do" anything, certainly little that is useful. Americans tend to "put up with" the oft-repeated stories of the old folks, of grandparents. "There he goes again . . . the good old days."

To be just to the aging, to be faithful to a whole set of relationships, it would help us to recall how the attitude to the elderly in other cultures differs significantly from ours. For southern Ghana's Akans, knowledge is power, but aging is wisdom—a wisdom that calls for reverence, for respect. In the Native American tradition, to honor the aging is to have life and wisdom. To Confucius, respect for elders is the supreme principle of morality, for it can define the very meaning of our being in the world, is a powerful binding force for stable society, is a source of world peace and order. The Hindu tradition stresses not the physical weakness and disabilities of the elderly, but their spiritual maturity and wisdom, models of an authentic human life serving all humanity disinterestedly. How keen of Buddhists to regard aging not as diminishment but as increase, a movement toward fuller life.

In a special way, we need to utilize the Hebrew Testament and rabbinic reflection thereon. The elderly transmit their experience of the past not as sheer knowledge but as a living witness to God's presence. Because life is a gift of God and all moments of life are equally sacred, the period of deterioration in aging demands special concern to preserve life with dignity. Aging can mean growth, celebration, fresh experience of God's presence. We need to recapture Abraham Joshua Heschel's insight, that the elderly need not only recreation but a vision, not only a memory but a dream. And his startling reminder, "Just to be is a blessing, just to live is holy."[6]

In one sense I am uncommonly fortunate. At 89 I no longer have to pretend. Bones become brittle, oxygen reaches the heart more slowly, and sauerkraut makes for diarrhea. All the more reason to be a living witness to God's presence.

In the context of biblical justice, the Christian will not accept the more classical idea that adult maturity is a finished state, that at a certain point, at the peak of physical and intellectual manhood or womanhood you are the complete person, you have it made, you have reached perfection. Nor will the Christian accept our American culture's conviction that as you grow older, you have less and less to give, are less and less a person. No, life is an endless pilgrimage. The perfection of a Christian is total conformity to the humanness of Christ—and that is a ceaseless process, never achieved here below.

In the process two words are of high importance, words that at first glance seem mutually exclusive: kenosis and growth. Essential to the pilgrimage is a kenosis, literally an "emptying," similar to the "self-emptying" of Jesus (Phil 2:7). For the journeying to go forward, I have to let go—let go of where I've been, let go of the level of life where I am now, so as to live more fully. Whether it's turning 21, 40, or 65, whether it's losing my health or my hair, my looks or my lustiness, my money or my memory, a person I love or a possession I prize; whether it's yesterday's applause or today's rapture; whether it's as fleeting as Malibu's surf or as abiding as God's grace—I have to move on. And to let go is to die a little. It's painful, it can be bloody; and so we hang on, we clutch our yesterdays like Linus' blanket, we refuse to grow.

But what is it that we the aging are growing into? All of us, believer and unbeliever alike, can grow into love. A quieter love, of course, perhaps without the passion of yesterday; but surely richer, possibly deeper, because mellowed by every face I've seen or touched, softened from the anger and fear of yesteryear, more understanding of difference and diversity, more tolerant of the sinner in all of us. A love that has learned to listen, learned to forgive. A love that, in the perception of St. Paul, "is patient and kind, not jealous or pompous, not arrogant or rude, does not seek its own interests, is not quick-tempered, does not brood over injury, does not rejoice over wrongdoing but rejoices with the truth" (1 Cor 13:4-6).

For Christians, it is our living faith that concretizes this love. As a Christian, my burden and my glory are to grow into Christ. Kenosis, self-emptying, is not its own end. I let go because only by letting go can I grow gradually into Christ, come to be conformed to his dying and rising, fashioned to his passion and resurrection. It is in this way that I reach oneness, not with abstract transcendence but with Someone transcendent, with the triune personal Love we call God. The "eternal life" that Jesus said consists in "knowing the true God and the one [He] sent, Jesus Christ" (Jn 17:3) is not primarily intellectual; it connotes immediate experience and intimacy. It involves a loving communion with God, with God's human images on earth, with every work of God's hands. In a word, God's justice.

Aging and the losses of aging often press kenosis, letting go, to its nadir, its low point. Loss is heaped on loss, even at times indignity upon indignity—social and psychic, physical and intellectual. Like Christ, I am stripped naked, for all the world to see—if it cares to look. What is left is not what I have achieved or amassed; what is left is who I am. Linked to the cross of Christ with torturous nails, the person with Alzheimer's is still an image of God, in a special way an image of the crucified Christ. With my mental faculties reasonably alert at 89, I am differently graced: Life can still delight me, people of all ages can still turn me on, injustice anger me, love leave me aglow. Now, perhaps more than ever before, I am aware that it is "Christ who lives in me" (Gal 2:20).

What does biblical justice demand of our culture? Respect for the aged and care for the aged. Not because we have discovered that they form a powerful voting bloc. Rather because "just to be is a blessing." Because they are the source of our life, cocreators with God. Because they are living witnesses to God's presence—if we have eyes to see. It is a caustic commentary on our culture when the aged are made to feel they are a burden on the economy; when men and women languish in nursing homes hoping their children will spend one hour with them; when life-preserving medicines are beyond their ability to pay; when life has no longer any meaning because there is no longer anyone who cares. Skewed relationships indeed; for even though God is always there, I suspect that, with the exception of certain saints, "God alone" fails to satisfy our very human yearning, our just desire, to be loved.

Immigrants

A somewhat unexpected arrival on the justice scene. To see the immigration issue in the context of God's justice, I suggest three stages for profound reflection: the people of Israel, Jesus the Christ, and our American situation.

The people of Israel began as nomads.[7] Simply to survive, they had to move from one place to another—migration after migration, until they found themselves in Egypt. Not of their own will, they were slaves for a good century, from about 1300 to 1200 B.C.E. This period of enslavement was characterized by suffering, persecution, agonizing toil. It was followed by the unexpected Exodus from Egypt, a divine liberation that was not only "freedom from" but "freedom for." Freedom from slavery indeed, but even more importantly, freedom to fashion a contrasting society, a community in sharp divergence from oppressive Egypt, a community characterized by compassion, enlivened by love. Entrance into the Promised Land sealed this movement into a people, for this land was God's own gift to Israel. And yet, twice more Israel suffered domination, much of the population driven into exile, first to Assyria (722 B.C.E.), then to Babylon (587 B.C.E.). "This agitated history of enslavement, exile, and domination explains the Israelites' attitude toward all strangers who attempt to dominate, and one of openness and hospitality toward the foreign immigrant because they themselves had experienced that same situation."[8]

Actually, as Carolyn Osiek has pointed out, the relationship between citizen and resident alien was not, strictly speaking, a question of hospitality, which had to do with guests and was directed by different rules.[9] Here it was treatment of non-Israelites living in Israelite territory. This treatment clearly fell under biblical justice, specifically right relationships to people, that stemmed from a covenant with Yahweh. Two powerful texts from the Torah summarize the prevailing legislation, the ideal attitude. "You shall not oppress an alien; you well know how it feels to be an alien, since you were once aliens yourselves in the land of Egypt" (Exod 23:9; see 22:21). Over and above not oppressing, "You too must befriend [love] the alien, for you were once aliens yourselves in the land of Egypt" (Deut 10:19; see 24:17). What lay behind such ordinances? The land actually is God's; all humans, even Israelites, are aliens. "The land is mine; and you are but aliens who have become my tenants" (Lev 25:23). In God's view, theologically, Israel was an alien, a permanent resident alien dwelling in the land of Yahweh, in a land that was not its own.

Although there are indications that resident aliens were often mistreated, they were granted equal rights with the Israelites before the law. Said Moses to the judges, "Listen to complaints among your kinsmen, and administer true justice to both parties even if one of them is an alien" (Deut 1:16). It seems that the resident aliens were not bound to military service, although they could hire themselves out as mercenary soldiers. Despite only limited rights to land ownership, it was possible for them to become wealthy. Immigrants could not take part in the deliberations of the assembly, whether clan, tribe, or city. They were obliged to follow the Israelite laws of sexual morality: "Whether natives or resident aliens, you must keep my statutes and decrees forbidding all such abominations by which the previous inhabitants defiled the land" (Lev 18:26-27).

Even though nonoppression of the stranger, and love besides, were guaranteed by law, behind the law lay the covenant, "the Lord of lords, the great God, mighty and awesome, who has no favorites, accepts no bribes; who executes justice for the orphan and the widow, and befriends [loves] the alien, feeding and clothing him" (Deut 10:17-18). Behind the law was the Lord who dealt thus with Israel when the people were aliens, strangers, in a hostile land.

Move now to Jesus the Christ, his approach to the stranger. To a Samaritan woman coming to draw water at a well in Samaria Jesus says, "Give me a drink" (Jn 4:7). It is difficult to exaggerate how unusual, how unexpected, how scandalous that request was. For one thing, this was foreign territory. True, Jews as well as foreign colonists lived in the district called Samaria. But these Jews of the north and the Jews of the south were intensely at odds; for the Jews in Samaria refused to worship in Jerusalem. Recall the words of the woman to Jesus, "Our ancestors worshiped on this mountain [Gerizim], but you people say that the place to worship is in Jerusalem" (v. 20). Recall her response to his request for water: "How can you, a Jew, ask me, a Samaritan woman, for a drink?" And John adds tersely, "For Jews use nothing in common with Samaritans" (v. 9).

More startling than that, Jesus was speaking to a woman. Notice the reaction of his disciples when they returned from gathering supplies in town: "They were amazed [shocked] that he was talking with a woman" (v. 27). Apparently more shocked that he was talking with a woman than because he was talking with a Samaritan.

Pertinent here is a scene Luke records when Jesus had set his face toward Jerusalem and his destiny. He sent messengers ahead of him to make arrangements for his lodging. When they came to a village of the Samaritans, the villagers "would not welcome him because the destination of his journey was Jerusalem." It was then that James and John asked Jesus, "Lord, do you want us to call down fire from heaven to consume them?" (Lk 9:51-54). Not only did Jesus rebuke the sons of Zebedee (v. 55), the "sons of thunder" (Mk 3:17). In his parable of the man who fell among robbers on the way down from Jerusalem to Jericho, he proposed as an example of neighborly love, as neighbor to the half-dead Jew, not another Jew—a Samaritan. Recall, too, how Jesus cured ten lepers and the only leper who returned to fall at Jesus' feet in gratitude was a Samaritan. Jesus' reaction is sobering: "Ten were cleansed, were they not? Where are the other nine? Has none but this foreigner returned to give thanks to God?" And Jesus said to him, "Stand up and go; your faith has saved you" (Lk 17:11-19).

Scripture scholar John McKenzie put it bluntly almost four decades ago: "There was no deeper breach of human relations in the contemporary world than the feud of Jews and Samaritans, and the breadth and depth of Jesus' doctrine of love could demand no greater act of a Jew than to accept a Samaritan as a brother."[10] It is Jesus' approach to the foreigner, to the stranger, that in largest measure inspired the posture of the early Church. "The attitude of the primitive Church toward the foreigner was revolutionary, and the large number of foreigners who joined the community soon outnumbered the Jewish members."[11] Christians, Paul told the Ephesians, "are no longer strangers and sojourners [aliens], but fellow citizens with the holy ones and members of the household of God" (Eph 2:19). With reference to this present world, however, the First Letter of Peter declares that Christians, who are citizens of the kingdom of heaven, are "aliens and sojourners" here below (1 Pet 2:11; see 1 Pet 1:17).

Turn now to our American situation. Back in 1996 an *Atlantic Monthly* article by historian David M. Kennedy intrigued me. What first seduced me was its title, "Can We Still Afford To Be a Nation of Immigrants?"[12] What followed was a swift lesson on America and its immigrants.

Historically the United States "has benefited handsomely from its good fortune as an immigrant destination."[13] Over a century ago, in the proclamation that made Thanksgiving Day a national holiday, President Abraham Lincoln thanked God for having "largely augmented our free population by emancipation and by immigration."[14]

When Lincoln spoke, there were 42 million Americans and half the country remained to be settled. Today's (2000) population is 291 million and the country has developed beyond Lincoln's power to imagine. Since the passage of the Immigration and Nationality Act of 1965, some 20 million immigrants have entered the United States. Two sets of questions that engaged historian Kennedy are equally pertinent today: (1) Why did people migrate to America in the past, and what were the consequences? (2) Why are people migrating to America today, and what might be the consequences?

Why migration in the past? There is the standard explanation: Immigrants were "noble souls," early- and mid-nineteenth century, mainly from northern and western Europe, "tugged by the lodestone of American opportunity, whose talents and genius and love of liberty account for the magnificent American character." A radically different explanation has the "new" immigrants, mostly from northern and western Europe, regarded as "degraded, freeloading louts, a blight on the national character—the kind of people described all too literally . . . by Emma Lazarus's famous inscription on the base of the Statue of Liberty: 'your tired, your poor . . . the wretched refuse of your teeming shore.'"[15]

Kennedy found these views inadequate as explanations of the movement of 35 million over the course of a century. Essential to movement on such a scale was *disruption*. Two convulsively disruptive developments had their historical dynamic within the context not of American but of European history: population growth and the Industrial Revolution. In the nineteenth century the population of Europe more than doubled, from some 200 million to more than 400 million, "a product of aspects of European historical evolution, especially improvements in diet, sanitation, and disease control."[16] The Industrial Revolution shook people loose from traditional ways of life: "in the typical transitional phase some workers who had left artisanal or agricultural employments could not be reabsorbed domestically in European cities. Thus they migrated overseas."[17]

An intriguing question: How did tens of millions of newcomers manage to accommodate themselves to America, and America to them, without more social disruption? How did American society make space so rapidly for so many people? Not, in Kennedy's view, wise social policy. Rather, three specific historical circumstances, taken together, go a long way toward answering the question. (1) For all their numbers, immigrants never made up a very large component of turn-of-the-century America. The census of 1910 records the highest percentage of foreign-born people ever resident in the United States: 14.7 percent, a decided minority. Here, then, is one circumstance accounting for the relative lack of social conflict. (2) Immigrants supplied the labor a growing economy demanded, and economic growth allowed the accommodation of newcomers without forcing the thorny questions of redistribution. (3) Pluralism: cultural, religious, national, linguistic—with wide geographical and political distribution. The states with the most immigrants had per capita incomes higher than the national average. Two crucial implications: (1) No immigrant group could realistically aspire to preserve its Old World culture intact for more than a few generations. (2) Neither any single immigrant group nor immigrants as a whole could realistically mount any kind of effective challenge to the existing society's way of doing things, for example, to dictate a new political order.

What is the new reality in immigration? Its sources: Latin America and Asia. Still, most of the countries now sending large numbers to the United States "are undergoing the same convulsive and economic disruptions that made migrants out of so many nineteenth-century Europeans: population growth and the relatively early stages of their own industrial revolutions."[18]

Take Mexico, the leading supplier of immigrants to the United States. Since World War II Mexico's population has more than tripled, touching off heavy internal migration, from rural to urban areas. Inmigration from countryside to Mexico City is estimated at a thousand a day. Since World War II the Mexican economy has grown at double the average rate, with rapid industrialization and widespread commercialization of agriculture. The "green revolution" has exacerbated the usual disruptions: depopulation of the countryside, urban in-migration, and movement across the national border. Since 1970 (into 1996) some five million Mexicans have moved to the United States; probably more than ten million have moved to Mexico City alone.

Can we still afford to be a nation of immigrants? (1) From numbers alone, says Kennedy, yes. The Census Bureau reports that as of 1994 the foreign-born represented 8.7 percent of the American population—just a little more than half the 1910 proportion. Surely the United States is resourceful enough to deal with an inflow proportionally half what it handled quite successfully early in the twentieth century. (2) From the needs and vitality of the economy, the issue is more complicated. After analyzing the complex factors, Kennedy concluded that, on balance, today's low-skill immigrants as a group make a positive economic contribution. It is no accident, he claimed, that today's immigrants are concentrated in the richest states (e.g., California), just as those of the 1920s were. Immigrants are not parasites on the "native" economy but participants therein. Most come for work, and most find it.

If the conclusion of a study by Stanford economist Clark W. Reynolds is correct—that "Mexico [the principal contributor of immigrants] and the United States need each other: the one to ease pressure on its employment markets, the other to find sufficient labor to sustain acceptable levels of economic growth"—then, said Kennedy, his original question may be wrongly put. The proper question may be, Can we afford *not* to be a nation of immigrants?

At this point we draw near to problems of justice. In spring 2000, Hispanics composed 28 percent of Texas, about 31 percent of California. It is now estimated that soon after the year 2050 non-Hispanic whites may form a minority of our population. And so, as I criss-crossed the country with my project Preaching the Just Word, I found controversy raging: Is the new migration actually doing harm to our economy? Is unskilled labor taking jobs from natives? And what will it do to our culture, our politics, our American way of life? As for Catholic Christians, we are already experiencing how difficult it is to merge Hispanics and Anglo Americans into a parish that is a single, well-knit, loving community. Not to mention the Vietnamese and the Koreans. On a somewhat humorous note, I am told that one of the serious problems in the construction of the new Catholic cathedral in Los Angeles was the question, How do we fit 40 or more Madonnas into one church structure?

A brief, if inadequate, word on the economics of immigration, which cannot be divorced from the issue of justice.[19] A new debate on immigration has been focusing on illegal immigrants and on welfare benefits to legal immigrants. Granted, economic factors should not and cannot decide the debate; still, economics raises important questions: Who gains? Who loses? In light of the answers, what should our immigration policy be?

In the 1920s the United States established a quota system on the basis of national origin that favored Germany and the United Kingdom. After its repeal in 1965, entry visas were granted mainly to applicants who had relatives already residing in the United States. In consequence, the number of immigrants rose rapidly. Whereas in the 1950s only about 250,000 entered the United States annually, by the 1990s more than 800,000 were admitted each year and some 300,000 entered and stayed illegally. What does economic research suggest for U.S. immigration policy, on the number to be admitted and the kinds of people to be admitted?

Some new perceptions. (1) The relative skills of successive immigrant waves have declined over much of the postwar period. (2) The earnings of the newest arrivals may never reach parity with the earnings of natives. (3) The large-scale migration of less-skilled workers has done harm to the economic opportunities of less-skilled natives. (4) The new immigrants are more likely to receive welfare assistance than earlier immigrants, and also more likely to do so than natives. (5) The increasing welfare dependency in the immigrant population may lay a substantial fiscal burden on the most-affected localities and states. (6) There are economic benefits (though small) from immigration, because certain skills they bring complement those of the native population.

A difficult question: Whose interests should U.S. immigration policy serve—natives, immigrants, the rest of the world affected by our policy, or all three? "The three groups may have conflicting interests, and economics cannot tell us whose interests matter most. The weight that we attach to each of the three groups depends on our values and ideology."[20]

How many and whom should we admit? Few mainstream studies have attempted to explore, purely on the basis of empirical evidence, how many immigrants should be admitted. Still, "a good case can be made for linking immigration to the business cycle: admit more immigrants when the economy is strong and the unemployment rate is low, and cut back on immigration when the economy is weak and the unemployment rate is high."[21]

> Economic research teaches a very valuable lesson: the economic impact of immigration is essentially distributional. Current immigration redistributes wealth from unskilled workers, whose wages are lowered by immigrants, to skilled workers and owners of companies that buy immigrants' services, and from taxpayers who bear the burden of paying for the social services used by immigrants to consumers who use the goods and services provided by immigrants. . . . The debate over immigration policy is not a debate over whether the entire country is made better off by immigration—the gains from immigration seem much too small, and could even be outweighed by the costs of providing increased social services. Immigration changes how the economic pie is sliced up—and this fact goes a long way toward explaining why the debate over how many and what kinds of immigrants to admit is best viewed as a tug-of-war between those who gain from immigration and those who lose from it. . . . Although the pendulum seems to be swinging to the restrictionist side, a greater danger to the national interest may be the few economic groups that gain much from immigration. They seem indifferent to the costs that immigration imposes on other segments of society. . . . In the short run these groups may simply delay the day of reckoning. Their potential long-run impact, however, is much more perilous: the longer the delay, the greater the chances that when immigration policy finally changes, it will undergo a seismic shift—one that, as in the twenties, may come close to shutting down the borders and preventing Americans from enjoying the benefits that a well-designed immigration policy can bestow on the United States.[22]

Without pretending to solve an immensely complex issue, let me develop two aspects of the problem: a Christlike attitude to the immigrant and a distressing fact within U.S. immigration policy.

I call the attitude Christlike because it comes close to the way Jesus dealt with the Samaritan woman at Jacob's well (Jn 4:5-42). My own meditation made for a powerful, provocative, at times humorous reflection as I experienced it and preached it in the capital city of our nation.

First, I don't have to *like* today's immigrants, be they from Mexico or El Salvador, from Vietnam or the Philippines. Nothing in the Gospel story suggests that Jesus liked the lady, this stranger at the well. Still, in his eyes she was a person, a woman, human, human as he was. Even more importantly, she had been shaped by God, shaped in the image and likeness of her Creator, gifted with intelligence and freedom, with a mind to know and a heart to love. And, for all her faults and fragility, she was still an image, a reflection, of God. Somewhat misshapen, like the rest of us, but still awfully precious in God's eyes, in Jesus' eyes. I ask myself: Is that the way I eye the immigrant, eye each immigrant?

Second, I don't have to *agree* with the immigrant, praise the legal immigrant's initiative, applaud the illegal alien's cleverness in crossing our borders. I may even vote, for serious reasons, to limit the number of legal immigrants. What in biblical and Christian justice I may *not* do is simply turn my back on them, take out my frustrations (as some legislators have done) on the children of the alien, refuse them medical care. Jesus held no brief for the Samaritan woman's lifestyle, told her frankly that her adventures in marriage were a farce. Yet he never said, "Skip the drink, lady; your hands are unclean"; he never made this a pretext for disowning her.

Third, it is the Christian's task, the Christian's privilege, to *reach out* to the stranger in trouble, the despised and the downtrodden, the bedeviled and the bewildered, the lonely and the unloved—the immigrant. Jesus took the initiative, the first step, with the Samaritan woman. It was he who started the conversation; *he* asked *her* for water—even though his disciples would be shocked to find him talking to a woman in a public place. I may not on principle wait for the stranger to make the first move. The age-old Christian virtue called "hospitality" is not primarily coffee and doughnuts after the Sunday service; it is the warm hand of welcome to the stranger, to those who are different, to those who do not look, talk, smell as I do.

Fourth, I dare not forget that the *gift I bring* to the stranger is not simply bread or water, a peanut-butter-and-jelly sandwich or a glass of sparkling Burgundy. Think back on Jesus. In return for the Samaritan woman's graciousness, her willingness to give a cup of cold water to a traditional enemy, he held out to her a promise, "living water," "a spring of water gushing up to eternal life" (Jn 4:10, 14), the Holy Spirit to refresh and quicken her sluggish spirit. The welcome I give to a stranger, to an immigrant, may well be the prelude to God's grace.

God's way of using my very ordinary humanness to draw down light, strength, courage, and peace into a struggling human frame—even beyond the individual in front of me. Somewhat as one fascinating conversation turned the Samaritan woman from sinner to apostle, apostle to the people in her town, so too for me. It's Presbyterian novelist and preacher Frederick Buechner's inspired insight: Humanity is like a gigantic spider web. Touch it anywhere and the whole thing trembles. For as we move about our world, a kind word here, an ugly act there, what we do for good or ill will touch this person, this person will touch another person, and so on and on, until who knows where the whole thing ends. No man, no woman, is an island. Might not the pre-Christian writer Terence serve as inspiration for today's Christian? "Naught that is human is alien to me."

Regrettably, U.S. Catholics have a checkered record on immigration. "The history of the Catholic Church in the United States is one of immigrant people creating a new spiritual home for themselves while seeking to maintain links to their religious traditions. It is the story of outsiders becoming insiders and then failing to welcome those who come after them, a process that repeats itself again and again with each succeeding group."[23] Witness the history of the Hmong in St. Paul, Minnesota; Puerto Ricans in New York and New Jersey; Mexicans in Texas; Japanese in California; African Americans in the South; Germans and Poles across our country.

Turn now to a distressing fact within U.S. immigration policy. I have in mind immigrants in detention. In 1999 there were 200,000 in varying lengths of detention; by the end of 2001, it was estimated, there would be over 302,000—not to mention the massive detentions that occurred after September 11. For lack of bed space in facilities owned and operated by the U.S. Immigration and Naturalization Service, 60 percent of detainees are currently housed in city and county jails. Once there, they are routinely housed with inmates held on criminal charges or those with criminal histories. In remote areas contact with attorneys is difficult, language always a problem. In San Pedro, California, a husband and wife were held in separate units for 16 months. Never were they allowed to visit each other or write directly. While in custody, they lost their home. Their three children, the oldest only 15, were left to fend for themselves in Los Angeles.

Listen to excerpts from a letter of a Jesuit friend of mine, Thomas L. Sheridan, retired professor of theology at St. Peter's College in Jersey City. He helps the Jesuit Refugee Service (JRS) with English and Bible classes in a detainee center in Elizabeth, New Jersey.

There are no windows; they never breathe fresh air or see the light of day except through one skylight. One woman has been there for almost three years. It would break your heart to see them. They have such a lost and hopeless look on their faces. . . .

When one of the English teachers failed to erase the board after her last class, the INS people interpreted this as disruptive of good order, canceled the English classes until further notice, and sent a monitor in to observe the Bible classes the following night. The Gospel reading for the following Sunday was Matthew 25:31ff., including "I was in prison and you visited me." The INS regarded this and some of the questions for reflection as disruptive. The Bible study was canceled too.

Subsequently, according to a volunteer with JRS, officials claimed that in programs like the Bible study and English classes JRS volunteers were creating a security problem by "offering unreasonable hope to detainees" and teaching them "to think on their own." But according to INS district director Andrea J. Quarantillo, the INS "has no objection to Matthew 25 or any other Bible passage and does not seek to censor them. We only request that detention issues not be included in the lesson plans." It is not my intention to condemn the INS; its task is monumental, its resources are limited, and even the perils from terrorism are never far away. I am simply convinced that when thousands of immigrants, many fleeing from persecution, are lodged with criminals, when years pass before good people are released from a detainment that is virtual imprisonment, sheer justice cries for improvement.

Pertinently, before me lies a copy of the *New York Times* from January 2, 2001. Descending column heads on the first page proclaim "Policy To Protect Jailed Immigrants Is Adopted by U.S.," "I.N.S. Acts To Halt Abuse," "Critics Say New Guidelines Fall Short of Resolving All Concerns for Detainees." In consequence of scores of complaints and lawsuits concerning the physical and mental abuse of immigrants detained in county jails and other detention centers, the new standards, covering everything from visiting policies to grievance procedures, propose to "provide safe, secure and humane conditions of detention for all aliens in I.N.S. custody." Still, "critics say the agency has fallen far short of that goal, especially in county jails in states like Louisiana, Texas, New Jersey and Florida, where detainees and their lawyers say inmates are beaten, solitary confinement is imposed for trivial offenses, and water and food are often inadequate." Advocates for immigrants claim that conditions may not improve because the new standards are not regulations, do not have the weight of law, and so could prove impossible to enforce, and would not allow legal challenges for lack of compliance. Further, the new standards do not address important issues such as the frequent transfers of detainees without the notification of their lawyers.

Immigration and Terrorism

Since September 11, 2001, immigration has attracted unparalleled attention, prodded fresh questioning. That morning terrorists from abroad crashed three hijacked American planes into the World Trade Center in New York City and the Pentagon near Washington, D.C., reducing to rubble the twin towers of America's business and setting aflame the symbol of America's military might. Fatalities, estimated early on as near or over six thousand, have more recently been lowered to below three thousand. Two years later, fear continues to hound much of the nation as the U.S. government wages war against agents of global terrorism, particularly suspected fundamentalist Islamic extremists, takes unprecedented security measures at airports, reports the loss of approximately 9.4 million jobs, and continues to find itself almost without clues about the source of anthrax attacks that not only contaminated postal offices and structures as massive as the Hart Senate Office Building but also took lives.

The critical issue of immigrant detention, exacerbated by September 11, leaves much to be resolved.[24] "The scope and terms of such detention are one of the sticking points in the antiterrorism legislation before Congress. Attorney General John Ashcroft favors broad powers to detain noncitizens indefinitely and remove them from the United States, while civil liberties advocates on both sides of the aisle urge a more calibrated approach."[25]

Punitive or Restorative Justice?

In this and the section that follows I am concerned, intellectually and emotionally, over two realities: life in prison and death in prison; incarceration and execution.

Life in Prison

Over two decades ago, Fr. Michael Bryant started as the District of Columbia jail's full-time minister. At that time he believed that the

U.S. justice system was fair, impartial, and balanced. After listening to thousands of men and women in that jail, he now recognizes that "our system of criminal justice is not fair, is not impartial, and is not balanced."[26] African Americans make up only 13 percent of our national population, Hispanics 9 or 10 percent; yet 48 percent in prison are black, 18 percent Hispanic. What do they have in common with the whites? They are poor, addicted, undereducated, and jobless. Our sentencing is more and more punitive: no more parole on the federal level, minimum-sentencing legislation, "three strikes and you're out" in California. Two-thirds return to prison: 70 percent of juveniles, 63 percent of adults. Listen to Pat Nolan, president of Justice Fellowship:

> I got a view of things after serving fifteen years in the California legislature. I also served 25 months in a federal penitentiary and four months in a halfway house. And I had a chance to see, first hand, the impact of the policies that I'd advocated as a legislator. God really took the scales from my eyes and I'm grateful for my time in prison, because he did expose me to what was going on.
>
> [The system is] horribly broken. We lock up two million Americans. That's one out of every 125 people in the United States of America. If you add parole and probation, the people who are on supervised release, that's six million. That's one out of every 42 Americans either directly behind the walls of a prison or with a probation or parole agent to whom they report. One in every 42. And yet victims aren't healed from their wounds. Our communities aren't any safer. The crime rate is down, but there's growing evidence that officials are "cooking the books," misreporting crimes to artificially drop it.[27]

Our criminal system is "horribly broken" on another level: the methods of all too many criminal investigations. A lead article in the *Sunday New York Times* for June 10, 2001, told the story of Michael S. Race, a detective-sergeant who retired in 1993 after serving during one of Brooklyn's bloodiest eras.[28] He had 750 murder cases behind him, had sent hundreds of handcuffed people into the criminal courts, usually, he admitted, after rushed investigations and often on the word of a single eyewitness—sometimes a lying informer or a crack addict seeking reward money. Only one of the 750 cases was "done the correct way, from A to Z." As a private investigator, after two years of digging, Race cleared two men, Anthony Faison and Charles Shepherd, who had spent 14 years in prison for murder, and led the authorities to a new suspect whose fingerprints had been found at the crime scene and never processed.

Not impertinent here is an added problem. On February 16, 2001, in Little Rock, Arkansas, for a weekend on justice with permanent deacons and their wives, I picked up the *Arkansas Democrat Gazette*. An article on the first page by Cathy Frye has for its column head "Prison firm can't afford to run units, calls it quits." Wachenhut Corrections Corp., the company operating the state's only two private prisons, simply could not afford maintaining the Grimes and McPherson units in Newport. "Most crippling were the unexpectedly high costs of caring for the state's entire female population. [O]ne woman cost the company more than $300,000 last year."

More troubling to me was the fact that Arkansas's Board of Correction and Community Punishment was already considering whether to turn the lockups over to the state. Why? Dangerous staffing shortages, unsanitary living conditions, poor maintenance, a lack of work and educational programs. "The units were dirty, broken or malfunctioning equipment was left in disrepair, women were deprived of underwear, their uniforms were shredded and rotting; inmates were not getting to their school classes or drug-abuse programs, close quarters and boredom were fuel for fights and other kinds of trouble." Not necessarily pervasive, and in this case largely a financial matter. Still, an indication of what is more likely to be tolerated when inmates are seen simply as criminals.

In the December 1998 issue of the *Atlantic Monthly* Eric Schlosser wrote a highly informative article on "The Prison-Industrial Complex."[29] The details are too many and too complex to be reproduced here, but three lengthy, closely packed paragraphs of Schlosser's summaries demand exact quotation.

Three decades after the war on crime began, the United States has developed a prison-industrial complex—a set of bureaucratic, political, and economic interests that encourage increased spending on imprisonment, regardless of the actual need. The prison-industrial complex is not a conspiracy, guiding the nation's criminal-justice policy behind closed doors. It is a confluence of special interests that has given prison construction in the United States a seemingly unstoppable momentum. It is composed of politicians, both liberal and conservative, who have used the fear of crime to gain votes, impoverished rural areas where prisons have become a cornerstone of economic development, private companies that regard the roughly $35 billion spent each year on corrections not as a burden on American taxpayers but as a lucrative market, and government officials whose fiefdoms have expanded along with the inmate population. Since 1991 the rate of violent crime in the United States has fallen by about 20 percent, while the number of people in prison or jail has risen by 50 percent. The prison boom has its own inexorable logic. Steven R. Donziger, a young attorney who headed the National Criminal Justice Commission in 1996, explains the thinking: "If crime is going up, then we need to build more prisons; and if crime is going down, it's because we built more prisons—and building even more prisons will therefore drive crime down even lower."

The raw material of the prison-industrial complex is its inmates: the poor, the homeless, and the mentally ill, drug dealers, drug addicts, alcoholics, and a wide assortment of violent sociopaths. About 70 percent of the prison inmates in the United States are illiterate. Perhaps 200,000 of the country's inmates suffer from a serious mental illness. A generation ago such people were handled primarily by the mental-health, not the criminal-justice, system. Sixty to 80 percent of the American inmate population has a history of substance abuse. Meanwhile, the number of drug-treatment slots in American prisons has declined by more than half since 1993. Drug treatment is now available to just one in ten of the inmates who need it. Among those arrested for violent crimes, the proportion who are African-American men has tripled. Although the prevalence of illegal drug use among white men is approximately the same as that among black men, black men are five times as likely to be arrested for a drug offense. As a result, about half the inmates in the United States are African-American. One out of every fourteen black men is now in prison or jail. One out of every four black men is likely to be imprisoned at some point during his lifetime. The number of women sentenced to a year or more of prison has grown twelvefold since 1970. Of the 80,000 women now imprisoned, about 70 percent are nonviolent offenders. About 75 percent have children.

The prison-industrial complex is not only a set of interest groups and institutions. It is also a state of mind. The lure of big money is corrupting the nation's criminal-justice system, replacing notions of public service with a drive for higher profits. The eagerness of elected officials to pass "tough-on-crime" legislation—combined with their unwillingness to disclose the true costs of these laws—has encouraged all sorts of financial improprieties. The inner workings of the prison-industrial complex can be observed in the state of New York, where the prison boom started, transforming the economy of an entire region; in Texas and Tennessee, where private prison companies have thrived; and in California, where the correctional trends of the past two decades have converged and reached extremes. In the realm of psychology a complex is an overreaction to some perceived threat. Eisenhower no doubt had that meaning in mind when, during his farewell address, he urged the nation to resist "a recurring temptation to feel that some spectacular and costly action could become the miraculous solution to all current difficulties."

Restorative Justice

Granted that the retributive model of justice—a model that punishes people, is based on vengeance and fosters nationwide corruption—is inadequate, even unjust. Is there another model? Recent years have witnessed a growing movement in America and abroad. It takes its rise from a conviction based on wide experience: The retributive system of justice is counterproductive. It does not rehabilitate, is enormously expensive, and leads speedily to recidivism, to relapse. Recommended in its place is a system called restorative justice. In harmony with biblical justice, its aim is to heal. It brings offender and victim together with mediators and representatives of the court. It has begun to show promise in New Zealand, was used in South Africa by the Truth and Reconciliation Commission, and can point to early stages in about 600 U.S. jurisdictions.

Take New Zealand. There the juvenile system is currently 100 percent focused on restorative philosophy and practice. In 1989, after a 15-year trial-and-error period, a law was passed mandating that the restorative justice process would be the direction for dealing with offenders under 17—while maintaining an ever-shrinking traditional system for those who plead not guilty. With that legislation, the government closed down all juvenile institutions; a few have reopened to cope with juveniles guilty of frightful crimes.

The approach? Within days of an arrest a facilitator from the

Department of Youth Justice tries to arrange a family-group conference: the offender, his/her family, and the victims. The offender admits the offense, explains relevant circumstances. A support person may add certain clarifying information. The victims are asked to express what they feel: anger, grief, greater understanding. Important here is the human face both sides bring to the situation. The victim is central. In the retributive system the victim can only testify; in the restorative system the victim is to some degree re-empowered, a balance is restored. And the offenders assume much more responsibility for their harmful actions. Group participation—herein we have the dynamics of the process.

Then the matter goes to a judge; in 95 percent of the cases he accepts the group's recommendations. There are sanctions, but it is the community that does the restorative part. The offender signs a contract to fulfill what is required, for example, payment, return to school, alcohol or drug treatment. If the terms are fulfilled, no conviction is entered into the record.

Does it always work? No. All that is claimed is that the restorative justice philosophy offers better opportunities than retributive justice for opening a healing process for the victim and the offender alike. Encouraging to me is one instance where restorative justice is actually working: the Indiana Women's Prison, the oldest adult female prison in the United States.[30] For 27 years Dana Blank has been active here, the last 11 as superintendent. Here she is busy creating a safe place for 400 convicted felons. Her facility holds several populations. There are juveniles sentenced as adults. There are women with medical and/or psychiatric conditions. And the prison is the entry point for all newly sentenced female offenders. No one of these is simply doing time. "No one," says Miss Blank, "sits around here and watches television all day." This superintendent is committed to rehabilitation.

Miss Blank is aware of discouraging statistics reported November 2000 in *Time* magazine. In the past two decades the number of women in U.S. prisons has risen 650 percent. Of the more than 149,000 female inmates currently in local jails and state and federal penitentiaries, 70 percent have at least one child under eighteen. Half of the 1.5 million children with an incarcerated parent will commit a crime before they turn eighteen. The superintendent does not deplore statistics; she is there to change them. She takes pride in the prison's Family Preservation Center. There mothers can spend time alone with their children in an enormous indoor play area with a range of toys and activities, comfortable chairs and rockers. Brightly painted, filled with light, it is a place any mother would be happy to take her child. Not only does the center encourage visits between mothers and children; it sponsors day camps and holiday parties. Not only does it have a program for pregnant offenders, teaching parenting skills and helping with child placement; it co-ordinates contacts between the offender and agencies assisting with the child. The staff, Dana Blank insists, are not guards; guards "keep people at bay." This staff spends a good deal of time in counseling, tutoring, working in summer camp.

As Dana Blank sees it, most women in prison share five realities: a history of sexual and/or other abuse, below-average education, a substance-abuse problem, motherhood, and low self-esteem. In her prison these women have an opportunity to cope with their history, grapple with their addictions, get an education, and in consequence strengthen self-esteem. Blank encourages self-expression—in a practical way by allowing prisoners to wear their own clothing. Each week 100 volunteers come to the prison. Some lead 12-step groups in craft work, painting, clowning, and yoga. Volleyball and softball teams come to compete against the offenders' teams.

Here indeed is restorative justice. For Dana Blank supports the concept of community-based corrections, including work release and other alternatives to incarceration for nonviolent offenders. She is convinced that the weakest part of the prison system is the transition back into civilian life. It needs to be extended in length and expanded in depth.

Pertinent here is the 1995 pastoral letter of the New Zealand bishops, *Creating New Hearts: Moving from Retributive to Restorative Justice.* The letter resulted from efforts on the part of prison chaplains, who felt that the Church had to connect with the movement, especially in view of its proven success. Toward the close of the letter the bishops commented on the retributive system as having "little room for forgiveness or reconciliation," whereas a fair criminal justice system should reflect compassion, healing, and forgiveness as mirroring gospel values.

In 1998 New Zealand's minister of justice presented a paper to the cabinet requesting approval of funding for pilot restorative-justice programs for adult offenders. He listed as potential benefits reduced costs to the criminal-justice system, decrease in the use of incarceration, decrease in the lengths of sentences, less repeat offending, and more meaningful victim and community participation.

Is a ground swell in favor of restorative justice apparent in the United States? Perhaps, at least among some faith-based communities.

I much fear, however, that public opinion still cries loudly for vengeance. Hence the two million and more Americans behind bars, with little hope for rehabilitation, because there is no effort at rehabilitation, relatively little interest. The only growth? The prison industry.

Of high potential significance is a statement of the Catholic bishops of the United States, "Responsibility, Rehabilitation, and Restoration: A Catholic Perspective on Crime and Criminal Justice."[31] In response to the "current trend of more prisons and more executions, with too little education and drug treatment," the bishops "are convinced that our tradition and our faith offer better alternatives that can hold offenders accountable *and* challenge them to change their lives; reach out to victims *and* reject violence; restore a sense of community *and* resist the violence that has engulfed so much of our culture" (p. 2). They are aware that "it is reported that more than thirty-seven thousand federal prisoners (30 percent of the federal inmate population) are baptized Catholic, many more Catholics are in local jails and state prisons, and hundreds of thousands are on probation or parole. Catholics can also be found among white-collar criminals whose illegal actions in businesses, financial markets, and government halls seriously damage our common life and economic stability." All those consulted "seemed to agree on one thing: the status quo is not really working—victims are often ignored, offenders are often not rehabilitated, and many communities have lost their sense of security" (pp. 5-6).

Striking and uncommon is the bishops' section on our scriptural, theological, and sacramental heritage. It includes our daily Lord's Prayer to forgive as we are forgiven, St. Paul's call to affirm the demands of both justice and mercy, the place of punishment and forgiveness, and the reality of free will and poor choices. It recalls a paradoxical Catholic vision: on the one hand, belief in responsibility, accountability, and punishment; on the other, respect for the lives and dignity of victims and offenders, preference for justice over vengeance, encouragement for models of restorative justice.

The bishops are impressed by the Hebrew Bible's rich tradition on God's justice and mercy, on the covenant that calls for punishment, demands reparations, insists on restoring relationships. This tradition is expanded in the New Testament, in Jesus' disappointment with those who oppress others or defile sacred spaces; his rejection of revenge and retaliation; his hope for the transformation of sinners; his call to feed the hungry, house the homeless, clothe the naked, visit the sick (including victims of crime) and the imprisoned. The bishops find in the Good Samaritan (Luke 10) a model for helping strangers and the victims of crime; in the Parable of the Prodigal Son (Luke 15), God's love for us and a model for loving the lost and seeking out the straying.

Here the bishops find the four traditional elements of the sacrament of penance instructive: *contrition*, genuine sorrow over wrongdoing and a serious resolution not to repeat it; *confession*, acknowledgment of, and acceptance of responsibility for, the hurtful behavior; *satisfaction*, the external sign of a desire to amend one's life through prayers or good deeds—compensation or restitution; *absolution*, forgiveness of the sin and welcome back into the community.

At this point the bishops recall a number of pertinent elements from Catholic social teaching: (1) The life of every human person has an inviolable dignity and value, including the most wounded victim and the most callous criminal. (2) Every human person has rights and responsibilities, at the intersection of which are crime and correction. (3) Human life is social, is lived out in relationships to family and community, calls for participation, for example, by victims needing to be heard and healed. (4) Punishment for criminal activity should serve three purposes: preservation and protection of the common good of society, restoration of public order, and restoration or conversion of the offender. To these the bishops add redress, repair of the harm done to victims and society. (5) Every public policy must be assessed by how it will affect the poorest and most vulnerable people in our society: the abused, the mentally ill, those discriminated against. "Unaddressed needs—including proper nutrition, shelter, healthcare, and protection from abuse and neglect—can be steppingstones on a path towards crime" (p. 25). (6) Subsidiarity and solidarity. Subsidiarity calls for problem solving, initially at the community level, encouraging communities to be more involved. Solidarity recognizes that "we are all really responsible for all."[32] We are obligated to work for justice beyond our boundaries, to see Jesus in the face of everyone, including victims and offenders.

The next section, fashioned from broad and rich experience, is devoted to policy foundations for "new approaches that understand crime as a threat to community, not just a violation of law; that demand new efforts to rebuild lives, not just build more prisons; and that demonstrate a commitment to reweave a broader social fabric of respect for life, civility, responsibility, and reconciliation" (p. 13). I can do no more here than list the foundations from their headings:

(1) protecting society from those who threaten life, inflict harm, take property, and destroy the bonds of community; (2) rejecting simplistic solutions such as "three strikes and you're out" and rigid mandatory sentencing; (3) promoting serious efforts toward crime prevention and poverty reduction; (4) challenging the culture of violence and encouraging a culture of life; (5) offering victims the opportunity to participate more fully in the criminal-justice process; (6) encouraging innovative programs of restorative justice that provide the opportunity for mediation between victims and offenders and offer restitution for crimes committed; (7) insisting that punishment has a constructive and rehabilitative purpose; (8) encouraging spiritual healing and renewal for those who commit crime; (9) making a serious commitment to confront the pervasive role of addiction and mental illness in crime; (10) treating immigrants justly; (11) placing crime in a community context and building on promising alternatives that empower neighborhoods and towns to restore a sense of security.

Insisting that the challenge of curbing crime and reshaping the criminal-justice system is not only a matter of public policy but also a test of Catholic commitment, the bishops develop seven calls to the community of faith. (1) Teach right from wrong, respect for life and the law, forgiveness and mercy. (2) Stand with victims and their families. (3) Reach out to offenders and their families, advocate more treatment, and provide for the pastoral needs of all involved. (4) Build community. (5) Advocate policies that help reduce violence, protect the innocent, involve the victims, and offer real alternatives to crime. (6) Organize diocesan and state consultations, that is, processes of engagement and dialogue with crime victims, former inmates, jail chaplains, judges, police officers, community leaders, prosecutors, families of victims and offenders, and others. "Ask them to share their faith, stories, hopes, and fears" (p. 53). At the state level, hold similar meetings under the auspices of state Catholic conferences. "These key Catholic public policy organizations can share their message with influential lawmakers and help shape new policies" (ibid.). (7) Work for new approaches.

Capital Punishment

Turn now to capital punishment. During the 1990s America was awash in a new crusade. Its background was a frightening escalation of violence. One significant reaction was an angry, demanding cry for capital punishment that stemmed in large measure, but not entirely, from a twin conviction: (1) that only execution is appropriate punishment for a number of particularly brutal crimes, for example, abuse of children, treason, a Hitlerian butchery of the innocent; and (2) that capital punishment is an effective way to combat the contemporary trend to savage violence.

Extensive research and reflection have brought me to the conclusion that capital punishment cannot be justified in America today. My argument begins with the experience of highly competent law enforcers. It was summarized for me in a 1995 OpEd column in the *New York Times* by Manhattan District Attorney Robert M. Morgenthau: "Prosecutors must reveal the dirty little secret they too often share only among themselves: The death penalty actually hinders the fight against crime." In summary he declared that "capital punishment is a mirage that distracts society from more fruitful, less facile answers. It exacts a terrible price in dollars, lives and human decency. Rather than tamping down the flames of violence, it fuels them while draining millions of dollars from more promising efforts to restore safety to our lives."[33]

Effectiveness? In 1975, when Morgenthau became district attorney, there were 648 homicides in Manhattan; in 1994 there were 330—a significant reduction, without executions, through more fruitful methods. Cost? A Duke University study in 1993 found that for each person executed in North Carolina, the state paid over $2 million more than it would have cost to imprison the convict for life. In New York the death penalty would cost the state $118 million a year; a fraction of that sum can finance an array of other solutions to crime. Justice? No one disagrees that innocent people have been executed; the only argument is, how many? "A 1987 study in the *Stanford Law Review* identified 350 cases in [the twentieth] century in which innocent people were wrongly convicted of crimes for which they could have received the death penalty; of that number, perhaps as many as 23 were executed. New York led the list with eight."[34]

That fact introduces another reason for surrendering capital punishment: its potential for irreversible injustice. Focus on just a single state. Texas executes more people than any other state. From January 1, 1977, to December 31, 2000, 683 executions took place in 31 states. Sixty-five percent of the executions occurred in five states: Texas (239), Virginia (81), Florida (50), Missouri (46), and Oklahoma (30). During the governorship of George W. Bush, from 1995 to 2000, there were 152.[35] The current rate is just under two executions a month. Most capital defendants are too poor to hire their own lawyers; under the Constitution the state must provide one. But some of the lawyers appointed to represent Texas defendants have done notoriously incompetent jobs. At least three slept while their clients were on trial for their lives; others were drunk. One judge turned down an appeal on the ground that the Constitution makes provision for a lawyer but does not demand that he be awake.[36] Listen to Stephen Bright, director of the Atlanta-based Southern Center for Human Rights, an organization that has provided extensive help to defendants in capital cases: "At least four people—Randall Dale Evans, Clarence Earl Bradley, Ricardo Adalpe Guerra and Frederico Martínez-Macía—were released from death row in Texas after journalists or volunteer lawyers conducted exhaustive investigations which established their innocence."[37]

One reason for the failures of indigent defense in Texas appears to be a cozy relationship between certain judges and the lawyers they appoint as counsel. Judges have to run for re-election every four years. Their campaigns cost thousands, even millions, of dollars, and much of the money is contributed by lawyers. Judges have appointed contributors as defense counsel.

In 1999 the Texas Legislature passed—unanimously in both the Republican-controlled Senate and the Democratic-controlled House —a bill to reform modestly the system for providing counsel to poor defendants. Because it had sometimes been weeks before an accused person even saw a lawyer, the bill also required that one be provided within 20 days after arrest. Most states put that limit at 72 hours. The proposed legislation brought an outcry from judges. Governor George Bush vetoed it.[38] And still, as President of the United States, he insists that during his governorship no one was unjustly executed. No hesitation, no doubt, no response to specific charges (save for a 30-day reprieve so that a more sophisticated DNA test could be performed in a rape and murder case). As probing a reporter as Bob Herbert has concluded that "justice in Texas is a joke."[39] As respected a columnist as Margaret Carlson questions the system's infallibility in the light of "the lightning speed at which executions are carried out, the lack of an adequate public-defender system, the closing of an office that aided inmates' appeals and a disturbingly high rate of innocence found in other states when death-penalty cases have been independently investigated."[40]

An unexpected development took place in Texas less than a year after the paragraphs above were written. The Texas legislature "passed a measure addressing a central complaint about Texas criminal justice: that indigent defendants are too often given bad lawyers to handle their cases. The lawmakers also approved legislation providing for DNA testing for many criminal defendants and prisoners, as well as a bill to increase payments to prisoners wrongfully imprisoned."[41]

Governor Rick Perry signed the DNA bill but vetoed perhaps the most controversial measure, a bill that would have made Texas the fourteenth state to ban the execution of retarded prisoners. This veto came despite a similar bill, supported by Gov. Jeb Bush, being passed in the Florida Legislature. Like former Texas governor George W. Bush, Perry indicated there are enough safeguards in place to protect mentally retarded criminals.[42] Most of the lawmakers who had supported the proposed Texas ban were motivated largely by the intense negative attention, national and international, focused on the state's death penalty during the presidential campaign of George W. Bush.[43]

Virginia, second to Texas in the number of criminals it has killed since the death penalty returned in 1976, is the per capita execution champion among large states. And why not? After all, Virginia enjoys a 21-day rule that excludes new evidence offered more than three weeks after a conviction. On Jan. 31, 2002, the Senate Courts of Justice Committee in Virginia reversed itself and killed, at least for the year, efforts to soften that controversial rule, despite testimony from the fiancée of a Roanoke man sentenced to 38 years in prison for a crime his accuser now says he did not commit—molestation of her ten-year-old daughter. The previous week, the committee had voted 8-6 to report a bill that would allow the Virginia Supreme Court to review nonbiological evidence of a convicted person's innocence after the statutory 21-day appeal window had passed. (Current law allowed the state's highest court to consider only appeals based on new DNA evidence after 21 days.) Afterwards, however, the committee chairman, Sen. Ken Stolle (R-Virginia Beach), who opposed the measure, met privately with several members and persuaded them to reconsider the vote. In consequence, bill supporters failed to receive enough votes to send it to the full Senate. More recently, in early December 2002, the Virginia Supreme Court revealed that it was contemplating changes in the 21-day rule. As an editorial in the *Washington Post* for December 11 stated, "It is long overdue. Allowing the evidentiary mosaic to freeze at any particular moment only guarantees that injustices become irremediable."

In Maryland on March 13, 2002, a conservative Senate committee killed a proposal that would have made it more difficult for juries to impose the death penalty, effectively dashing any hope for legislation in 2002 to delay executions. Only minutes after hearing testimony from proponents and opponents of a bill to increase the burden of proof in the sentencing of death-penalty cases, the Senate Judicial Proceedings Committee voted it down 7-4. Less than a year before, April 9, 2001, a bill to halt executions while researchers determined whether racial bias plays a role in Maryland's use of capital punishment died as the General Assembly adjourned for the year. I find it cruelly humorous that on the same night delegates and senators could agree on how many crabs someone should be allowed to catch without a license.

In its January 6, 2003, issue, the *Washington Post* reported that a University of Maryland study had uncovered a large racial disparity in executions in Maryland. "Maryland prosecutors are far more likely to seek the death penalty for black suspects charged with killing white victims, a racial disparity that mirrors national trends and raises questions about whether capital punishment is being administered fairly." Pending the completion of the study, outgoing Governor Paris N. Glendening in May 2002 halted all executions. Before his election, current governor Robert L. Ehrlich Jr. pledged to lift the moratorium regardless of the findings and to review cases on an individual basis. A *Post* editorial claims that Mr. Ehrlich misses the point. These data demonstrate that a given case can be rock solid and still be no more worthy of death than one in which capital punishment was never even sought. It is possible, in other words, for the state to be both rigorous and discriminatory. Is this really the Maryland that Mr. Ehrlich wants?[44]

The increasing dissatisfaction with the death penalty received uncommon support in late January 2000, when Governor George Ryan of Illinois, a moderate Republican and a supporter of the death penalty, ordered a temporary halt to executions. The criminal-justice system in Illinois, one commentator has remarked, "has proved to be both tragic and farcical. Real killers roamed free while the wrongfully convicted were handed tickets to eternity. In some cases ignorance and incompetence were the culprits. In other, more chilling instances the innocent were deliberately betrayed."[45] Illinois has exonerated 13 men who had been condemned to death.

Two years later, a bipartisan commission the governor had established called for a sweeping overhaul of capital punishment in the state. In a report released April 15, 2002,

   . . . the 14-member panel recommended 85 ways to prevent unwarranted executions, including videotaping all interrogations of suspects in capital cases, to prevent coerced confessions; reducing the number of factors making a crime eligible for the death penalty to 5 from 20; submitting all such cases to a state board for review, and establishing a statewide DNA database and an independent forensics lab. . . .

The commission also called for a ban on executing murderers who are mentally retarded, as well as those whose convictions had been based solely on the testimony of a single eyewitness, prison informer or accomplice. . . .

The report includes detailed analysis of all 275 death penalty cases since Illinois re-established capital punishment in 1977. More than half of the sentences were reversed, it says, because of trial court errors and mistakes by prosecutors and defense lawyers. Nearly 60 percent of the sentences came in cases where a murder was committed in the course of a felony, one of the criteria that the commission proposes dropping; 46 percent involved multiple murders, and in 10 percent children were the victims. . . .

Though the abolition of capital punishment is not among the commission's recommendations, the report says "a narrow majority" of its members would support its demise. . . .[46]

In the same year, Chicago lawyer Scott Turow published his latest novel, *Reversible Errors* (Farrar, Straus and Giroux). Though fiction, the book harks back to a similar case he had handled in 1991, a case that proved quite traumatic for him. Halfway through writing *Errors,* the governor had appointed him to the commission mentioned above. Following up on the highly critical report, the governor declared in October 2002 that the flawed state system could not be trusted and launched a mass hearing of clemency appeals from 142 of the 158 people then on Illinois's death row. Although Turow is not morally opposed to the death penalty, "the mounting evidence of unfair application of the ultimate penalty to minorities, along with sloppy defense counsels, prejudiced juries and forensic errors, finally persuaded Turow and most of the commission that the present system was not fixable. . . . [N]owhere does *Errors* deliver a clear judgment on the death penalty. Instead it conveys a deep sense of unease."[47]

On January 11, 2003, outgoing Governor Ryan commuted the death sentences of 167 people to life imprisonment without the possibility of parole. This action followed a day after the governor had pardoned four death row inmates who he said had been tortured into false murder confessions.

As I write in 2003, more than 100 prison inmates have had their convictions overturned thanks to DNA evidence. But often at a dreadful cost. One example. An Oklahoma junior high school science teacher, Dennis Fritz, was convicted of raping and murdering a 21-year-old neighbor. No criminal record; flimsy circumstantial evidence; testimony of a jailhouse snitch who claimed Fritz confessed while awaiting trial. His conviction by a jury, his sentencing for life, separated him from his 13-year-old daughter, whom he was raising as a single father. A DNA test requested by his lawyers excluded him as well as a codefendant, implicated someone else who had never been charged with the crime. He was freed—after 12 years behind bars.

A personal note. Adjoining my former lodgings in Washington, D.C., is the McKenna Center, named after the late Horace McKenna, S.J., and continuing his extraordinary service to the poor, the homeless, the hungry. The cook at this Jesuit-run center is African-American Joseph Brown, known to his friends as Shabaka. Shabaka spent almost 15 years on Florida's death row. There, as in most other states that subscribe to capital punishment, a majority of his cellmates were from minorities; some were retarded, and almost all were poor. Shabaka was eventually found to be innocent—after almost 15 years behind bars. In his experience, "Racism plays a big part in [the criminal-justice system]. . . . If you'd been at my trial in Florida, you'd have thought you were at a K.K.K. meeting and I was the guest of honor. I was the only black person in the whole courtroom. The jury was all white."[48]

Richard Dieter, director of the Death Penalty Information Center in Washington, D.C., has pointed out that while African Americans comprise about 12 percent of the U.S. population, they account for 40 percent of prisoners on death row, and 36 percent of those executed; of the 510 executed since the Supreme Court returned the question to the individual states in 1977, at least 34 were designated as retarded. Though holding only one half of one percent of death row inmates, the federal government recently concluded a study of the 19 convicts involved. The conclusion was that despite serious efforts to ensure fairness in seeking the death penalty for defendants convicted of federally eligible crimes, 14 of the inmates were African American.[49]

Dissatisfaction with capital punishment is being expressed on surprisingly high levels. In June 2001, nine highly regarded veterans of the American Foreign Service called for an end to the death penalty for the mentally retarded. As President George W. Bush was preparing for his first visit to Europe, "the diplomats, whose combined service in 18 countries under Republican and Democratic presidents totals nearly 200 years, say the practice puts the United States at odds with the rest of the world, creates diplomatic friction, especially with European allies, tarnishes America's image as the champion of human rights and harms broader American foreign policy interests."[50] I believe that the former Soviet republic Kyrgyzstan and Japan are the only other countries where the mentally retarded are put to death.

A case in point here. In 1983 Earl Washington Jr., both brain-damaged and mentally retarded, was taken into police custody in rural Virginia, waived his Miranda rights, and confessed to all sorts of crimes—burglary, rape, murder. A string of eyewitnesses told police he was the wrong person. Still, prosecutors went ahead and charged him with the murder of a young woman, Rebecca Williams. Serious discrepancies in his "confession" made no difference; after a three-day trial he was convicted and sentenced to death. In 1985 he came within nine days of being executed. Early DNA testing seemed to offer evidence of his innocence; in 1984 his sentence was reduced to life imprisonment. In 2000 more sophisticated tests showed conclusively that Earl Washington had not attacked Rebecca Williams. He was pardoned by Gov. James L. Gilmore III and was freed from prison in February 2001.[51]

Unexpectedly, in a speech to a meeting of Minnesota Women Lawyers on July 2, 2001, Supreme Court Justice Sandra Day O'Connor said "serious questions are being raised" about the death penalty. Noting that 90 death-row inmates have been exonerated by new evidence since 1973, she said that "the system may well be allowing some innocent defendants to be executed." She went on to describe the noxious influence of poor defense lawyers on capital cases—arguing that those who can afford to hire their own lawyers are less likely to be convicted and less likely, if convicted, to be sentenced to death. She said that Minnesota, which does not have a death penalty, "must breathe a big sigh of relief every day." Justice O'Connor's remarks were seen as significant because she often casts the deciding vote in close cases, and she has generally supported the death penalty during her two decades on the court, has voted to permit the death penalty for teenagers convicted of murder, and has joined or written key opinions that made it more difficult for capital defendants to have their state sentences overturned in federal court. She has, however, expressed ambivalence about cases in which the defendant may be mentally retarded.[52]

Another argument against capital punishment is the sanctity of all human life. Here we touch a dreadfully complex issue. If every human life is so sacred that every homicide is unethical, immoral, is not every war an abominable injustice? If we argue to a just war on the basis of self-defense, must we not submit that we humans have developed in our humanity to a point where killing as punishment is unnecessary, where there are more effective ways of preserving the moral order, of defending society? Here Pope John Paul II has argued that "as a result of steady improvements in the organization of the penal system, such cases [i.e., where only through execution is defense of society possible] are very rare, if not practically nonexistent."[53] Even more strongly in St. Louis in 1999: "The dignity of human life must never be taken away, even in the case of someone who has done great evil."

In our Preaching the Just Word retreat/workshops, John Carr of the United States Catholic Conference points to a strange succession of events: A medical doctor kills a fetus, an antiabortionist kills the doctor, the state kills the antiabortionist to show that killing is wrong. It is sheer vengeance, retribution, an eye for an eye.

Powerful in this regard is the fact that the European Union and the 41-member Council of Europe bar admission to any nation that has not banned the death penalty. Whereas in this country capital punishment is viewed primarily as a criminal-justice issue, in other democracies it is regarded as a human-rights matter.

In summary: If (1) capital punishment actually hinders the fight against crime; if (2) capital punishment drains millions of dollars from more promising efforts to restore safety to our lives; if (3) people have in fact been executed for crimes they did not commit; if (4) convicts charged with capital crimes frequently do not have adequate defense counsel; if (5) prisoners have spent as many as 15 years on death row before being found innocent; if (6) a disproportionate number of those on death row are African Americans or Hispanics, poor, uneducated, even retarded; if (7) states are declaring or considering a moratorium on capital punishment because of acknowledged injustices in the system; if (8) virtually every country across Europe has outlawed it; if (9) astute persons such as Pope John Paul II, not lacking in compassion for the families of victims, are convinced that humanity has reached a stage where capital punishment is no longer necessary to protect society; if (10) the primary motivation behind capital punishment is vengeance; if (11) execution only rarely if ever brings genuine closure to the agony of the bereaved; if (12) a good case can be made for the sanctity of all human life, even the life of the murderer or rapist; and if (13) restorative justice can at times effect a transformation in the life of even the most hardened criminal—must we not seriously consider whether capital punishment is itself an unjust system?

Rigid proponents of capital punishment call such as me bleeding hearts, with a strange affinity for the criminal rather than for the bereaved. I beg to differ. Nerves in my body twitch in revulsion against the serial killer, the violator of women and little children, the hate-filled terrorist, the bomber of buildings and their occupants. It is not easy for me to live the age-old distinction "condemn the sin, love the sinner." But loving the sinner is not a matter of wine and roses, of tender feelings. To love a criminal is to want with all my will what is best for him or her—in a genuine sense, what God would want or at least approve, as far as we can read God's mind from the way God has spoken to us in God's written Word, and the way God speaks to us in the signs of the times. Should it not profoundly disturb men and women of compassion, especially Christians enjoined by Jesus to promote the good of even their enemies, when a jolt of electricity or a fatal injection cuts off for ever any possibility of regret, of remorse, of rehabilitation, of conversion? Isn't it ironic that some of those who were allowed to witness the execution of Timothy McVeigh (whose 7,000-pound bomb ripped apart the lives and limbs of 149 adults and 19 children in Oklahoma City) were hoping for some sign of sorrow on his face as he died? They will never see it.

Capital Punishment
and Mentally Retarded Defendants

At this point I find it imperative to explore more fully the injustice of this country's executing mentally retarded persons. On June 21, 2002, the front page of the *New York Times* reported that on the previous day the United States Supreme Court declared (*Atkins* v. *Virginia*) that the Constitution bars the execution of mentally retarded defendants. This landmark death-penalty ruling was based in large measure but not exclusively on the majority view that a "national consensus" now rejected such executions as excessive and inappropriate.

Of the 38 states that have a death penalty, 18 now prohibit executing the retarded, up from two when the court last considered the question in 1989. Writing for the majority (6-3), Justice John Paul Stevens wrote in part:

A claim that punishment is excessive is judged not by the standards that prevailed in 1685 when Lord Jeffreys presided over the "Bloody Assizes" or when the Bill of Rights was adopted, but rather by those that currently prevail. As Chief Justice Warren explained in his opinion in *Trop* v. *Dulles,* 350 U.S. 86 (1958): "The basic concept underlying the Eighth Amendment is nothing less than the dignity of man. . . . The Amendment must draw its meaning from the evolving standards of decency that mark the progress of a maturing society."

It is not so much the number of these states [now prohibiting execution of the retarded] that is significant, but the consistency of the direction of change. Given the well-known fact that anti-crime legislation is far more popular than legislation providing protections for persons guilty of violent crimes, the large number of states prohibiting the execution of mentally retarded persons (and the complete absence of states' passing legislation reinstating the power to conduct such executions) provides powerful evidence that today our society views mentally retarded offenders as categorically less culpable than the average criminal. The evidence carries even greater force when it is noted that the legislatures that have addressed the issues have voted overwhelmingly in favor of the prohibition. Moreover, even in those states that allow the execution of mentally retarded offenders, the practice is uncommon. . . . And it appears that even among those states that regularly execute offenders and that have no prohibition with regard to the mentally retarded, only five have executed offenders possessing a known I.Q. less than 70 since we decided Penry [v. *Lynaugh,* 1989]. The practice, therefore, has become truly unusual, and it is fair to say that a national consensus has developed against it.

Our independent evaluation of the issue reveals no reason to disagree with the judgment of "the legislatures that have recently addressed the matter" and concluded that death is not a suitable punishment for a mentally retarded criminal. We are not persuaded that the execution of mentally retarded criminals will measurably advance the deterrent or the retributive purpose of the death penalty. Construing and applying the Eighth Amendment in the light of our "evolving standards of decency," we therefore conclude that such punishment is excessive and that the Constitution "places a substantive restriction on the State's power to take the life" of a mentally retarded offender. *Ford,* 477 U.S., at 405.[54]

An editorial in the *New York Times* observed importantly that "Judge Stevens also signaled that the question of what constitutes 'cruel and unusual punishment' is not one that is answerable solely by coldly analyzing opinion polls and surveying state legislatures. It inevitably engages the moral sensibility of the individual justices. Indeed, the court had no business in the first instance relying so heavily on public sentiment. . . ."[55]

From the dissent came a typically acerbic opinion registered by Justice Antonin Scalia. "Seldom has an opinion of this court rested so obviously upon nothing but the personal views of its members." After noting the high importance traditionally attached by the court to "objective factors" informing its decisions, especially "the statutes passed by society's elected representatives," Scalia claimed that in the present case the court "pays lip service to these precedents as it miraculously extracts a 'national consensus' forbidding execution of the mentally retarded." He declares that "the prize for the most feeble effort to fabricate 'national consensus' must go to its appeal (deservedly relegated to a footnote) to the views of assorted professional and religious organizations, members of the so-called 'world community' and respondents to opinion polls." He agrees with Chief Justice Rehnquist that such appeals are irrelevant.

Although I agree with the majority opinion, I do wish that Justice Stevens had spent far more time on "objective factors" than he gave to the national consensus. What are the moral insights, the "objective factors," that lie behind the growing consensus? "Categorically less culpable than the average criminal," yes. But all too little on this; not enough on retribution and deterrence, the social purposes allegedly served by the death penalty. I much fear that Justice Stevens' presentation leaves him at times somewhat open to the probing wit of his dissenting colleague. An editorial in the *Washington Post* for June 21, 2002, expressed my own reaction with admirable clarity:

> . . . the court majority yesterday could not bring itself simply to repudiate the earlier holding. Rather, the opinion by Justice John Paul Stevens argues that the national consensus that did not exist in 1989 does exist now. A practice, in other words, that the Constitution only recently permitted has, without any change in the document, become repugnant to it. Where does the court find this new consensus? Since 1989 the practice has become increasingly disfavored, and 18 states have now restricted or aban-

doned the execution of retarded people. Yet, as Justice Antonin Scalia points out in dissent, more than half of all states that permit capital punishment still also permit executing the retarded. So it is a stretch to argue that this shift of opinion—which could prove temporary—represents a change of constitutional magnitude. Rather, it seems to be a convenient gloss for the justices' own change of heart. We're grateful for that rethinking. A more candid account would have made the decision more to be admired.

On one point I discover general agreement: In the years ahead there will be hard debate on who must be regarded as retarded and who gets to decide; little if any help here from the court. Still, a giant step forward has been taken on capital punishment in the United States. A giant step since 1989, when the Supreme Court held that executing the mentally retarded did not fall under the "cruel and unusual punishments" forbidden by the Eighth Amendment to the Federal Constitution.

Healing the Wounds of Murder

One of the most moving books I have recently been privileged to read is Antoinette Bosco's *Choosing Mercy*.[56] On August 19, 1993, in her Connecticut home, Ms. Bosco received a telephone call from Montana's Lake County sheriff, informing her that her son John and his wife, Nancy, had been found shot to death in their new home. From the evidence of a stopped electric clock police estimated that they had been killed a week earlier, August 12, about two in the morning.

I found myself screaming, sometimes aloud, sometimes with silent cries tearing at my insides. I tormented myself, wanting to know who was the faceless monster that had brought such permanent unrelenting pain into my family. I wanted to kill him with my own hands. I wanted him dead.

But that feeling also tormented me, for I had always been opposed to the death penalty. I felt now I was being tested on whether my values were permanent, or primarily based on human feelings and expediency. With God's help, I was able to grasp the truth again, that unnatural death at the hands of another is always wrong, except in a case of clear self-defense.

The state is no more justified in taking a life than is an individual. And so armed, I found myself speaking out on a national platform, pleading against the death penalty for anyone.[57]

"On a national platform." Antoinette was aware that Americans were beginning to feel discomfort over some troubling facts: over 3,600 currently on death row; more than 675 killed in the past 24 years—"some surely innocent"; 88 death-row inmates freed in that time (new trials, convictions overturned on appeal, DNA proof of innocence); more than 65 on death row, even though their crimes were committed when they were juveniles (eight executed in Texas since 1985); 26 states allowing execution of the mentally retarded; application of the death penalty skewed racially and by income.[58]

Unexpectedly, the Bosco killer was discovered: Joseph Shadow Clark, the 18-year-old son of the people from whom John and Nancy had purchased their home, a first-year student at a Quaker college. Capital punishment had been reinstated in Montana for heinous murders. But Antoinette made it clear that she opposed the death penalty, and Shadow was sentenced to 220 years in Montana State Prison, with no eligibility for parole until age sixty.

Antoinette's life is a remarkable story of growth in forgiveness. She joined Survivors of Homicide, whose members help one another to cope with rage, despair, hopelessness—what she calls the Fellowship of the Wounded. She was almost alone in her opposition to capital punishment; most of them wanted the "justice" she saw as vengeance: "fry them slowly." She came to see that

> forgiving doesn't mean to give in; it means to let go, and letting go is a precondition to becoming free. If you don't forgive, you give the one who hurt you ever more control over you. If I didn't forgive Shadow Clark, I would be emotionally handcuffed to him, bound to him in a destructive way. Jesus said that he had come "to set us free," and he showed us the way. In a word—forgiveness. It was a contradictory path for his times, and has remained so in our time.[59]

Important in her experience was the execution in Texas of Karla Faye Tucker. "I had seen clips showing Karla as gentle, caring, a lover of God. She had caught my attention in a very personal way before that fateful day. I had read about her complicity in a gruesome murder of two in 1983. Could the twenty-three-year-old drug-soaked prostitute who wielded an axe that day to steal the breath of two people be the same person as the thirty-eight-year-old woman I was seeing on television? No, no way." But the Supreme Court turned down her appeal, and then-Governor George W. Bush refused a stay of execution. When the prison spokesman came out to report that Karla was dead, Antoinette "wasn't expecting the gleeful reaction [she] saw from so many people. . . . It was a dark circus—a strange dance of death, where people were whooping and hooting to celebrate the murder of a fellow Texan."[60]

From meeting with people who had been hurt and doing healing services with churches Antoinette moved in another direction: the mission of being a voice for life—"square in the anti-death penalty pulpit."[61] She knew she had a major conflict before her, with people on both sides, and politics very much in evidence. Catholic Governor Mario Cuomo of New York, outspoken against capital punishment, lost his bid for re-election in 1994 to Catholic George Pataki, adamantly for the death penalty. In 1995 New York reinstated capital punishment.

Antoinette's experiences multiplied. One example must suffice. Methodist minister Walter Everett, filled with painful anger at Mike Carducci, the murderer of his son, wrote to Mike in prison to thank him for his expression of sorrow in court, and concluded, "As hard as these words are to write, I forgive you." In so writing, he found that his burden was beginning to lift. "By offering forgiveness, I freed myself from that hurt." When Mike read the letter, it changed his life. He fell to his knees to pray for his own forgiveness. He told Everett that the forgiveness had given him "the will to live." They met in prison, and Everett offered Carducci friendship and love; they hugged each other and cried. Then an amazing turn. Released from prison, Mike fell in love and asked Everett to officiate at his wedding; he did. Now a truck driver, Mike and the minister still get together to talk with groups about forgiveness, about personal feelings, about ending the death penalty. Antoinette's broad experience has convinced her that the death penalty "actually prevents families from grieving, that by encouraging families to hate, it prolongs their rage, that it is not a solution to violence, but an escalation of violence."[62]

Over and over again Antoinette sees in the group Murder Victims' Families for Reconciliation (MVFR) a living-out of a definition from the Vietnamese Zen master Thich Nhat Hanh: "Reconciliation is to understand both sides, to go to one and describe the suffering being endured by the other side; then to go to the other side and describe the suffering endured by the first side."[63]

On that note I leave Antoinette. She represents a growing number of Americans who have been deeply wounded by the murder of loved ones, yet fortunately are struggling not only for the abolition of capital punishment as an unjustified assault on life, but also for a *genuine* "closure" to the hurt and rage that ravage the families of the murdered. That closure, they are convinced, should not come, cannot come, from the destruction of another life, from vengeance, from retribution; only from reconciliation, from mercy, from forgiveness. The conviction stems not so much from abstract reasoning as from the experience of men and women who, like Antoinette, actually moved from heart-rending pain and acute anger to profound peace.

For Christians, such forgiveness and reconciliation, in so extraordinarily difficult circumstances, are a striking response to the prayer Jesus bequeathed to us: "Forgive us as we forgive" (Mt 6:12). It is also a remarkable example of biblical justice, loving as Jesus loved, Jesus the Just One.

Ecology

During my early decades as a theologian, two realities absorbed my professional and personal interest: God and people. Here were the relationships that counted for a Catholic Christian: loving God above all else, and loving every man, woman, and child as an image of God. In those two directions lay theological reality, for myself and for those thousands of women and men whose lives I touched from the pulpit and in the confessional, in lectures and seminars, through books and articles.

The early 1970s introduced a third factor. I became aware that back in 1967 historian Lynn White Jr. had authored an influential article in *Science* magazine focusing the blame for the world's environmental problems squarely on Christianity. Specifically, White argued that the West's ecologic fall from grace began with the first creation account in Genesis (1:27-28), the Priestly version wherein God sets humans off from other creatures and then gives us dominion over other creatures. Using this account as paradigmatic of the whole Bible, White argued that no religion has been more anthropocentric than Christianity, none more rigid in excluding all but humans from the realm of divine grace and in denying any moral obligation to the lower species. The Christian axiom? Nature has no reason for existing save to serve humanity.[64] Although its immediate influence on me was only a brief effort in the classroom to refute the thesis, a new seed had been planted.

More significant for my future was a series of six radio addresses I delivered on the NBC radio program "Guideline" in January and February 1974. The focus of the addresses was reconciliation: with God, within ourselves, with one another, and with nature.[65] On the issue of nature, I had been stimulated by a *New York Times* interview on December 15, 1973, with social philosopher and psychoanalyst Erich Fromm. He had come to this country in the early 1930s, an exile from Hitler's Germany, his hopes high for life and work in a vibrant America. Forty years later he felt profound fear for his adopted country. "The United States is not entirely in hell. There is a very small chance of avoiding it, but I am not an optimist."

Why the gloom? One reason was our "unrestrained industrialism." As Fromm saw it, after World War II America's industrial machine spewed an endless flow of motor cars and pleasure boats, refrigerators and air conditioners, barbecue pits and heated swimming pools. Such incredible excess of material things, Fromm claimed, the machine process, has minified man and woman, made our own lives seem unimportant to us. "We have grown soft from it at a sacrifice of, what shall I call it, the soul." In the process we have become the world's most destructive society. Not only had we bombed Vietnam back to the Bronze Age. "Our society is also internally destructive. In the last decade or so a million people have been killed in highway accidents. We produce cars with built-in obsolescence. Knowing the possible dangers, we continue to pollute the environment. And we subsidize violence on the screen—movies in which human life is depicted as brutish and cheap."

Since Fromm's jeremiad, the destruction has hardly diminished. As America turned into the 1990s, continuous chemical emissions from 100 million refrigerators, 90 million air conditioners, and 100,000 central air conditioning units in large buildings were the major causes for the depletion of the world's ozone layer—a critical factor for cancer.[66]

A number of my homilies in the 1980s touched on environmental issues. But it was only when I discovered biblical justice in 1990 that my theology became a passionate search for a right relationship not only with God and God's human images, but also with God's material creation, with the earth and sea and sky that God had "found very good" (Gen 1:31).

I suspect that my own late involvement in matters ecological was in part due to a relative inattention to the environment in Catholic scholarship and from the Church's magisterium. Not only were biblicists somewhat sluggish in stressing the intimate, indispensable relationship between nature and humankind as evidenced in their own field of specialization, but only in recent decades have theologians made profound efforts to shape systematic foundations for ecological theology, to make a theology of the environment an integral facet of the search for justice, for community. Official documents, whether universal or regional, had rarely given sufficient attention to the "things" of God, save (justifiably) to condemn their misuse. Welcome exceptions were Vatican II's Pastoral Constitution on the Church in the Modern World and John Paul II's address prepared for World Peace Day 1990, "Peace with God the Creator, Peace with All Creation."[67]

Why such a magisterial and theological lag? In the first section, I stressed Joseph Sittler's explanation: Christians have separated creation and redemption, nature and grace.[68]

Fortunately, the last three decades have witnessed a growing call for a new theology of nature and a new ethic for the earth. The literature is so enormous that only a separate book would do justice to it. For clarity's sweet sake, I have found it useful to follow H. Paul Santmire's division of the material into the three most formidable schools of thought: reconstructionists, apologists, and revisionists.[69]

For reconstructionists, our time demands an entirely new theological word about nature. Traditional Christian thought, they claim, offers people of faith few if any viable theological resources for responding to our global environmental crisis. We must design a new edifice of thought from the ground up, with new foundations and new categories. Some have turned away from Western religious traditions, have embraced insights from primal and Eastern religions. Others, particularly Matthew Fox, draw extensively from mystical traditions in the Christian West, as well as from the spiritualities of primal religions. Others, such as Rosemary Radford Ruether and Sallie McFague, draw on feminist insights, often breaking away from an alleged patriarchal tyranny in classical Christian theology. Mary Daly has opted for a total deconstruction. In each approach "the result is the same: a conscious or unconscious rejection of the classical kerygmatic and dogmatic traditions of Christianity as the primary matrix of theological knowing."[70]

In contrast to the reconstructionists, the apologists underscore what they consider to be the Christian faith's positive ecological implications, above all the tradition's encouragement of "good stewardship of the earth." The apologists work out their insights in terms of theological anthropology and ethics. They define environmental issues by referring to the themes of social justice. Their primary concern is for wise management of the resources of the earth for the sake of the people of the earth, especially "ecojustice" for the poor.[71]

Such, among others, was the World Council of Churches' call for a just, participatory, and sustainable society.

Santmire finds both approaches inadequate for a Christian political engagement or serious theological dialogue with other faith traditions. Reconstructionists lack a Pauline cosmic Christology, typically advocate a "christic cosmology." Some play down or reject "the scandal of particularity," the Word becoming flesh in Christ Jesus; it is the cosmos that is the body of God. Apologists work mainly with an anthropological framework that stresses good stewardship, an idea too functional, too manipulative, too tied in with money to awaken new hearts, new minds. An anthropocentric focus has outlived its usefulness. In summary, "The reconstructionists fail to connect with the core convictions of the Christian community, while the apologists fail to address that community's need for a theology of nature shaped by central Christian faith commitments."[72]

Santmire insists that a third approach is possible, is urgently needed, and already exists. It is a revisionist tradition of theological reflection about environmental issues, orthodox but innovative, flourishing since the 1960s. Here the highest priority is given to biblical interpretation. At the same time, the tradition itself stands in need of reformation for the twentieth century. Central to the revision is the re-emergence of creation theology, paralleled by renewed scholarly interest in a biblical theology of wisdom.

What will such a revisionist theology of nature look like? It must be (1) biblical, but a more critical encounter than ever before with the written Word of God; (2) Christocentric, but highlighting with Joseph Sittler the cosmic creational and salvific purposes of God with all things (Paul's *ta panta*); (3) ecological, in that the vision will be holistic, humanity and nature each with its own integrity; (4) ecclesiological, incarnate in the life of the Christian community, whose identity and activity are formed in its worship.

I have room only for the seventh of Santmire's nine specific theological insights for the shape and content of a revisionist Christian ecology:

> Since the divinely covenanted, universal good for all things is *shalom,* the divinely mandated life for humans in this world is a life of *shalom,* with God, with each other and with all creatures, in anticipation of the dawning of the great and glorious seventh day, the eternal sabbath of God, when all the hungry shall finally be fed and all relationships of domination will finally be overcome, when the lamb will lie down with the lion, death shall be no more, and all things shall be made new.[73]

My own revisionist approach to the ecological crisis runs basically along the lines of Santmire's four characteristics. It is thoroughly biblical; it highlights Sittler's grace-link between redemption and creation; it integrates humanity and nature in a holistic vision; and it is incarnate in the worship and life of the Christian community. The difference may be verbal rather than substantive; it lies in the singular stress I place on biblical justice, precisely as fidelity to relationships that stem from our covenant with God cut in the blood of Christ. Salvation takes place within a single, all-embracing community. My salvation depends on fidelity to three relationships: Do I love God above all else, above all human idols? Do I love every human being, friend and enemy, as Jesus has loved and loves me? Do I touch each "thing," everything that is not God or the human person, with reverence, as a gift of God?

Worth mentioning here are two reassuring realities, one broadly Christian, the other specifically Catholic. The broadly Christian reality is the biblical reality, the answer to Lynn White Jr.'s thesis blaming Genesis and Christianity for our ecological crisis. From a careful study of that thesis, David Toolan has concluded:

> In retrospect, it is clear that Lynn White's indictment of the biblical worldview was too sweeping by far. By and large, with the exception of the apocalyptic Book of Daniel, the Hebrew Bible exhibits no dualism that would oppose two distinct ontological orders, human vs. world, history vs. nature, spirit vs. body, mind vs. matter. The Bible does not limit redemption to human beings, as the primordial "rainbow" covenant with Noah makes clear. It conceives of redemption reaching out to embrace "every living

creature to be found with you, birds, cattle and every wild beast with you, everything that came out of the ark, everything that lives on the earth" (Gen 9:10). In short, nature is included within salvation history.

The separation of history from nature or redemption from creation is largely a modern phenomenon, something that nineteenth century exegetes took over from influential idealists like Hegel. Within the Hebrew Bible itself, such dichotomies are not to be found. . . .[74]

John Paul II has carried ecology beyond any of his predecessors, beyond Vatican II. The earth, nature, things, the nonhuman entered pre-1978 documents of the magisterium in their relation to the development and progress of man and woman. Take the Second Vatican Council as it urges Christians, while on pilgrimage to a heavenly city, to construct a more human world:

For when, by the work of their hands or with the aid of technology, man and woman develop the earth so that it may bear fruit and become a dwelling worthy of the whole human family, and when they consciously take part in the life of social groups, they are carrying out God's design, manifested at the beginning of time, that they subdue the earth, bring creation to perfection; and develop themselves.[75]

In his message for the World Day of Peace, January 1, 1990, "Peace with God the Creator, Peace with All of Creation," John Paul set the ecological crisis within the broader context of the search for peace within society. He linked two principles essential for a solution to the ecological crisis, for a peaceful society: an ordered universe and a common heritage. "Theology, philosophy and science all speak of a harmonious universe, of a 'cosmos' endowed with *its own integrity.* . . . On the other hand, the earth is ultimately a common heritage, the fruits of which *are for the benefit of all.*"[76] He insisted that the Christian vision is grounded in religious convictions stemming from revelation: not only the story of creation and the sin that resulted in earth's rebellion against the human, but a subjugated earth's mysterious yearning for liberation with all God's children (Rom 8:21-23)— all things made new in Christ (Rev 21:5).

As John Paul saw it, the solution to so profound a moral problem calls for responsibility: a new solidarity between developing nations and the highly industrialized; a world's address to the structural forms of poverty, to exhaustion of the soil, to uncontrolled deforestation; a serious look at lifestyles, consumerism, instant gratification. John Paul called for contemplation of nature's beauty, recognition of its restorative power for the human heart. He made bold to assert that Christians must "realize that their responsibility within creation and their duty toward nature and the Creator are an essential part of their faith."[77] In conclusion he commended to our imitation St. Francis of Assisi, who loved all of God's creatures—not only the poor but also animals and plants, natural forces, even Brother Sun and Sister Moon.

An essential part of our faith. Rarely if ever has a Christian leader spoken so clearly and so boldly about the relationship between humans and our earth. And John Paul's examples, for all their generality, lay down specific areas that challenge our faith: exhaustion of the soil, uncontrolled deforestation, consumerism. In this context I think it advisable to specify at some length several of the ecological issues that are particularly confrontational in our time and raise questions of justice, biblical and ethical.

Environment

I begin with the environment. My example of choice is the Columbia River watershed. The core of the 259,000 square miles of the Columbia watershed is the 1,200 miles of the Columbia River. It begins in British Columbia, is fed in the United States by tributaries in Montana, Idaho, Washington, and Oregon, and flows to the Pacific Ocean. This network of rivers, the region's lifeblood, is an extensive ecosystem that transcends national, state, and provincial borders.

On January 8, 2001, the Catholic bishops in this watershed of Canada and the United States issued a pastoral letter "because we have been concerned about regional economic and ecological conditions and the conflicts over them in the watershed." The letter is addressed not only to the Catholic community but "to all people of good will. We hope that we might work together to develop and implement an integrated spiritual, social, and economic vision for our watershed home, a vision that promotes justice for people and stewardship of creation."[78]

The letter does not intend to criticize efforts to provide adequate living for families and is hopeful that commercial and industrial enterprises are concerned about the environment.

It is important for those with deeper concerns about the environment to recognize that farmers, ranchers, and other landowners and workers are not their enemies. It is equally important that the latter groups seek to better understand environmental concerns. Protection of the land is a common cause promoted more effectively through active cooperation than through contentious wrangling.

We call for a thorough, humble, and introspective evaluation that seeks to eliminate both economic greed that fails to respect the environment and ecological elitism that lacks a proper regard for the legitimate rights and property of others.[79]

The effort of the bishops is to explore what Scripture and the Catholic Church have to say about (1) stewardship, (2) the need to respect nature, and (3) the need to recognize and promote the common good.

First, however, the current condition of the region. Industrial development has provided needed goods and jobs. But at times the development has resulted in harm. Some selective facts. U.S. dams provide irrigation, but north of the border dams have flooded Canadian lands, depriving families of their homes, farms, and businesses. Agricultural chemicals control pests and increase profits but can also pollute land and water. Mining provides jobs and funds schools but at times leaves land and waters tainted. Forestry provides needed lumber for homes and industry, jobs for loggers, mill workers, and truckers, but in some places timber harvesting and road construction cause increased runoff and sedimentation.

On these issues and many more, the bishops see signs of hope: a realization on the part of many that their own or others' actions have caused harm; scientific studies of agricultural, fishing, transportation, and energy needs; a new consciousness among government officials and business entrepreneurs about the impact of past abuses, and the expressed intention to avoid such abuses in the future; various proposals for a responsible cleanup of past devastation; efforts to use profits from U.S. dam operations to compensate Canadian communities most heavily impacted; greater community involvement and exchange of ideas.

Here a key concept is respect: respect for one another, for God, and for the environment; respect for the rights of others. This demands an increasing awareness of the needs of our neighbors; of the sanctity of life from conception to natural death; of the integrated ecosystem. We are called not only to relate to people as neighbors and to our shared place as our common home, but also to recognize our responsibility for this place—a responsibility to God and to the community.

Consumerism

Relevant here is John Paul II's strong condemnation of a "super-development"

which consists in an excessive availability of every kind of material goods for the benefit of certain social groups [and] easily makes people slaves of "possession" and of immediate gratification, with no other horizon than the multiplication or continual replacement of the things already owned with others still better. This is the so-called civilization of "consumption" or "consumerism," which involves so much "throwing-away" or "waste." An object already owned but now superseded by something better is discarded with no thought of its possible lasting value in itself, nor of some other human being who is poorer.[80]

What John Paul has expressed in such personal terms can be expanded worldwide.

- The richest 20% of the world's population earn 86% of the world's income, consume 80% of the world's resources, and create 83% of the world's waste. The poorest 20% of the world's population earn under 2% of the world's income.

- Globally, about a billion people are malnourished. Every day an average of 20,000 children die from hunger-related causes—about one child every six seconds. A child in the poorest countries is ten to fifteen times more likely to die before the age of five than a child in the United States.

- Each U.S. inhabitant consumes each day his/her weight in "stuff" (minerals, wood products, food, energy, etc.)—just over 100 kilograms per person.

- Per capita water use in the United States: 1,300 gallons per day—100 gallons of this in households, the remainder in agriculture and industry (it takes eight gallons of water to grow one tomato in an irrigated field). Around the world, 1.2 billion people do not have easy access to clean water.

- The United States consumes 25% of all fossil fuels consumed in the world. Two billion people around the world do not have access to electricity.

- Since colonial times, the United States has lost 50% of wet-lands, 90% of prairies, 95% of virgin forests; one quarter of all large mammals are endangered, 14% of birds, 12% of plants; we have lost 33% of all topsoil through erosion.

- The United States and other developed countries, with a small percentage of the world's people, consume 84% of the paper. The average U.S. inhabitant consumes about 730 pounds of paper products a year; the world average is 125 pounds. Seventy or more pounds per person is considered the minimum needed to ensure basic literacy and communication.[81]

The United Nations, with a similarly shocking set of statistics on consumption disparities, concludes:

Today's consumption is undermining the environmental resource base. It is exacerbating inequalities. And the dynamics of the consumption-poverty-inequality-environment nexus are accelerating. If the trends continue without change—not redistributing from high-income to low-income consumers, not shifting from polluting to cleaner goods and production technologies, not promoting goods that empower poor producers, not shifting priority from consumption for conspicuous display to meeting basic needs—today's problems of consumption and human development will worsen.[82]

In her highly practical, down-to-earth book *Guests of God: Stewards of Divine Creation,*[83] Monika K. Hellwig suggests that, before we consider our consumption patterns, most of us must pay attention to what we waste and what we do with our waste. She notes how troublesome recycling can be, how much of a nuisance to separate biodegradable materials into a compost heap in the backyard or the community gardening lot.

But this is precisely the kind of issue in which personal convenience is at odds with the common good. At the present stage of industrial and economic development and in view of the present consumption patterns of the wealthy nations, recycling is an important factor in long-term ecological balance, even though the individual person or a particular family has little direct gain from it. Recycling efforts are unselfish gestures costing a small amount of inconvenience, yet many good people do not see it as a matter of spirituality, a matter affecting their relationship to God.[84]

Underlying all specific issues is a critical question: Are we faced with an environmental crisis—a crisis that involves justice human and divine? Serious observers are convinced of it. They point to global warming, soil erosion, declines in food production, the worldwide threat to or absence of clean water, the ceaseless destruction of forests, the steep decline in biodiversity, that is, the multimillion species that share the earth with us and perform functions that are in many instances indispensable for human living. All this in the context of the consumerism summarized above. Other scholars are less pessimistic. Gregg Easterbrook, in particular, has spelled out what he calls an "ecorealism,"[85] which recognizes what the doomsayers pass over: how much progress we have made. He admits that skeptical debate is good for the environmental movement, but it must be reasonable, or else it will discredit itself. A number of his claims make sense. For example, resources must indeed be diverted to ecological protection in the developing world; nature "makes pollutants, poisons, and sufferings on a scale so far unapproached by men and women except during periods of warfare"; nature still rules much more of the earth than does genus *Homo;* nature appears to enjoy fostering life and evolving. Environmentalists do not help their cause by exaggerating threats and damages; nature is less fragile than environmentalists assume. Still, as Toolan points out,

Easterbrook's critique is itself skewed. First, his picture of the current situation can be optimistic because he concentrates his attention on progress in the United States, while almost wholly ignoring the bleak situation in the developing countries of Africa, Latin America, and south and southeast Asia. Second, his attack on environmental catastrophism skews the analysis. Real environmental problems are minimized and shorn of any urgency. Nowhere is this more evident than in the chapter on global warming. At the start of that chapter, Easterbrook briefly acknowledges that an "artificial greenhouse effect is the most disturbing ecological prospect of our moment on the Earth," and he offers that it is a prospect "against which women and men are well advised to take immediate steps." But nowhere does Easterbrook make a concerted case for these steps, and the point is quickly lost in the following thirty-eight pages, which make the case that scientific models of climatic change are uncertain, that Mt. Pinatubo's eruption in 1991 put much more carbon dioxide in the air than industry and automobiles do, and, in any case, warming might improve the agricultural production of Canada and Siberia. Easterbrook is so busy beating up environmentalists for the exaggerations of their "worst case" scenarios that the reader finally forgets the last line of this chapter, which asserts that "any reasonable policy that reduces the odds of climate change is more than worth the price."[86]

I dwell on this because any intelligent, promising approach to a complex environmental issue demands a thorough grasp of both sides. I experienced this need in embarrassing fashion when we took our retreat/workshop Preaching the Just Word to the clergy and laity of the Diocese of Helena, Montana. For my homily on the first full day, August 5, 1999, I had decided to be quite relevant, touch biblical justice to an environmental issue in that state. I titled my homily "Water, Wilderness, and Grizzly Bears."[87] I had done a fair amount of homework. With the help of the Greater Yellowstone Coalition in Bozeman, Montana, I presented the environmentalist position on those three issues. Put more briefly here:

- *Water.* The request of the American Smelting and Refining Company for a permit to build an enormous underground copper/silver mine in northwest Montana, 25 miles upstream of Idaho's largest fresh-water lake, involved a treatment of mine wastewater using unproven, experimental technology and discharge of three million gallons per day into the lower Clark Fork River—consuming all the allowable pollution, thereby precluding other forms of growth and development in the area.

- *Wilderness.* The vast majority of Montanans want to preserve the unique spaciousness of the state and to protect its great expanses of wild lands, the critical watersheds, the free-roaming wildlife habitat. The ecological, economic, and spiritual values of these roadless areas merit permanent protection as wilderness.

- *Grizzly bears.* There is serious talk of taking the grizzly off the threatened list, but grizzlies are dwindling and could disappear. Their habitat is disappearing steadily through logging, road building, sprawling subdivisions, and development by the oil and gas and recreation industries. We are told that to delist the grizzly would loosen habitat protections that are keeping the entire Yellowstone ecosystem patched together in the face of tremendous pressures.

All well and good, save that my three examples presented *only* one side of the problem. Only afterwards was I made aware of the complexity of the issues: for example, the arguments of loggers respectful of the land but baffled by the intransigence of environmentalists. Unhappily, this information reached me too late to be incorporated into the homily. A lesson in scholarly patience.

Ecologists

Happily, there are men and women entrepreneurs more interested in protecting the environment than in profits. One such person struck me powerfully several years ago: Yvon Chouinard, age early 60s, president and founder of Patagonia, an outdoor clothing and gear company based in Ventura, California. From its beginnings in the early 1970s, the entire goal of the company was to do the right thing. At first this meant making the most useful and durable products. The company produced aluminum chocks instead of the old steel pitons for climbing, so that rocks would not be scarred. It was also the first outdoors company to introduce modern synthetic fleece. In 1984 Chouinard directed his operation to pledge a percentage of sales (which reached $180 million in 1998) for activist environmental groups. In 1996 Patagonia decided to use in its clothing organic cotton only, that is, cotton grown without artificial pesticides or fertilizers.

In 1999 Chouinard was leading a struggle to dismantle some of the nation's hydroelectric dams, once essential for people, now destructive of spawning salmon. He was instrumental in the taking down of the Edwards Dam on the Kennebec River in Maine. In the state of Washington, the government, egged on by Chouinard, was looking for ways to put such dams as the Little Goose out of service.[88]

Could Chouinard have made much more money without such a focus? Yes indeed. "But part of the process of life," he declares, "is to question how you live it."[89]

Another uncommonly effective ecologist is Albert J. Fritsch, a Jesuit with a doctorate in chemistry. From a simple green house in Mt. Vernon, Kentucky, he directs Appalachia-Science in the Public Interest (ASPI). The Central Appalachian region, the bioregion where ASPI is based, includes eastern Kentucky, eastern Tennessee, West Virginia, western Virginia, and western North Carolina. What Father Fritsch and his staff of 12 (mostly part-time) do is assist in environmental and economic preservation, recovery, and renewal. Every day, on farms, in forests, gardens, and homes, they demonstrate the value of solar energy, the fruitfulness of the land, and the possibilities of connecting technology and science in ways that serve Appalachia's residents. In fact, ASPI's worldview has taken the staff to Haiti, Peru, and the Dominican Republic, where harnessing the sun's energy has enriched lives.[90] Three Rs sum up Fritsch's life: rethinking, restoring, respecting.

Here an all-important word is sustainability, defined as self-sufficient, simple living with minimal reliance on outside fossil fuels and food. Solar energy is a principal project. A striking example is the recycled 1988 Mitsubishi/Dodge Colt of Fritsch's associate Joshua Bills. It makes no noise, needs no oil, no coolant, no spark plugs. Under the hood are eight batteries. Twelve more are stashed in the trunk, whose exterior sports a 20-watt solar panel to power the car's electrical accessories, after the manner of an alternator. Electrical power is gathered from solar collectors on a carport attached to ASPI headquarters. The car conversion cost $6,000; the cost of using it is less than two dollars a month. (Admittedly, the car's energy is used up after about 80 miles, and it takes nine hours to recharge the batteries fully; but it is a commuter car, and there is more renewable energy where the Colt's comes from.) On March 15, 2002, after five months of negotiation with Kentucky Public Service Commission, ASPI was finally allowed to connect its solar-powered system to Kentucky Unity Company's electric grid.

Other solar applications include food dryers, water heaters, solar photovoltaic electrical applications, and solar greenhouses. The green house that is ASPI's headquarters has its own greenhouse, which harnesses the sun to raise out-of-season carrots, garlic, Swiss chard, and herbs. Since 1997, their raised-bed gardens, installed where pavement once covered the soil, have yielded over 7,000 pounds of vegetables. The gardener? Al Fritsch.

An unexpected discovery. The ginseng herb grows almost everywhere in Appalachia. But when checking on ginseng in my still useful *Webster's New International Dictionary of the English Language* (2nd ed., 1958), I read that ginseng "is of little use except as a demulcent." And yet, in 1999, ASPI began the Appalachian Ginseng Foundation (AGF), which calls ginseng "the silver bullet and the key to liberation of the Appalachians from the shackles of the extractive coal, timber, oil, and wood-fiber industries." How so?

International buyers will pay $400 a pound for mature, wild ginseng roots. Ginseng, a medicinal herb highly regarded in Asia, is appreciated more and more in the United States for its therapeutic uses. It's a "lucrative source of income that does not destroy the forest canopy," says ASPI's Web site (www.a-spi.org). Wild ginseng could prove a powerful incentive not to sell those trees or mining rights.

But poachers and overzealous harvesters must be discouraged from decimating an already endangered species. AGF, while it neither defends nor debates ginseng's health benefits, is working hard to protect, produce and market virtually wild ginseng for its contributions to environmental and economic health in Appalachia. (ASPI is assisting university studies on ginseng's effectiveness in treating prostate cancer.)

Right now, AGF is focusing a lot of energy on a ginseng-marketing system, with a possible model in the tobacco-allotment system, which Al Fritsch calls a "good system superimposed on an unhealthy product." The system would not be to limit production (as with tobacco) but to certify and protect growers. At this point, ginseng growers are extremely secretive, because in one afternoon a single poacher could wipe out a crop five or more years in the making—and fail to harvest in a way that ensures future crops.[91]

A concluding word from Al Fritsch, written after 9/11, tells us succinctly how intimately linked are his work and the terrorist attacks on the World Trade Center and the Pentagon. "The highly subsidized, nonrenewable energy economy is simply unsustainable and cannot be secured by any amount of military power. . . . Tell [your children] the world cannot continue to exist divided between the haves and the have-nots, especially since the have-nots are realizing their power. . . . We need to do as much soul-searching as flag-waving."[92]

Homeless Veterans

Homeless veterans? An area of injustice? Yes, and yes. Unknown to the vast majority of Americans, and therefore doubly tragic. I must confess, I myself touched it for the first time when preparing a homily for May 27, 2001. The occasion was the annual Memorial Day concert on the Washington Mall. Before the evening concert, Jerry Colbert, mastermind and organizer of the concert, had a Mass celebrated by me at the Washington Court Hotel for relatives, some of the participants, and other friends. The heart of the concert, seen live by perhaps a quarter million spectators, watched on TV by untold millions, was the homeless veteran who became the heart of my homily after I had unearthed some chilling facts.

Who are these homeless veterans? Mostly male (2% are women), the vast majority are single, most come from poor communities; 45% suffer from mental illness; half have substance-abuse problems. Where have they served? World War II, the Korean War, the Cold War, Vietnam, Grenada, Panama, Lebanon. 47% served during the Vietnam era. More than 67% served at least three years; 33% were stationed in a war zone.

How many homeless veterans are there? No national records are kept. VA estimates? On any given night, more than 275,000. Over the course of a year, more than half a million—one of every four homeless males.

Why are these veterans homeless? Not only because affordable housing, a livable income, healthcare are often unavailable. A large number of displaced and at-risk veterans live with lingering effects of post-traumatic stress disorder and substance abuse, compounded by a lack of family and social support networks. And most housing money in federal programs for the homeless goes to families or homeless women with dependent children.

The Department of Veterans Affairs? It is indeed the nation's largest provider of services; but with an estimated half million veterans homeless at some time during a year, the VA reaches less than 10% of those in need—leaving 460,000 still without services.[93]

Beyond doubt, a matter of justice, human and divine. Sheer logical reasoning, ethical argument, lays an obligation on the rest of us—government and citizenry—to rescue homeless veterans from their degradation; for they have put their lives on the line for us, were willing to die for us. And only God knows how many of them would not be homeless today, had they not offered their flesh and spirit for our defense.

Biblical justice lifts that obligation to a still higher plane for Jew and Christian, speaks to us through our respective covenants with God. Here Isaiah's God brooks no compromise:

> This, rather, is the fasting that I wish:
>   releasing those bound unjustly,
>   untying the thongs of the yoke;
> Setting free the oppressed,
>   breaking every yoke;
> Sharing your bread with the hungry,
>   sheltering the oppressed and the homeless;
> Clothing the naked when you see them,
>   and not turning your back on your own.
>   (Isa 58:6-7)

Jesus, the Just One par excellence, has our homeless veterans very much in mind when he still tells us whereon our salvation depends: "I was hungry and you gave me food, I was thirsty and you gave me drink, I was a stranger and you welcomed me, naked and you clothed me, ill and you cared for me, in prison and you visited me" (Mt 25:35-36). "You welcomed me"; more literally, "you invited or received me as a guest." To all of us who claim to follow Jesus, each of these homeless veterans *is* Jesus, to be welcomed as you would welcome the Son of God in our flesh. Such is New Testament justice; this is what fidelity to our covenant demands. Not invites; demands.

Happily, a Roman Catholic in the House of Representatives, Christopher H. Smith of New Jersey's 4th District, is the prime sponsor of a bill, H.R. 2716: Homeless Veterans Comprehensive Assistance Act of 2001, that was enacted by the Senate and House of Representatives, "To amend title 38, United States Code, to revise, improve, and consolidate provisions of law providing benefits and services for homeless veterans." The Act was signed into law by President George W. Bush on December 21, 2001 (P.L. 107-95). The Act:

- Authorizes 2,000 additional HUD low-income housing vouchers for homeless veterans.

- Authorizes ten new Domiciliaries for Homeless Veterans programs.

- Authorizes $285 million for the Homeless Grant and Per Diem Program.

- Authorizes $250 million for the Department of Labor's Homeless Veterans Reintegration Program (HVRP).

- Requires the VA to provide technical assistance to nonprofit community-based organizations seeking federal funding for homeless programs.

- Requires the VA to provide mental health programs wherever primary care is provided.

- Earmarks $10 million for medical care for homeless veterans with special needs, including older veterans, women, and substance abusers.

Twenty closely packed pages of detail follow. The national goal: "to end chronic homelessness among veterans within a decade of the enactment of this Act." In this context the Act encourages "community-based organizations, faith-based organizations, and individuals to work cooperatively" to end this homelessness within a decade.

Two other veterans' bills sponsored by Congressman Smith have been passed by the Congress:

- H.R. 1291, Veterans Education and Benefits Expansion Act of 2001, which authorizes more than $3.1 billion over five years to expand and increase educational, housing, burial, and disability benefits. The Montgomery GI Bill (MGIB) college educational benefit will increase by 51% over the current levels. H.R. 1291, as amended in the House, contains provisions from four previously approved House bills: H.R. 801, H.R. 1291, H.R. 2540, and H.R. 3240. This was signed into law by President George W. Bush on December 27, 2001.

- H.R. 2540, Veterans Compensation Rate Amendments of 2001, which boosts compensation payments for disabled veterans by $2.5 billion over the next five years. This was signed into law by President George W. Bush on December 21, 2001.

Indeed the government responded with landmark legislation, in harmony with ethical and legal justice, a response of gratitude to a long-lived human need. Imagine my dismay when less than two years later—on the very day we dropped the first bomb on Iraq in 2003—to see federal budget hearings being aired on C-SPAN. A Democrat exclaimed his horror at reducing veterans' benefits, especially during wartime; a Republican retorted that the proposal was not to cut benefits to veterans . . . "only" to cut benefits to veterans' hospitals! A few months later I heard from a friend who had been wounded in Vietnam and recently had applied for benefits to help pay for his prescriptions. He was angry and incensed with a sense of betrayal that his request was denied. Why denied? Because on January 16th, the VA had suspended enrollment for the rest of the year (2003) for all veterans in his group not already enrolled. Such benefits are administered through VA hospitals.

What might be a specifically Roman Catholic response, in harmony with biblical justice? As of 2003, there were 19,081 Catholic parishes in the United States.[94] If each Catholic parish were to find several homeless veterans within the parish boundaries, get to know them, have them invited to homes for food and conversation, discover needs not yet met, we would add a measure of love to generous but impersonal government bills. If we expanded parish nursing programs or helped ill persons find access to "compassionate use" programs available at most pharmaceutical companies, we would live out patriotism beyond flag waving, faith beyond creeds.

A Just War?

As I write, most Americans are struggling with two urgent questions. One lies in the realm of theory: In our time is a just war legitimate, and if so, under what conditions? The other is frighteningly concrete: Granted war can be justified, does the Bush administration's plan for a pre-emptive strike against Iraq fulfill the required conditions?

First the sheer possibility of a just war. This issue has troubled Christianity throughout its history. Back in 1959 Jesuit theologian John Courtney Murray expressed the heart of the problem in one of his typically insightful sentences: "The effort of the moral reason to fit the use of violence into the objective order of justice is paradoxical enough; but the paradox is heightened when this effort takes place at the interior of the Christian religion of love."[95] But the very struggle to make violence serve the purposes of rational policy and Christian living has an important result: development of the just-war theory. "Rather than man being a set of static rules, this synthesis represents a dynamic and flexible attempt to limit both the purposes and conduct of warfare."[96]

Nevertheless, there is a serious problem here. To clarify the contemporary problem, let me begin with the traditional Catholic expression of a just war as summarized by first-rate moral theologian Richard McCormick in 1967.[97]

First, *wars of aggression* as a solution of international disputes or as an instrument of national aspirations are immoral. Explicit in this regard was Pope Pius XII's Christmas message of 1944.[98] "The concept of aggression constitutes a problem in itself. It is a notion not adaptable to modern strategic and technological realities, since these are characterized not so much as the 'crossing of borders' but as the use of enormous force from great distances. From a military standpoint, 'aggression' has become an almost meaningless term."[99]

Second, *defensive war* is morally justifiable. Failure in this regard, especially in an era familiar with weapons of mass destruction, would give free rein to brutal violence, would be unconscionable. In summary, war is justifiable not to punish an offense or to recover things, but only to repel injury and aggression.

Third, *preparations for defensive war* are morally justifiable. This is a logical consequence of the second proposition. It simply means that a people threatened with unjust aggression may not remain passively indifferent. In the absence of an international authority capable of arbitrating disputes and thus preventing threats, a posture of defense cannot be denied. This does not condone or promote the arms race.

Fourth, *conscientious objection* is morally indefensible. Pius XII's reasons? His judgment, paraphrased by John Courtney Murray, was "premised on the legitimacy of the government, the democratic openness of its decisions, and the extremity of the historical necessity for making such defense preparations as would be adequate in the circumstances."[100]

Fifth, to be morally justifiable, war must be the *last resort.* Every other reasonable means must have been exhausted. The reason? The enormity of the physical and moral evils inflicted by war. It calls for a thorough exploration of the means available: for example, diplomacy and foreign aid.

Sixth, the *principle of proportion* must be applied. Two points here. (1) It means weighing the evils of the injustice committed against the destruction and suffering inseparable from war. At times the damages caused by war may not be comparable to those of tolerated injustice. (2) One must weigh the solid probability of success against the horrors of war. "Without hope of success, resort to warfare would but surround the existing and continuing injustice with violence and bloodshed, hence would be an irrational response. . . ."[101]

Seventh, there are two *limitations to the use of force* in defensive actions: the immunity of noncombatants and the general principle of proportionality. The immunity of noncombatants asserts a fundamental moral principal unanimously accepted by Catholic moralists: It is immoral to take innocent human life directly, that is, to perform a lethal action with the intention that death should result. Underlying this principle is the assumption that in war there *are* "innocents." And indeed there are: children, for example, and those not engaged in military action or in activity that promotes or aids military action. That is why "total" warfare and obliteration bombing cannot be justified on moral grounds. "Total warfare implies the assumption that all, or practically all, citizens of a warring nation may be considered as combatants, hence as objects of the defendants' intent to kill." No, "there are many, even the vast majority, who are technically innocent," because their co-operation in violent war making is not sufficiently close.[102] Obliteration bombing suffers from the same dreadful, deadly immoral assumption. That is why I cannot justify, why I deplore with all my mind and heart, the atomic destruction wreaked by the United States on Hiroshima and Nagasaki during World War II, despite the continuing justification attempted by many on the grounds that the bombings saved untold American lives. I may not do an evil act because good will come of it.[103]

Attacks on this traditional teaching as irrelevant rather than erroneous were common and strong a generation ago and have been summed up by McCormick with his customary fairness and lucidity.

> It is pointed out that historically it was not a relevant teaching in World War II, in which there was area bombing, e.g., of Hamburg, London, Berlin, Hiroshima and Nagasaki, and unconditional surrender was forced. It is claimed that Catholic moral teaching was not made relevant by Catholic spokesmen, an indication of its abstractness and impracticality. The distinction between combatant and noncombatant does not fit the present realities. . . . The teaching renders effective defense impossible, hence is no longer applicable to the type of deterrence and war that Christians are called on to wage. The twofold effect is stigmatized as "utter nonsense." . . . The teaching is preoccupied with taxonomical casuistry in the field of military morality . . . hence it shows a lack of moral revulsion for war. And so on.[104]

John Courtney Murray's response to such attacks is worth reading in its entirety.[105] He declares that the initial relevance of the teaching lies in its value as solvent of false dilemmas. First, there are the two extreme positions: "a soft sentimental pacifism and a cynical hard realism—both 'formative factors in the moral climate of the moment.'" The second false dilemma casts up desperate alternatives: universal atomic death versus complete surrender to communism. The traditional teaching refuses to move between such alternatives. Its relevance is twofold: remotely, "its power to form the public conscience and to clarify the climate of moral opinion in the midst of today's international conflict"; proximately, "its capacity to set the right terms for national debate on public policies bearing on the problem of war and peace in this age, characterized by international conflict and advanced technology." This, Murray claimed, "is no mean feat. . . . The Church does not look immediately to the abolition of war. Her doctrine still seeks to fulfill its triple traditional function: to condemn war as evil, to limit the evils it entails, and to humanize its conduct as far as possible."[106]

In this connection I have never forgotten Murray's observation that

on grounds of the moral principle of proportion the [traditional] doctrine supports the grave recommendation of the greatest theorist of war in modern times, von Klausewitz: "We must therefore familiarize ourselves with the thought of an honorable defeat." Conversely, the doctrine condemns the hysteria that swept Washington in August 1958 when the Senate voted, eighty-eight to two, to deny government funds to any person or institution who ever proposes or actually conducts any study regarding the "surrender of the government of the U.S."

In a footnote at this point Murray penned these classic sentences:

When "Washington" thinks of "surrender," it apparently can think only of "unconditional" surrender. Thus does the demonic specter of the past hover over us, as a still imperious *rector harum tenebrarum.* Thus patriotism, once the last refuge of the scoundrel, now has become the first refuge of the fool. It is folly not to foresee that the United States may be laid in ruins by a nuclear attack; the folly is compounded by a decision not to spend any money on planning what to do after that not impossible event. There is no room today for the heroic romanticism

of the apocryphal utterance, "The Old Guard dies but never sur-
renders." Even Victor Hugo did not put this line on the lips of
Cambronne; he simply had him say, "Merde." For all its vulgar-
ity, this was a far more sensible remark in the circumstances.[107]

Murray's final comment on the moral problem of war will bring us
three decades closer to contemporary developments. "It may be that
the classical doctrine of war needs more theoretical elaboration in
order to relate it more effectively to the unique conflict that agitates
our world today, in contrast with the older historical conflicts upon
which the traditional doctrine sought to bear, and by which in turn it
was shaped."[108]

The Persian Gulf War 1990-91

A pertinent, if partial, endeavor in that direction came from Jesuit
John Langan in connection with the Persian Gulf War of 1990-91.[109]
The article is too dense to summarize. It seems best to examine with
Langan three basic lines of objection to applying just-war theory to
situations such as the Gulf War. (1) The theory is theologically unacceptable and is incompatible with basic Christian values. (2) The theory effectively leaves out of consideration some aspects of either the
particular situation or the general character of modern warfare that
need to be considered if a satisfactory and conclusive verdict on the
morality of a given war is to be reached. (3) The theory contains so
many indeterminate elements and potentially contradictory considerations that we should not be surprised that applying it does not yield
a determinate result.

The first objection stems from pacifists or from people moving in a
pacifist direction. Here Langan deals at some length with a controversial editorial in the Roman journal *La civiltà cattolica*.[110] Among
the editorial's 18 principal theses: Modern war is radically different
from war in the past; it is total; since Benedict XV (1914-22) the
Church's opposition to war has been absolute; the conditions for a
just war cannot be met today; war always produces more harm than
good; injustices can always be solved through peaceful means; and
(unexpectedly) the only acceptable kind of war is a war of pure
defense against ongoing aggression—which makes it clear that the
position being proposed is not pacifism. In response, Langan suggests
(1) that "the intensity the editors feel in registering their reasonable
dismay at the human cost of the Gulf War and their skepticism about
beneficial effects has impeded their ability for careful argumentation

that would reveal respect for the probity and intelligence of those who disagree"; (2) that "it is not clear how the editors would deal with the position that the Gulf War was a defensive war of the sort they should recognize as legitimate"; and (3) that "the editors are attempting a revision and repositioning of official church teaching so that the strong denunciations of warfare issued by recent popes would clearly count as the center of the teaching, and defensive war against ongoing aggression would count as a remote peripheral exception. Such a revision naturally raises questions about continuity in church teaching, which is a very delicate point."[111]

The second objection is incompleteness. Even very vehement critics of the Gulf War—such as the editors of *30 Days*, who characterized it as "a 'just' extermination"[112] acknowledged that Iraq's seizure of Kuwait violated international law and was condemned by the United Nations. "But the critics could point to a variety of more or less relevant considerations which cast serious doubts about the consistency of U.S. policy in the Middle East generally and about the credibility of allied claims."[113]

The question as it relates to the Gulf War is "whether we should allow some set of these considerations to overturn the generally acknowledged affirmation that Kuwait and its allies had a just cause for waging war with Iraq. The point in this case is whether Iraq in invading Kuwait committed an unacceptable act of injustice, an inadmissible breach of international order, not whether Iraq does or does not have some legitimate territorial claims against Kuwait, much less whether Iraq's general course of conduct can find some support in some moral considerations."[114] Still, such broader considerations, while not excusing Saddam Hussein, might lessen a tendency to self-righteousness on the part of Americans and their allies, and contribute to "a delicate blending of sympathy and scepticism" that in many ways is more difficult than applying just-war theory.[115]

Third, the indeterminacy theory claims that the various criteria of just-war theory do not so cohere as to provide definite and convergent results in the hands of different theorists. In dispute are terms like "just cause" and "legitimate authority," and how to measure proportionality. The theory itself gives very little guidance where one affirms both the justice of the cause and the disproportion of the means.[116]

The Persian Gulf War 2003-
In the course of his State of the Union address, January 29, 2002, President George W. Bush for the first time used "Axis of Evil" to

describe Iran, Iraq, and North Korea. The effect was expressed neatly in a *Time* magazine column by Michael Elliott:

> ... the phrase instantly entered the lexicon of contemporary politics. For the President's fans, the words cleverly linked memories of World War II to Bush's belief that the contest with terrorists and the states who succor them is a war of moral clarity. For his foes, the term was cheap and illogical nonsense; there was no "axis," it was said, for the three nations posed different and discrete threats. As for branding them evil, that just proved once again that Bush was an ignorant cowboy who saw a multihued world in monochrome.[117]

Evil or not, Elliott declares, the programs are "mighty dangerous." What should the Bush administration do? "Whatever it can, without searching for a spurious consistency in its approach to widely differing situations." Because Mr. Bush's primary focus is on making Saddam Hussein disarm or disappear, I shall concentrate on the Iraqi crisis. I find it interesting that the United States began the year 2003 "eyeball to eyeball with a paranoid, ruthless regime hell-bent on obtaining nuclear weapons to complement an army the Pentagon rates among the most formidable in the world." The nation? North Korea.[118] An additional reason for alarm: On January 10, 2003, North Korea announced that it was pulling out of the Treaty on the Non-Proliferation of Nuclear Weapons, the cornerstone of global efforts to halt the spread of atomic weapons; besides, it has refused to allow a return of U.N. inspectors to a reactor capable of producing nuclear materials that could be used to build a bomb.

Here, as Michael Duffy noted in September 2002, the fundamental issue is Mr. Bush's "new national-security strategy, a long-range plan for the U.S. overseas, which argues that the strongest nation in the world has the right to pre-emptively attack anyone who seeks to harm its people or interests."[119] He closed his column with this shrewd insight:

> Logic says it will take better intelligence—far better than we have now—to make a pre-emptive doctrine war. Congress last week held hearings on what went wrong last year [9/11/01]— and why the President did not act on the wisps of information his Administration had gathered in the months leading up to

Sept. 11. Bush's critics imply that if all the warnings and indications had been pulled together in advance, the President or his
aides could have discerned the plot and launched a pre-emptive
strike on Osama bin Laden last summer. That is a charge the
White House dismisses. But Bush's pre-emptive doctrine assumes
that we may never have all the intelligence, we may be able to
make only educated guesses about our enemies' arsenals and
intentions, and we'll need to rely on wisps and warnings and our
guts. Bush may be comfortable making decisions that way.
Whether the country is ready to go to war on instinct is another
question.[120]

Shortly before Duffy's column appeared questioning the advisabil-
ity of a pre-emptive strike against Iraq from a tactical, practical
assessment of probable success with our current limited intelligence, a
September 13 letter intended for President Bush was hand-delivered
September 16 at the White House to National Security Adviser Con-
doleezza Rice by Bishop Wilton Gregory of Belleville, Illinois, president of the United States Conference of Catholic Bishops. This letter
stemming from the 60-member U.S. bishops' Administrative Committee affirmed traditional Catholic just-war principles to assess the
morality of a just war, in this instance to assess a pre-emptive strike
against Iraq.[121]

On November 8, 2002, the United Nations, after recalling a number of pertinent activities with regard to the problem of Iraq, determined to secure full compliance with its decisions, decided that Iraq
has been and remains in material breach of its obligations under relevant resolutions. Nevertheless, it afforded Iraq a final opportunity to
comply with its disarmament obligations under relevant resolutions of
the Security Council, and accordingly set up an enhanced inspections
regime with the aim of bringing to full and verified completion the
disarmament process established by resolution 687 (1991) and subse-
quent resolutions of the Council.[122]

Aware of this resolution, the United States Conference of Catholic
Bishops issued its Statement on Iraq on November 13, 2002.[123]

As we Catholic Bishops meet here in Washington, our nation,
Iraq and the world face grave choices about war and peace,
about pursuing justice and security. These are not only military
and political choices, but also moral ones because they involve

matters of life and death. Traditional Christian teaching offers ethical principles and moral criteria that should guide these critical choices.

Two months ago, Bishop Wilton Gregory, President of the United States Conference of Catholic Bishops, wrote President George Bush to welcome efforts to focus the world's attention on Iraq's refusal to comply with several United Nations resolutions over the past eleven years, and its pursuit of weapons of mass destruction. This letter, which was authorized by the U.S. Bishops' Administrative Committee, raised serious questions about the moral legitimacy of any pre-emptive, unilateral use of military force to overthrow the government of Iraq. As a body, we make our own the questions and concerns raised in Bishop Gregory's letter, taking into account developments since then, especially the unanimous action of the UN Security Council on November 8th.

We have no illusions about the behavior or intentions of the Iraqi government. The Iraqi leadership must cease its internal repression, end its threats to its neighbors, stop any support for terrorism, abandon its efforts to develop weapons of mass destruction, and destroy all such existing weapons. We welcome the fact that the United States has worked to gain new action by the UN Security Council to ensure that Iraq meets its obligation to disarm. We join others in urging Iraq to comply fully with this latest Security Council resolution. We fervently pray that all involved will act to ensure that this UN action will not simply be a prelude to war but a way to avoid it.

While we cannot predict what will happen in the coming weeks, we wish to reiterate questions of ends and means that may still have to be addressed. We offer not definitive conclusions, but rather our serious concerns and questions in the hope of helping all of us to reach sound moral judgments. People of good will may differ on how to apply just war norms in particular cases, especially when events are moving rapidly and the facts are not altogether clear. Based on the facts that are known to us, we continue to find it difficult to justify the resort to war against Iraq, lacking clear and adequate evidence of an imminent attack of a grave nature. With the Holy See and bishops from the Middle East and around the world, we fear that resort to war, under present circumstances and in light of current public information, would not meet the strict conditions in Catholic teaching for overriding the strong presumption against the use of military force.[124]

Just cause. The *Catechism of the Catholic Church* limits just cause to cases in which "the damage inflicted by the aggressor on the nation or community of nations [is] lasting, grave and certain" (#2309). We are deeply concerned about recent proposals to expand dramatically traditional limits on just cause to include preventive uses of military force to overthrow threatening regimes or to deal with weapons of mass destruction. Consistent with the proscriptions contained in international law, a distinction should be made between efforts to change unacceptable *behavior* of a government and efforts to end that government's *existence*.

Legitimate authority. In our judgment, decisions concerning possible war in Iraq require compliance with U.S. constitutional imperatives, broad consensus within our nation, and some form of international sanction. That is why the actions by Congress and the UN Security Council are important. As the Holy See has indicated, if recourse to force were deemed necessary, this should take place within the framework of the United Nations after considering the consequences for Iraqi civilians, and regional and global stability (Archbishop Jean-Louis Tauran, Vatican Secretary for Relations with States, 9/10/02).

Probability of success and proportionality. The use of force must have "serious prospects for success" and "must not produce evils and disorders graver than the evil to be eliminated" (*Catechism*, #2309). We recognize that not taking military action could have its own negative consequences. We are concerned, however, that war against Iraq could have unpredictable consequences not only for Iraq but for peace and stability elsewhere in the Middle East. The use of force might provoke the very kind of attacks that it is intended to prevent, could impose terrible new burdens on an already long-suffering civilian population, and could lead to wider conflict and instability in the region. War against Iraq could also detract from the responsibility to help build a just and stable order in Afghanistan and could undermine broader efforts to stop terrorism.

Norms governing the conduct of war. The justice of a cause does not lessen the moral responsibility to comply with the norms of civilian immunity and proportionality. While we recognize improved capability and serious efforts to avoid directly targeting civilians in war, the use of military force in Iraq could bring incalculable costs for a civilian population that has suffered so much from war, repression, and a debilitating embargo. In assessing whether "collateral damage" is proportionate, the lives of Iraqi men, women and children should be valued as we would the lives of members of our own family and citizens of our own country.

Our assessment of these questions leads us to urge that our nation and the world continue to pursue actively alternatives to war in the Middle East. It is vital that our nation persist in the very frustrating and difficult challenges of maintaining broad international support for constructive, effective and legitimate ways to contain and deter aggressive Iraqi actions and threats. We support effective enforcement of the military embargo and maintenance of political sanctions. We reiterate our call for much more carefully-focused economic sanctions which do not threaten the lives of innocent Iraqi civilians. Addressing Iraq's weapons of mass destruction must be matched by broader and stronger non-proliferation measures. Such efforts, grounded in the principle of mutual restraint, should include, among other things, greater support for programs to safeguard and eliminate weapons of mass destruction in all nations, stricter controls on the export of missiles and weapons technology, improved enforcement of the biological and chemical weapons conventions, and fulfillment of U.S. commitments to pursue good faith negotiations on nuclear disarmament under the Nuclear Non-Proliferation Treaty.

There are no easy answers. Ultimately, our elected leaders are responsible for decisions about national security, but we hope that our moral concerns and questions will be considered seriously by our leaders and all citizens. We invite others, particularly Catholic lay people—who have the principal responsibility to transform the social order in light of the Gospel—to continue to discern how best to live out their vocation to be "witnesses and agents of peace and justice" (*Catechism*, #2442). As Jesus said, "Blessed are the peacemakers" (Mt 5).

We pray for all those most likely to be affected by this potential conflict, especially the suffering people of Iraq and the men and women who serve in our armed forces. We support those who risk their lives in the service of our nation. We also support those who seek to exercise their right to conscientious objection and selective conscientious objection, as we have stated in the past.

We pray for President Bush and other world leaders that they will find the will and the ways to step back from the brink of war with Iraq and work for a peace that is just and enduring. We urge them to work with others to fashion an effective global response to Iraq's threats that recognizes legitimate self defense and conforms to traditional moral limits on the use of military force.

I find myself in full agreement with the Administrative Committee and with the bishops as a whole in their presentation of traditional Catholic just-war principles. Nevertheless, if only in fairness to President Bush, I must confess that I appreciate a significant dilemma confronting him. On the one hand, he may not respond with military force unless Iraq's threat is "imminent." On the other hand, does it make sense to restrict "imminence" to the moment when weapons of mass destruction intended for the United States or another country are actually in the air?

In a London *Tablet* article, an American specialist on just-war principles, J. Bryan Hehir, conceded that

there are reasons for believing that an attack on Iraq is both strategically persuasive and morally legitimate. But there are too many other factors which urge the United States to step back from the brink of armed action to make these reasons decisive. So we are left, lastly, with the issue of necessity. Is it *necessary* to solve the problem of "radicalism and technology" in this way, by a military assault on Iraq? Not, "is it achievable, desirable, and simpler than the alternatives?", for these criteria are not enough to begin a war. Rather, is it the *only* way, the *last* resort? This must be the test. So far it has not been met.[125]

The *New York Times* for March 9, 2003, carried four pieces rejecting President Bush's projected attack on Iraq: an editorial and three OpEd pieces by Thomas L. Friedman, former President Jimmy Carter, and Maureen Dowd.

The editorial, "Saying No to War," stated flatly, "if it comes down to a question of yes or no to invasion without broad international support, our answer is no." The editors insisted that "by adding hundreds of additional inspectors, using the threat of force to give them a free hand and maintaining the option of attacking Iraq if it tries to shake free of a smothering inspection program, the United States could obtain much of what it was originally hoping to achieve." In their opinion, Mr. Bush "has talked himself into a corner where war or an unthinkable American retreat seem to be the only alternatives visible to the administration." Moreover, "despite endless efforts by the Bush administration to connect Iraq to Sept. 11, the evidence simply isn't there." As for the United Nations, "if the United States ignores the Security Council and attacks on its own, the first victim of the conflict will be the United Nations itself." Finally, the United States needs to demonstrate by example that there are certain rules that everybody has to follow, one of the most important of which is that you do not invade another country for any but the most compelling of reasons. Where the purpose is fuzzy, or based on questionable propositions, it's time to stop and look for other, less extreme means to achieve your goals.[126]

Friedman's column, "Fire, Ready, Aim," began with a Bush line that captured for the globalism expert all the things that troubled him about the President's approach to Iraq: "When it comes to our security, we really don't need anybody's permission." Why troubling? First, "our security." "Because Saddam Hussein has neither the intention nor the capability to threaten America." When Bush turns a war of choice into a war of necessity, people suspect that the real reason must be his father, or oil, or some right-wing ideology. Second, no need for permission? Not for a war of necessity, as against the 9/11 terrorists in Kabul. But for a war of choice in Iraq, we need the world's permission, because we cannot rebuild Iraq without allies. The world does not want to be "led by a president ideologically committed to war in Iraq no matter what the costs." We need allies not to win the war but to win the peace.[127]

Carter's column, "Just War—or a Just War?", claimed "it is clear that a substantially unilateral attack on Iraq does not meet [the criteria for a just war]": a last resort, with all nonviolent options exhausted; discrimination between combatants and noncombatants; violence proportional to the injury we have suffered; legitimate authority sanctioned by the society the attackers profess to represent (specifically, absence here of international authority for the goals of a regime change and a Pax Americana in the region); and a peace established that is a clear improvement over what now exists. "American stature will surely decline further if we launch a war in clear defiance of the United Nations. But to use the presence and threat of our mil-

itary power to force Iraq's compliance with all United Nations resolutions—with war as a final option—will enhance our status as a
champion of peace and justice."[128]

Dowd's column, "The Xanax Cowboy," drew its title from her
sense that in his "call to war" in a news conference on March 6 the
President "seemed tranquilized." "[B]ouncing from motive to
motive" for a preemptive invasion, he "made it clear that Saddam is
going to pay for 9/11," even though "this administration concedes
there is no evidence tying Iraq to the 9/11 plot." "It still confuses
many Americans that, in a world full of vicious slimeballs, we are
about to bomb one that didn't attack us on 9/11 (like Osama); that
isn't intercepting our planes (like North Korea); that isn't financing Al
Qaeda (like Saudi Arabia); that isn't home to Osama and his lieu-
tenants (like Pakistan); that isn't a host body for terrorists (like Iran,
Lebanon and Syria)." Genuinely concerned to protect Americans,
Bush finds no cost too high—"shattering the U.N., NATO, the European alliance, Tony Blair's career and the U.S. budget." In closing,
Dowd cites a 1997 "statement of principles" signed by Jeb Bush and
future Bush officials (e.g., Rumsfeld, Cheney, and Abrams) that
"exhorted a 'Reaganite policy of military strength and moral clarity,'
with America extending its domains by challenging 'regimes hostile to
our interests and values.'"[129]

An unexpected adversary of war against Iraq was Gen. Norman
Schwarzkopf. The famed "Stormin' Norman," who commanded U.S.
forces in the 1991 Gulf War, said "he hasn't seen enough evidence to
convince him that his old comrades Dick Cheney, Colin Powell and
Paul Wolfowitz are correct in moving toward a new war now [Jan.
28, 2003]. He is worried about the success of the U.S. war plan, and
even more by the potential human and financial costs of occupying
Iraq. . . . He worries about the Iraqi leader, but would like to see some
persuasive evidence of Iraq's alleged weapons programs."[130]

Not surprisingly, the President's approach had strong popular support (60 percent at a late stage), and influential men and women
expressed their prowar convictions with intelligence and feeling. Let
wordsmith William Safire stand as an impressive example. One may
reject his arguments for discontinuing "the Phony War," what Tony
Blair derided as "perpetual negotiation." It is pertinent to recall with
him and the President that March 10, 2003, "was the 15th anniversary of Saddam's poison-gas massacre of Kurds in Halabja." I am particularly intrigued, however, with Safire's prediction of what would
happen if Bush were simply to answer legitimate disagreement by get-

ting on with the war and helping to create a dictator-free confederation: "As the U.S. does that, dissent will decline. Tragic mistakes will be revealed, but most of the embedded media will focus on heroes. Smoking guns and hiding terrorists will be found. European non-allies and Arab potentates will find ways to forgive us and our new alliances will be rewarded with security. And American voters next year will remember who offered fear and who offered hope."[131]

On Monday, March 17, 2003, President Bush delivered his ultimatum to Saddam Hussein: Leave Iraq within 48 hours or war will begin. On Wednesday, March 19, bombs burst over Iraq.

III

JUSTICE SACRAMENTALIZED

The title of this section, "Justice Sacramentalized," raises four issues. (1) There is the problem of a critical relationship: liturgy and justice; liturgy and social action. What is the connection between our worship on Sunday and how we act the rest of the week—more exactly, how we act when we leave the church building? (2) There is an issue intimately related to, indispensable for, a liturgy that does justice: the transformative power of the Eucharist, the significance of this sacrament for changing the human heart. Attention must be directed briefly to (3) liturgy of the world and to (4) challenges posed by inculturation.

Liturgy and Justice

For background, I must leap back into history. Then I shall attempt a contemporary integration of liturgy and justice. Finally, some attention to practical problems that hinder integration, and examples of success in such efforts.

History

I begin with a fairly large segment of liturgical history, actually from 1833 to the new millennium. Reach back, first, to the European roots of the liturgical movement between 1833 and 1925.[1] Not all the details; simply some of the more notable moments. Following the French Revolution and the disarray of the Church, Prosper Guéranger re-established the Benedictine Abbey of Solesmes, centering monastic life on the liturgical year and its important feasts and seasons, and advocating a return to Gregorian chant as the official liturgical music of the Roman Church. Despite a highly subjective approach and a somewhat limited vision, his passion for the liturgy and for a Christian life with liturgy as its source was so influential that a strong critic, Louis Bouyer, was convinced there is no achievement in the contemporary liturgical movement that did not originate in some way with Guéranger.

The German liturgical movement traces its origins to the Benedictine monastery of Beuron (1863). Greatly influenced by Solesmes, Beuron contributed influential texts on the liturgy, as well as a famous art school that promoted a harmonious relationship between art and liturgy. Further shape and direction for the movement were provided by Beuron's daughter house Maria Laach (1893). Here the prominent names were Abbot Ildefons Herwegen and two of his monks, Kunibert Mohlberg and Odo Casel, in collaboration with diocesan priest Romano Guardini, and with the help of two remarkable professors, Franz Josef Dölger and Anton Baumstark. One aspect of Casel's work merits explicit mention here, if only for its influence on the future:

> Casel's major contribution was the classic text, *Das christliche Kultmysterium*. In this work, he spoke of the sacraments as mysteries, believing that pagan mystery cults were a preparation for the Christian mysteries. While this theory is no longer held by sacramental theologians, his interpretation of the sacraments gave way to a very positive and rich view of the Church as the Mystical Body of Christ which expresses itself relationally and symbolically through sacramental participation. This concept of the Church as the Mystical Body of Christ would become an important element in the European liturgical movement and one of the founding principles of the liturgical movement in the United States.[2]

In Belgium the liturgical movement traces its roots to 1872, when Abbot Maurus Wolter of Beuron founded a monastery at Maredsous, whose liturgical publications, in collaboration with the newer monastic community of Mont César at Louvain, were powerful forces. It was out of Mont César that the pastoral liturgical movement grew, through the prophetic vision and leadership of Dom Lambert Beauduin. Ordained a presbyter of the Diocese of Liège in 1897, he entered Mont César in 1906. Known for a strong social consciousness and a genuine compassion for the oppressed, he believed that entrance into a religious community would provide the atmosphere of prayer and support he needed to become an effective preacher. Convinced that the liturgy alone could provide the grounding necessary for

Christian social activism, he proclaimed it shameful that the liturgy was the endowment of an elite, insisted that it must be democratized, made nourishment for everyone. He envisioned the Mystical Body of Christ overflowing with a passion for justice—the vision that would soon captivate Virgil Michel and through him the liturgical movement in the United States. Put simply, Beauduin's purpose and desire in founding the liturgical movement were to help God's people to live out their baptism through worship and social action.

A similar pastoral, pragmatic approach was evident in Austria, emerging at the Augustinian monastery of Klosterneuburg, thanks in large part to the imagination of one of its canons, Pius Parsch. Not far from the monastery, in a small church that was a testing ground for his ideas, he called for a liturgical participation that was full and active, that connected liturgy and daily life. What was developing in Austria was an integrated movement that promoted the union of Word and worship.

The passage of the liturgical movement from Europe to the United States is a fascinating story. While young Benedictine Virgil Michel was studying philosophy at Sant' Anselmo in Rome in the 1920s, he immersed himself in the different schools of social, industrial, and economic ethics. There he was stimulated by Lambert Beauduin, especially his development and interpretation of the doctrine of the Mystical Body of Christ. Wrote Beauduin:

I knew [Michel] well at Rome, and when he discovered that I was concerned with the liturgical movement at Louvain, we became quite friendly, and he often came to talk to me in private; but liturgy was not for him just a matter of study; it was above all a powerful means of doing apostolic work, by increasing the faith and devotion of the faithful. His vocation for such work seemed part of himself. He asked me to arrange for him to spend the holidays in our monastery at Louvain, in order to become familiar with all the details of the organization of liturgical work. . . .[3]

Traveling extensively in Italy and Germany, in France and Spain, living close to the people, observing daily life in monasteries and churches, discussing philosophy with philosophers, farming with farmers, liturgy with liturgists—all this influenced Michel to encourage a Christian social order and to stay close to ordinary folk.

One of Michel's greatest discoveries in Europe, through his talks with Beauduin and the time spent in those monasteries, was the doctrine of the Mystical Body of Christ. Such a doctrine was virtually unheard of in the United States at the time. He began to recognize that a community transformed by its worship could ultimately be instrumental in the transformation of society. Thus, as early as 1925, Michel saw the liturgical movement as a means of countering the secularism and individualism of the modern age.[4]

It was Michel's suggestion to his abbot that launched the periodical *Orate fratres* (now *Worship*), to foster a deeper understanding of, and wider participation in, the prayer of the Church. Other seeds in his thinking were planted in Europe, to grow into major concerns on his return to Collegeville, Minnesota: the role of women in the world; liturgy and social justice; a series of texts for religious education that would be rooted in the liturgy; and the full and active participation of the laity in the liturgy. A splendid summary of Michel's integrated vision, the vision that characterized the founding of the liturgical movement in the United States, has been recaptured by Keith Pecklers from a paragraph by H. A. Reinhold in 1947, several years after Michel's death:

It is almost beyond human comprehension to grasp the completeness with which Michel absorbed everything that Austria, Belgium, and Germany had to offer. But greater yet was what he did with it. Instead of dragging his find across the border as an exotic museum piece, he made it as American as only an American mind can make it. He had seen the high sweep of German ecclesiology and sacramentalism; he had admired the Belgians for their clear grasp of a new spirituality and their critical awareness of all that stood in the way of liturgical, ecclesiastical piety from traditional carry-overs; he had learned in Austria what the common people could gather from the Church's treasure without fright, but he did not come back to force these foreign and incoherent moulds on the American church. Besides, his clear realism and his burning apostle's heart had one urge none of the great masters in Europe seemed to see: the connection of social justice with a new social spirituality. For Virgil Michel the labor encyclicals of Leo XIII and the liturgical reforms of Pius X did not just by accident happen within one generation, but were responses to cries of the masses for Christ, who had power and gave the good tidings. They belonged together.[5]

Very simply, the bridge over which the liturgical apostolate came to America was Virgil Michel.

In 1935 Michel argued that "liturgy is the indispensable basis of Christian social regeneration."[6] It was actually in the 1930s and 1940s that the connection between liturgical and social reform became strong. It was then that liturgy became a significant concern for men and women involved in such movements as Catholic Action, the Catholic Worker, Friendship House, and the Grail Movement.[7] Each merits comment.

Integrative Movements

Catholic Action was established in the United States as an organ of the National Catholic Welfare Council, to mobilize Catholic laity to work co-operatively with the hierarchy in social justice, to renew American culture, secular society, through apostolic, social activism. The local chapters, specifically the parishes, were called "cells," since parishes were seen as the Mystical Body in miniature. Despite the emphasis on a spiritual grounding of the movement, largely through retreats, in its early years Catholic Action did not recognize the intrinsic link between liturgical action and social action. The absence of a liturgically based spirituality suggested that Christians through personal piety and good works sanctified the Church and built the reign of God. Happily, as Catholic Action expanded in the 1930s, the doctrine of the Mystical Body became its unifying factor, specifically the realization that genuine Catholic Action must spring from the Church's worship, particularly from the Eucharist: Catholic Action must issue from the altar and lead back to the altar. Here passive participation that neglected the corporate dimension of liturgy was seriously challenged.

Almost from the beginning of Catholic Action, Virgil Michel and his associate editors on *Orate fratres* had recognized its importance for the goals of the liturgical movement. Throughout the volumes of the journal, therefore, many articles reveal Catholic Action as prolonged worship, a continuation in daily life of the sacrifice offered to God at the liturgy. The movement's growth was intensified by the involvement of the young: the Chicago Student Catholic Action

(1936), which at one point included 60 high schools, colleges, and universities in the Chicago metropolitan area; and the Young Christian Workers (1938), under liturgical leaders such as Reynold Hillenbrand and John J. Egan, taking up the challenge to be a new youth for a new world, with its guiding principle the Mystical Body of Christ expressed liturgically and socially.

The Catholic Worker (CW) movement was founded by Dorothy Day and Peter Maurin. Steeped in the Church's liturgy, Day had a profound passion for justice that ignited others during the Depression. In the midst of her own problems before her conversion—an abortion following an unwanted pregnancy, a child out of wedlock, a communism that never actually satisfied her—she looked for ways to help those suffering under the American socioeconomic system. Following her baptism, she saw how people's religious practice and liturgical experience were divorced from daily life, particularly from the poor. Significant for her approach to justice was her friendship with Maurin, an itinerant French peasant and social visionary. Together they envisioned a life of Christian radicalism based on the gospel and rooted in the liturgy. Inescapable for Day was the relationship between the Eucharistic banquet and the hungers of the deprived on the streets. She was convinced that the gospel had *not* been preached to the poor.

Founded as just a newspaper, the Catholic Worker soon included houses of hospitality to shelter the street people and to teach the Church's social doctrine to workers, promoting discussion between workers and the intellectual community. Though a Church-based movement, CW functioned independently. It was founded on the doctrine of the Mystical Body, which it took from the liturgical movement. The Catholic Worker's concern was not simply with feeding the hungry and housing the homeless, not primarily social education. It was to be an organic community grounded in the liturgy, with liturgical prayer a daily practice for the unemployed and destitute. The movement was long misunderstood, slandered as communism in disguise—in Michel's rhetoric, a stone of scandal, like Christ, to the self-righteous.

Friendship House, founded in Toronto in the early 1930s by a Russian baroness, Catherine De Hueck, was a shelter for the poor and destitute—no questions asked; all were received as God's ambassadors. Discouraged by slow progress and resentment from local residents, De Hueck and her volunteers were ready to give up when Virgil Michel arrived, called them fortunate, urged them to persevere, told them that their vocation was to live the Mass, because between two Masses they could do everything. Their situation improved; they opened houses in New York City, Chicago, Milwaukee, Ottawa, and Ontario. Basic to the project was the baroness' conviction that liturgy could transform society, her ceaseless search for connections between the Christ encountered in the liturgy and the Christ encountered in the streets. Liturgical participation should improve our collective sight, the better to recognize the Christ who lives in the poor.

The Grail, founded as a women's movement in 1929 by Dutch Jesuit Jacques van Ginneken, was brought to the United States in 1940 by Lydwine van Kersbergen and Joan Overboss. From the beginning, they made contact with liturgical pioneers and promoters. Their training program had two primary goals: to make the liturgy come alive for participants and to carry the spirit of the Eucharist throughout the day. The lay apostolate must always be grounded in the liturgy. The Grail combined a deep formation in Christian spirituality with outreach to the needy. Projects included re-Christianizing the American culture, ecumenical work, a ministry to married persons, and a department of Catholic culture (e.g., press and film). Despite occasional brushes with the hierarchy and resistance from advocates of individualistic piety, the Grail continued to integrate liturgy and life, with the theology of the Mystical Body as a central principle. With such integration the primary focus of these women could be achieved: the social transformation of a materialistic culture that needed to hear the call to conversion in perhaps a new way. In 1944 the national headquarters of the Grail were permanently relocated in Loveland, Ohio.

For my purposes, the overriding significance of these and other movements was the integration of liturgy and life, the movement from church to world, from altar to people, from the Christ of the Eucharist to the Christ in the streets. And unifying all, the doctrine of the Church as the Mystical Body of Christ.

Of high relevance to Michel's thinking was the economic depression of that period; stimulating at the same time was Pius XI's 1931 encyclical *Quadragesimo anno* on reconstruction of the social order.

Pius XI had identified individualism and collectivism as two dangers that would have to be addressed in the task of social reconstruction, and he had compared a reconstituted social body with the Mystical Body of Christ. Michel had already appropriated an organic notion of the Church from his years of study in Europe, especially under the influence of Lambert Beauduin. It was in the image of the Mystical Body that he found the solution to these two problems.[8]

Here was the only answer Michel could see to the balanced harmony between the individual and the social. "There the individual retains his full personal responsibility, the fullest possibility of greater realization of his dignity as a member of Christ; yet he is ever a member of the fellowship of Christ, knit closely with his fellow members into a compact body by the in-dwelling Spirit of Christ. *There* is the pattern of all social life lived by individuals."[9]

It is precisely in the area of the historical relationship between liturgy and social action that I have uncovered an interesting disagreement among scholars. Bryan Hehir found that in the 1940s and 1950s the liturgical movement and social ministry in the United States enjoyed a close rapport. One of his first approaches to the systematic study of Catholic social teaching came through reading the *Proceedings* of the Liturgical Conference. There the names Diekmann, Hillenbrand, Sheehan, Reinhold, and Leonard complemented the names Ryan, Haas, Higgins, and Egan.[10] On the other hand, in a 1994 interview Msgr. John Egan expressed his conviction that this was rather the ideal than the norm.

> Those who bridged the gap between the liturgical and social movements were relatively few. Many liturgical leaders missed the social justice aspect in their promotion of a liturgical revival, in Egan's estimation. Virgil Michel, H. A. Reinhold, and Reynold Hillenbrand were, of course, exceptions to this, in that they labored tirelessly for an integration of these two important dimensions of ecclesial life.[11]

A similar divergence rears its head where the Second Vatican Council is concerned. Hehir is convinced that the efforts of Michel and others, the encyclicals *Mystici corporis* and *Mediator Dei,* and the social teaching of Leo XIII, Pius XI, and Pius XII bore fruit in Vatican II, for example, in the Constitution on the Sacred Liturgy (*Sacrosanctum concilium*) and the Pastoral Constitution on the Church in the Modern World (*Gaudium et spes*). "The Council provided the framework for the diverse movements of the 1940s and 50s to become central strands in the fabric of Catholic faith at the level of theological reflection and Christian life."[12] On the other hand, Margaret Kelleher notes that "One looks in vain throughout the Constitution on the Liturgy . . . to find an explicit connection between the liturgy and social reform. . . . The famous statement identifying the liturgy as 'the summit toward which the activity of the Church is directed' and 'the fount from which all her power flows' (SC 10) was a perfect context for making a connection between liturgy and the work of justice. But this was not done."[13]

In reflecting on the missed connection on the occasion of the twentieth anniversary of *Sacrosanctum Concilium* John Egan suggested that there were too few people who had really seen the liturgy as a source and paradigm for social reform and that the impact made by those who did was minimal. His reading of the situation in the United States was that cooperation between the liturgical apostolate and the social apostolate had virtually disappeared by the late 1950s. Thus it was not part of the planning before the council and "liturgy and justice went their own ways during and after the council."[14]

What is generally recognized is that the intimate link between liturgy and social justice, Michel's vision of liturgy as "the indispensable basis of Christian social regeneration,"[15] is a "potential largely unfulfilled in the Church in the United States."[16] In large measure, liturgists and social activists occupy two separate camps, and our Catholic people are tragically unaware that in the Catholic vision liturgy and justice belong together, that one without the other is not completely Catholic. My purpose at this point is to suggest why it is simply imperative that the link be restored.

Integration
This segment is not an effort at the ultimate systematization and integration, which calls for the wedding of many minds, a number of specialties, collaboration of clergy and laity, of liturgiologists and activists, experience as well as inspiration. Mine is a more modest effort, but to my mind indispensable. I mean an effort to show how biblical justice (a richer concept than our traditional "social" justice) might influence, and be influenced by, the Church's liturgy.

Recall from Section I the essentials of biblical justice. It is fidelity to relationships that stem from a covenant. Three relationships. To God: Love God above all human idols, with all your heart and soul, all your mind and strength. To people: Love every human being, friend and enemy, as an image of God, like another self, especially the less fortunate, the downtrodden, those summarized in the biblical "widows, orphans, and strangers." To the earth: As stewards and not despots, touch all of God's material creation, all that is not God or the human person, with respect, with reverence, as a gift of God. How might such justice invigorate our liturgies, and our liturgies help fashion a people of God's own justice?[17]

I begin with a basic fact: The justice the liturgy celebrates includes the ethical and the legal, but rises above them. Notre Dame's Mark Searle put it with striking clarity almost a quarter century ago: "The liturgy celebrates the justice of God himself, as revealed by him in history, recorded in the Scriptures, and proclaimed in the assembly of the faithful."[18]

But precisely how? Several years ago I declared that the liturgy does not supply us with practical wisdom in the social, political, and economic arenas. That broad statement must be modified. If the homily is liturgy, if, as Vatican II insisted, the homily is "part of the liturgical action,"[19] then a well-prepared homilist can, indeed should, link the liturgical readings, the prayers, and the symbols to what is going on in politics in the richest nation on earth, and in the moral climate of society and the cultures we inhabit. Still, a basic question remains. How does the liturgy of the Eucharist *as a whole* shape us into people, into Christians, who can recognize justice or injustice when we see it, stimulate us to live justly ourselves individually and as a church, to practice justice, to work for justice, to denounce and destroy injustice?

Recall, to begin, that the liturgy, specifically the Eucharistic liturgy, is the very presence of Jesus, the Servant of justice, in the people assembled, in the Word proclaimed, in the body and blood shared. Recall that biblical justice is a matter of relationships. And the three relationships? To God, to people, to the earth.

The Eucharist reveals and celebrates our relationship to *God*. Here I must confess my daily displeasure as I approach the Preface and I am instructed to pray, "We do well to give God thanks and praise." "We do well"—a dreadfully weak translation of, or substitution for, the old Latin "Vere dignum et iustum est." To praise God and thank God always and everywhere "is utterly fitting and a matter of justice." If I do not praise and thank God regularly, constantly, wherever I am, I am unfaithful to my covenant with God cut in the blood of Christ; I am guilty of biblical injustice.

The official prayer of the Christian community begins each day with the invitation from Psalm 95:6-7: "Come, then, let us bow down and worship, bending the knee before the Lord, our maker. For He is our God and we are His people, the flock He shepherds."

Praise and thanks are a matter of justice, of fidelity, because it is God to whom we owe our being, our existence, our life at every moment. Because it is God to whom we owe our salvation in Christ. Because it is "God's love [of us]" that "has been poured out into our hearts through the Holy Spirit that has been given to us" (Rom 5:5). Because it is God who is our last end, our hope, our destiny.

The Eucharist reveals and celebrates our relationship with *one another*, specifically our oneness as the Body of Christ. That is why we begin with a procession in song. As Jesuit J-Glenn Murray delightfully insists to Catholics across the country, the purpose of the opening procession "is not to get Father from A to B." It is a gathering song, a reminder that we are a people on a journey, on pilgrimage. Mary Collins has caught this and expressed it cogently:

We forget who we are, where we came from, where we are headed. So we assemble when it is timely, to invest ourselves as a community of Christians in liturgical anamnesis. The self-engaging activity of our liturgy not only causes us to remember who we are; it invites us to commit ourselves to a life congruent with our identity.

All liturgy is anamnesis. Sunday Eucharist is the center of Christian anamnesis. This is the weekly occasion on which the baptized assemble to reconstitute themselves publicly in their identity as the Church of Jesus Christ. . . .

But the Church acts most profoundly in the Sunday assembly to reconstitute itself as the Body of Christ. In Sunday eucharistic liturgy we move through public praise and thanksgiving for the mystery; we remember, and remembering dare to move even nearer to our shared identification in the mystery of Christ. Through sacramental communion in the body broken for the world's life and blood poured out for the world's forgiveness, each of us engages ourselves, each of us commits ourselves, and the Church is reconstituted by God's gifts to us.

Our constitution as Church is always partial, never exhaustive. So we must reassemble every Lord's Day. We are burdened by the limit of our comprehension of inexhaustible mystery. We are also limited by the inauthenticity which comes from having divided identities, dual commitments to serve our own purposes as well as God's.[20]

Like Jesus' parables, the Eucharist—homily and symbols—does not force decisions on people. It generates insight, gives fresh perspective, invites people to discover what God's kingdom is all about—and leaves the rest to their graced freedom. Once again Mark Searle has ventured a fresh perspective. In the Eucharist "We stand to one another not as the rich to the poor, the wise to the ignorant, the strong to the needy, the clever to the simple; we stand rather as the poor to the poor, the weak to the weak, the loved to the loved."[21] Back in 1981, a gifted and beloved Father Robert W. Hovda expressed in striking syllables the equalizing, leveling power of the Eucharist:

Where else [other than at Eucharist] in our society are all of us— not just a gnostic elite, but everyone—called to be social critics, called to extricate ourselves from the powers and principalities that claim to rule our daily lives in order to submit ourselves to the sole dominion of the God before whom all of us are equal? Where else in our society are we all addressed and sprinkled and bowed to and incensed and touched and kissed and treated like *somebody*—all in the very same way? Where else do economic czars and beggars get the same treatment? Where else are food and drink blessed in a common prayer of thanksgiving, broken and poured out, so that everybody, *everybody* shares and shares alike?[22]

Wondrously true, but even there we cannot help experiencing a torment and a tension.[23] For the liturgical assembly does not adequately reflect the justice of the kingdom; it reflects more obviously the divisions of social groupings. For all our Eucharistic equality, the tensions abide: rich and poor and the in-between, black and white and yellow and red and brown, men and women, the famous and the forgotten, CEOs and cleaning folk and the unemployed, Anglos and Hispanics, and so many more. How can the liturgy affect such divisions? How build up the single Body of Christ that Godfrey Diekmann rightly insisted was the soul of the pre-Vatican II pastoral-liturgical movement, the one image he believed can inspire us to grasp and live what it means to share the life of God?[24]

Many years ago John C. Haughey, a Jesuit colleague of mine at the Woodstock Theological Center in Washington, D.C., recaptured for me an unforgettable insight expressed by government people engaged in a Woodstock project on government decision making. As they saw it, good liturgy facilitates public responsibility not because it provides principles of solution, tells people precisely what to think about specific conflicts; rather because a celebrant who effectively celebrates the transcendent puts them in touch with that which transcends all their burning concerns, their particular perplexities. Good liturgy frees them to sort out the issues they have to decide, because it makes them aware of their addictions and their illusions, casts a pitiless light on myopic self-interest, detaches from a narrow selfishness, facilitates Christian discernment. In that sense liturgy is not so much didactic as evocative: Let *God* transpire; let *God* speak!

I agree, with one clarification. The effectiveness of the Eucharistic celebration is not limited to the priest celebrant who "effectively celebrates the transcendent." It is the whole assembly in its full, conscious, active participation that effectively celebrates the transcendent. Hence the significance of the double epiclesis: the invoking of the Holy Spirit on the bread and wine *and* on the people gathered, emphasizing not only the transformation of the elements into the body and blood of Christ but also the transformation of the community.

The liturgy reveals and celebrates our relationship to the *earth*, to material creation, to all that is not God or the human person. The point is, God's "things" can be used to build up relationships or to destroy them—from a jug of wine to nuclear energy, from bread shared generously to luxuries clutched feverishly. The breaking of the one Bread, our sharing in the undivided Christ, cries out against the varied ways we turn God's creation committed to our care into captives of our cupidity—yes, into weapons of power and destruction.

This is not a jeremiad against the wealthy, against today's "rich man dining sumptuously each day" and failing even to see the Lazarus "lying at his door covered with sores, who would gladly have eaten his fill of the scraps that fell from the rich man's table" (Lk 16:19-21). My concern is much broader. I mean a consumerist culture that infects our nation and does not spare the Christian. I mean an American value system that sees the material world as a giant cookie jar to be raided at our pleasure. I mean what John Paul II castigated as

an excessive availability of every kind of material goods for the benefit of certain social groups [that] easily makes people slaves of "possession" and of immediate gratification, with no other horizon than the multiplication or continual replacement of the things already owned with others still better. This is the so-called civilization of "consumption" or "consumerism," which involves so much "throwing-away" and "waste." An object already owned but now superseded by something better is discarded, with no thought of its possible lasting value in itself, nor of some other human being who is poorer.[25]

For the Catholic, such a culture is incompatible with reception of the Bread broken for all, broken in a special way for the broken.

I have focused on the Eucharist. But the liturgical symbols that involve our relationship to material creation are not limited to bread and wine. There is the water of baptism, simultaneously symbolic of death and rebirth, of dying and rising. There is the oil for healing, the oil for consecration, the oil for faith building. There is the wood of the cross, supreme paradox of life through death, symbol of reconciliation not only with God and neighbor but also with an earth ruptured from us by sin. There is the incense rising to heaven for forgiveness, for veneration, for exorcism. There is the ring, symbol of love and fidelity. There is darkness and there is light.[26]

On this connection between the natural world and liturgical symbols, I have been recently stimulated by an intriguing ambiguity uncovered by Fordham University's Elizabeth Johnson. It concerns the age-old Latin expression *communio sanctorum*. The word *sanctorum* could mean either "holy persons" or "holy things," participation in sacred realities, especially the Eucharistic bread and the cup of salvation, the meaning when the phrase was first used in the Eastern Church. Medieval theologians, she notes, "played with both meanings. Actually, there is no need to choose between the two, for they reinforce one another." And then Johnson's insight into a profound application today:

> In the light of the contemporary moral imperative to treat the evermore damaged earth as a sacred creation with its own intrinsic rather than instrumental value, the elusive quality of the phrase's original meaning is a happy circumstance. At its best, sacramental theology has always drawn on the connection between the natural world and the signs of bread, wine, water, oil, and sexual intercourse which, when taken into the narrative of Jesus' life, death, and resurrection, become avenues of God's healing grace. Now, in the time of earth's agony, the sancta can be pushed to its widest meaning to include the gifts of air, water,

land, and the myriad creatures that share the planet with human beings in interwoven ecosystems—the brothers and sisters of Francis of Assisi's vision. For the universe itself is the primordial sacrament through which we participate in and communicate with divine mystery. Since the same divine Spirit who lights the fire of the saint also fuels the vitality of all creation, then "communion in the holy" includes holy people and a holy world in interrelationships. By this line of thinking, a door opens from within the symbol of the communion of saints itself to include all beings, sacred bread and wine certainly, but also the primordial sacrament, the earth itself. Once again, this symbol reveals its prophetic edge as its cosmic dimension calls forth an ecological ethic of restraint of human greed and promotion of care for the earth.[27]

There are, of course, other ways of approaching the relationship between worship and justice. John Coleman, for example, has submitted seven ways in which the Eucharist is essentially a proclamation of social justice.[28] I have submitted an approach that has the advantage of linking liturgy specifically with *biblical* justice, and therefore with *all* of our relationships: to God, to God's people, and to God's material creation. Within that context, a set of conclusions directly related to the issue at hand: liturgy and justice reunited.

We Catholics claim to be servants of justice. But we are justified in doing so only if we do not sever social action from the most powerful source of grace at our command. Only if we recognize that our self-giving to God's justice draws its power primarily from a sacred hour, from the Servant who still proclaims to the world in and through us, "This is my body given for you" (Lk 22:19). Only if, as suffering servants, we are prepared to walk the way of the cross that is inseparable from proclaiming God's justice, prepared to follow the Servant who "was despised and rejected by others, a man of sorrows, one from whom others hide their faces" (Isa 53:3).

In season and out of season, I shall continue to insist that liturgists and worshipers at God's liturgy on the one hand, and social activists and practitioners of God's justice on the other hand, dare not constitute two utterly separate organizations, much less two constituencies in conflict. How can expert liturgists and devout worshipers claim to be men and women of biblical justice if they do not live the demands of Yahweh through Isaiah?

> Is this the manner of fasting I wish,
>   of keeping a day of penance:
> That a man bow his head like a reed,
>   and lie in sackcloth and ashes?
> Do you call this a fast,
>   A day acceptable to the Lord?
> This, rather, is the fasting that I wish:
>   releasing those bound unjustly,
>   untying the thongs of the yoke,
> Setting free the oppressed,
>   breaking every yoke;
> Sharing your bread with the hungry,
>   sheltering the oppressed and the homeless;
> Clothing the naked when you see them,
>   and not turning your back on your own.
> Then your light shall break forth like the dawn,
>   and your wound shall quickly be healed. . . .
> Then you shall call, and the Lord will answer;
>   you shall cry for help, and He will say: Here I am.
>   (Isa 58:5-9)

And how can social-justice practitioners do justice to their activism if they draw their power, their influence, from sheerly human competence and energy, and not from the most efficacious, most dynamic source of grace in our universe—from the Eucharist Vatican II declared "is the source from which all [the Church's] power proceeds"?[29]

A fact of liturgical history not sufficiently known: One of the (recently deceased) liturgical leaders long convinced that there is an intrinsic affinity between worshiping devoutly and living justly, that the liturgy itself is the pre-eminent school of justice, was Godfrey Diekman.[30] He participated in the 1963 protest march on Washington, stood about 50 yards from Martin Luther King Jr. during the unforgettable "I Have a Dream" address. Despite the unhappiness of the then bishop of Mobile-Birmingham, Godfrey joined other priests in the 1965 march on Selma, Alabama. In fact, the banner he carried continued to brighten his monastery room. It reads, "Selma is in Minnesota, too." Not himself a day-in-day-out social activist,

> Godfrey was one of a good number of liturgists caught in the crossfire of strategies of justice in the late sixties and early seventies [of the twentieth century], an inevitable dispute given the

early liturgical movement's presumption that a social agenda would be achieved by a *slow* and *organic* development, with the laity gradually becoming empowered through liturgy to assume their position as leaders in the marketplace. This strategy, according to Andrew Greeley, became unsatisfactory to promoters of justice. Instead of waiting for the liturgy to transform the laity, priests took over! Liturgical activities of the fifties promised great results if liturgy were modernized—but no one dreamt how far things would go, and there was no structure in place in terms of artists, musicians, scholars, resources at every level. "We need to realize," Greeley concluded, "that transformation is going to take a long, long time. Social activists demand short-term results; what Godfrey was predicting is necessarily long-term."[31]

I can only hope and pray that the vision of this commonsense Benedictine may draw together once again our liturgists and social reformers, our worshipers and activists. Not primarily to establish a single fraternity; rather that the Body of Christ may move more effectively from church to world, from altar to people, from Christ crucified on Calvary to Christ crucified at the crossroads of our earth. Only then are we likely to realize, bring to concrete actuality, what a perceptive, sympathetic Protestant put into a penetrating expression: "If you Catholics could get your act together, you'd be dangerous!"

Liturgy as Transformation

On January 8, 1999, Jesuit J-Glenn Murray, director of the Office for Pastoral Liturgy of the Diocese of Cleveland, stunned the community of John Carroll University with a celebration of the Eucharist that had the campus buzzing about the rare power of that liturgy. The university's magazine declared that "he brings to the Mass a creativity and intensity that work to pry the scales from your eyes so that you see the sacred ritual with something you imagine approaches its original power." In fact, the editor of the magazine said to anyone who would listen, "It was as if I had never been to Mass before." Two weeks later, during an interview at the same university, Murray said:

As awesome and beautiful as the preconciliar liturgy was, I believe the [Vatican Council] fathers understood that people could leave this beautiful liturgy we shared—this was my experience as a kid—and two blocks away had no problem calling me a "nigger." I think implicitly the leadership's insight was: "How can you pray this way and behave that way—there is something wrong here."[32]

John Carroll had a unique experience of liturgy because the celebrant had been transformed. If the experience is to carry over, not be lost with the passage of time, if an experience is to evolve into a transformation, what is needed is an ongoing Eucharistic spirituality. This might well begin with the Catholic tradition mentioned earlier, the tradition reaffirmed by Vatican II:

The liturgy is the summit to which the Church's activity is directed; at the same time it is the source from which all her power proceeds. . . . The renewal in the Eucharist of the covenant between the Lord and humans draws the faithful into the compelling love of Christ and sets them afire. From the liturgy, therefore, *and especially from the Eucharist,* as from a fountain, grace is channeled into us, and that sanctification of men and women in Christ and the glorification of God, to which all other activities of the Church stretch and strain as toward their goal, are most effectively achieved.[33]

Begin with that truth of Catholic theology, exaggerated as it may seem to untutored ears: From the Eucharist as from no other comparable source all the Church's power proceeds. It is the Eucharist that can transform us into eucharists. For what is the Eucharist? It is a presence; a presence of Christ; a real presence; a presence of the whole Christ, body and blood, soul and divinity; a presence that stems from love, the love of a God-man, and leads to love, a crucified love, a crucified love for every man and woman born into this world. This Eucharist can make of us, demands of us that we become, genuine eucharists. I mean that we be present to our sisters and brothers; really present; a presence of the whole person, not only mind and money but flesh and spirit, emotions and passions; a presence that springs from love and leads to love: "Love one another as I have loved you" (Jn 15:12).

Important for a Eucharistic spirituality is the sacrificial element. This comes through with incomparable power if we meditate on four words Matthew and Mark used in describing the bread Jesus changed into his body at the Last Supper: Jesus took, blessed, broke, and gave (Mt 26:26; Mk 14:22).[34]

First, Jesus "took" a loaf of bread. Not high Mediterranean cuisine; ordinary food. A staple of life indeed, but quite common. It reminds us how God chose for God's people a motley mob of unruly runaway slaves, culturally undistinguished, often rebellious, frequently unfaithful, unpredictable, unreliable. As Moses told them, "It was not because you are the largest of all nations that the Lord set His heart on you and chose you, for you are really the smallest of all nations. It was because the Lord loved you and because of His fidelity to the oath He had sworn to your fathers that He brought you out with His strong hand from the place of slavery, and ransomed you from the hand of Pharaoh, king of Egypt" (Deut 7:7-8). Similarly for Christians. God chose us to be part of God's people, specifically servants of justice. *God* chose us; we did not choose God. And God chose us not because we deserved it (what indeed recommends us?), simply because God wanted to, because such was God's mysterious will, God's mystery-laden love.

Second, Jesus "blessed" the bread. What incredible creative power in that blessing! What had been, a split second before, a common loaf is now, instantaneously, transfigured into the incarnate Son of God. It is such a blessing, God's word, that transformed those restless Hebrew tribes into God's people. A similar blessing, pronounced over us when God called us to serve justice, changed us into agents of the reconciling Christ. Each day should be a fresh creation, a ceaseless miracle of grace.

Third, Jesus "broke" the Bread. He divided the Bread so that there might be enough for all. In a sense deeper still, the body of Christ had to be broken if it was to bring life to the world. "Unless a grain of wheat falls to the ground and dies, it remains just a grain of wheat," cannot produce images of itself; "but if it dies, it produces much fruit" (Jn 12:24). We remember how God had to discipline God's own people time and again, from the exile in Egypt to the captivity in Babylon and beyond, to bring them to a deeper awareness of God, of themselves, of others. He had to "break" them. So too with us. To make us fit instruments for justice, Jesus has to "break" us, destroy the false self in us. Paradoxically, I am least myself when I make the world revolve around me—my successes and my failures, my hurts and my frustrations, my diaphragmatic hernia and my ingrown toenail. The "I" has to be transformed. And so God molds me in the fire of suffering. Not for its own sake; sheer suffering is neither good nor bad.

Rather to reshape me in the image of God's Son, the Jesus who "learned obedience from what he suffered; and when he was made perfect, he became the source of eternal salvation for all who obey him" (Heb 5:8-9).

Fourth, Jesus "gave" the Bread. He gave what he had blessed, what had been mere bread and wine, gave it to his dear friends and through them to all of us, for the world's salvation. It was strikingly symbolized on the cross, when Jesus flung his arms wide to embrace the world, and at the same time his hands were empty, for he had given us everything. He had given us himself in the sacrament of his flesh. Similarly, a gracious God poured life and love incessantly on the Hebrew people, till at the end God had only God's only Son to give. "God so loved the world" (Jn 3:16). We too, chosen and blessed and broken, are given to a little world for its life. In every Mass, in the Eucharist we celebrate, with the whole priestly people we offer the body of Christ, and on the same paten we offer ourselves. The profound meaning of our vocation as a "holy priesthood" (1 Pet 2:5) lies in this: We are given—given to others for their life. God changes into Christ not only bread and wine; God changes *us* into Christ—for the life of the world.

But precisely here a problem in justice raises a fairly ugly head. A liturgy that does justice is a liturgy that fashions community, destroys corroding divisions, brings ever closer the prayer of Jesus that those who believe in him "may be brought to perfection as one," one as the Father and Jesus are one (Jn 17:20-24). To broad distress, the Eucharist that traditionally has been the sacrament of unity is currently a center of discord. Should the celebrant mouth an ageless Latin or a prosaic vernacular? Do we chant an austere Gregorian or swing with the St. Louis Jesuits? Dare we cradle Christ in our hands or does reverence demand a mouth open and eyes closed? Is church still the scene of sacred silence or the arena for community sharing? Is a male celebrant God-given or gender injustice? For countless Catholics, these are not idle questions; they touch the very nerves of our worship.

Potentially even more divisive than any of the above is a growing movement for liturgical "restoration," a "reform of the reform." Rembert Weakland, O.S.B., former archbishop of Milwaukee, posed the problem neatly:

Few dispute the fact that the liturgical reforms of the Second Vatican Council have been implemented with mixed results.

There is a widespread sense that the liturgy can be improved and that the quality of liturgical practice is crucial to the life of the Church as a whole. What many lay Catholics may not realize is that the welcome desire for better liturgy has, in some quarters, taken a highly polemical and potentially divisive turn. Some proponents of this new wave of criticism like to describe their plan as a "reform of the reform" or, more accurately, a restoration— a return to the Vatican II documents and a new start at implementation. I fear, however, that the liturgical restoration envisaged by these proponents threatens the unity of the Church as well as the coherence of our common worship; and some of their thinking is now pervading Roman liturgical documents.[35]

I am not concerned here with Weakland's arguments against the restorationists, compelling though I find them. I resonate to his concluding suggestion: "Instead of fomenting acrimonious controversies over 'renewal' versus 'restoration,' Rome's Congregation for Worship might attempt to arrive now at a consensus in the Church on what has been truly beneficial about the renewal, and what is valid about the criticisms levelled against it."[36] In this connection I believe that, if Catholics are to engage productively in the discussion, if liturgy is to promote transformation, a specific type of conversion is necessary.

Conversion
I do not mean the sudden, swift turnabout from Saul to Paul, from strict Pharisee to Christian believer. I recommend a more complex approach, the systematic method Jesuit theologian Bernard Lonergan has left us. As believers, as faith-filled Christians, as reconcilers (2 Cor 5:17-20), our task is to help people to recognize, understand, value, and live accurately the various relationships they have to one another, so that they might heal the ruptures that alienate, that destroy relationships. In short, to promote justice.

Healing these ruptures is the function of conversion. But what precisely is the conversion? For Lonergan, a conversion to exact fidelity to four transcendental precepts. (1) Be attentive: Focus on the full range of experience. (2) Be intelligent: Inquire, probe, question. (3) Be reasonable: Marshal evidence, examine opinions, judge wisely. (4) Be responsible: Act on the basis of prudent judgments and genuine values. This last, for Lonergan, includes being in love: wholehearted commitment to God as revealed in Jesus Christ. Why are these precepts called transcendental? Because they are not limited to any particular genus or category of inquiry, for example, science or theology. They are simply a normative expression of the innate, God-given, spontaneous, and invariably unfolding operations of human intentional consciousness.

The transcendental method does not admit of easy explanation. One has to absorb Lonergan's *Method in Theology,* a challenging invitation to self-awareness, self-understanding, self-appropriation. For my purposes here—an aid to transformation—two aspects are especially significant. First, "in a sense everyone knows and observes transcendental method. Everyone does so, precisely in the measure that he is attentive, intelligent, reasonable, responsible."[37] Second, "in another sense it is quite difficult to be at home in transcendental method, for that is not to be achieved by reading books or listening to lectures or analyzing language. It is a matter of heightening one's consciousness by objectifying it," that is, "applying the operations as intentional to the operations as conscious."[38] Concretely, how does one do that with the four precepts? It is a matter of

1) *experiencing* one's experiencing, understanding, judging, and deciding, (2) *understanding* the unity and relations of one's experienced experiencing, understanding, judging, deciding, (3) *affirming* the reality of one's experienced and understood experiencing, understanding, judging, deciding, and (4) *deciding* to operate in accordance with the norms immanent in the spontaneous relatedness of one's experienced, understood, affirmed experiencing, understanding, judging, and deciding.[39]

In connection with those four precepts, Lonergan identifies three conversions I find highly pertinent for transformation: intellectual, moral, and religious.

Intellectual conversion is "a radical clarification" of experience. It eliminates a misleading myth about human knowing: that to know is to see, hear, touch, taste, smell, feel. On the contrary, "the world mediated by meaning is a world known not by the sense experience of an individual but by the external and internal experience of a cultural community, and by the continuously checked and rechecked judgments of the community. Knowing, accordingly, is not just seeing; it is experiencing, understanding, judging, and believing."[40] Liberation from the myth, discovering the self-transcendence proper to the human process of coming to know, is to break through ingrained habits of thinking and speaking. "It is a conversion, a new beginning, a fresh start. It opens the way to ever further clarifications and developments."[41]

Moral conversion involves shifting our criteria for decisions and choices from satisfactions to values. It "consists in opting for the truly good, even for value against satisfaction" when they conflict. But "deciding is one thing, doing is another." What remains? To root out biases in the self, in culture, in history; to keep scrutinizing our responses to values; to listen to criticism; to learn from others.[42]

> So moral conversion goes beyond the value, truth, to values generally. It promotes the subject from cognitional to moral self-transcendence. . . . He still needs truth . . . the truth attained in accord with the exigencies of rational consciousness. But now his pursuit of it is all the more secure because he has been armed against bias, and it is all the more meaningful and significant because it occurs within, and plays an essential role in, the far richer context of the pursuit of all values.[43]

Similarly, religious conversion goes beyond the moral. It occurs when we are "grasped by ultimate concern." It is a falling in love, unqualified self-surrender; it means loving "with all one's heart and all one's soul and all one's mind and all one's strength." It means accepting a vocation to holiness. "For Christians it is God's love flooding our hearts through the Holy Spirit given to us. It is the gift of grace." It involves replacing the heart of stone with a heart of flesh, and then moving gradually to a complete *transformation* of all my living and feeling, my thoughts and words, my deeds and omissions.[44] Gentle reader, note the high point of this conversion process: transformation.

Not a rigid order of conversions—first intellectual, then moral, then religious. Normally, religious conversion is prior to moral, which in turn is prior to intellectual. Nor is Lonergan's approach to conversion ivory-tower philosophical theology. It has to do with truth, with values, with love, with "the eros of the human spirit,"[45] with suffering, with a transformation not only of my innermost self but of my relationship to people and the earth, to culture and history. Its high point, religious conversion, is conversion "to a total being-in-love as the efficacious ground of all self-transcendence, whether in the pursuit of truth, or in the realization of human values, or in the orientation man adopts to the universe, its ground, and its goal."[46] It is critical not only for individual holiness but for the building of community.

The building of community. Here I return to where I began: A liturgy that does justice is a liturgy that fashions community, destroys corroding divisions, averts acrimonious controversies, specifically on the way we worship. I am not downplaying the power of the liturgy itself to effect community. I am strongly suggesting that a lifelong process of conversion, of self-transcendence, of transformation can be enormously helpful for Christian conversation, for peaceful discussion rather than angry debate, for the ability to differ without destroying love—yes, for an ultimate agreement on a reformed liturgy. Conversion in the Lonergan mode changes *me*.

Liturgy of the World

In this next segment on liturgy I want to move out from the sheer bread-and-wine offering to a liturgy that includes it but goes far beyond it. To do so effectively, I find it useful to begin with an uncommonly stimulating article, "Cosmological Liturgy and a Sensible Priesthood."[47] There David Fagerberg writes wittily, that is, wisely and amusingly, of the "synthetic cooperation between sense perception and the intellectual conception which is required for knowing." That this is frequently overlooked, he holds with philosopher Joseph Maréchal, "may be due to the disintegration of classic scholasticism in philosophers succeeding St. Thomas Aquinas." Noted Maréchal more than a half century ago:

> If this conception of the material function of the sense elements belongs to Kant, who established it against Cartesian ontologism, it had formerly been the common possession of all the scholastic philosophers, since the most stubborn "dissidents" among them have held the peripatetic tenet that "There is nothing in the intellect that was not first in the senses." . . . St. Thomas carefully avoids suggesting that the intelligence would only be a transposition and a duplicate of the senses. Sensation provides intellection with a starting point and some matter, nothing more. In his seemingly most "sensualistic" formulas he always safeguards the higher formal point of view of the intellect.[48]

After affirming, with philosopher Etienne Gilson, that "There is only one subject able to turn sense perceptions of particular objects into signs of general notions—namely, man,"[49] Fagerberg announces the liturgical conclusion of his "foray" into sensation and intellection:

. . . without *anthropos,* the sensible world would not be known intellectually, and the splendour of the created world would not be mediated into the cosmic praise of God. Without *anthropos,* this material cosmos would not serve sacramentally or be offered eucharistically to God. Angels can understand the sensible world, and animals can experience it, but only *anthropos* can both perceive and know the material world. Man and woman are the cosmic priests of the visible world, and add the splendour of the created matter to the celestial praise of God when they offer it up in "reasonable worship" (Rom 12:1—*logiken latreian*). "Alongside 'kosmos noetos' (the intelligible world) Holy Tradition sets 'kosmos aisthetos' (the sensible world). This latter encompasses the whole realm of what belongs to the senses in the sacraments, in the liturgy, in icons, and in the lived experience of God. . . . The beautiful then is as a shining forth, an epiphany, of the mysterious depths of being, of that interiority that is a witness to the intimate relation between the body and the soul." The liturgical role of man and woman depends upon the twin capacities of sense and intellect, body and soul. It is a liturgy which neither angel nor animal can celebrate.[50]

Such a liturgy of the world sees the creative *agapē* of God flowing through the whole of creation, and in response creation's *eucharistia.* The command in Genesis 1:28, "subdue . . . have dominion," is not an imposition of human will upon nature; "it is a liturgical command, and liturgy is hierarchical. It means that, filled with divine splendour, man and woman would rule in accordance with God's will and pass on this light generously to the worlds beneath them. Thus the material world would be in the Kingdom, i.e., under the rule of God."[51]

It is an awesome vocation to which our baptism introduces us, "eucharistic priests of the material cosmos."[52] This is not to downgrade *the* Eucharist, our thanksgiving par excellence, bread and wine transmuted into the body and blood, soul and divinity, of the risen Christ, offered to the Father in praise and gratitude from the rising of the sun to its setting. It simply extends our liturgy to worldwide dimensions, to all of created reality. Not only to the "matter" of each sacrament, to the water of baptism and the oil of healing. Not only to the wood of the cross. To "everything [God] had made and found very good" (Gen 1:31). So far-reaching a vision of liturgy can aid immensely the effort to touch biblical justice to the nonhuman creation that makes possible our pilgrimage to God.

Liturgy Inculturated

A fairly recent addition to my awareness of justice reached me from India. A professor of philosophy, Subhash Anand, has called for a renewed effort toward an inculturated liturgy, especially of the Eucharist.[53] He is aware of a significant paragraph in Vatican II's Constitution on the Sacred Liturgy:

Even in the liturgy the Church does not wish to impose a rigid uniformity in matters which do not involve the faith or the good of the whole community. Rather she respects and fosters the spiritual qualities and gifts of the various races and peoples. Anything in their way of life that is not unbreakably bound up with superstition and error she studies with sympathy and, if possible, preserves intact. Sometimes she even admits such things into the liturgy itself, as long as they harmonize with its true and authentic spirit.[54]

Two decades later the movement toward an Indian liturgy had come to an end. Why? Michael Amaladoss believed that the reason for the absence of adequate progress was that "earlier enthusiastic efforts have met official opposition."[55]

The Indian experience led me quite naturally to the United States, compelled me to investigate, at length and in depth, the extent to which this country's "way of life" has impacted our liturgy. I begin with a working definition of inculturation supplied more than a decade ago by theologian Peter Schineller, long active in the Jesuit Nigeria-Ghana mission, currently director of the Gaudium et Spes Institute in Nigeria.

Inculturation is the incarnation of Christian life and of the Christian message in a particular cultural context, in such a way that this experience not only finds expression through elements proper to the culture in question, but becomes a principle that animates, directs and unifies the culture, transforming and remaking it so as to bring about "a new creation."[56]

Why a particular emphasis on inculturation in our time? Schineller offers two reasons: First, we are living in an unprecedented "age of mission, with tremendous challenge to and activity on the part of the church." Second, "we are in an age of global awareness, which includes the awareness of cultural diversity."[57] On broad lines, this process of inculturation exhibits three stages. The first stage goes back to the Word of God taking flesh and dwelling among the Jewish people—the model par excellence of inculturation. "His entire life and ministry remain the central paragon for uncovering and inculturating gospel values of the kingdom into particular contexts."[58] The second stage begins with the conversion of Paul and his mission to non-Jews, for example, his presentation of the gospel to the Greek philosophies and religion of his day (see Acts 17:26-34)—the basic approach of Christianity for almost two thousand years. The third stage emerges clearly with Vatican II. Let Karl Rahner expose his own division of church history, which has certain similarities to Schineller's three stages of inculturation, especially in Rahner's emphasis on Vatican II and a world church.

[W]hile the Church must be inculturated throughout the world if it is to be a world Church, nevertheless we cannot overlook the fact that the individual cultures themselves are today involved in a process of change to a degree and at a rate previously unknown. As a result, it is not easy to say what content bearing importantly on the future the individual cultures can offer for a Church that is meant to become a world Church in the full sense. Whatever we may say about these and many other questions, it is incontestable that at Vatican II the Church appeared for the first time as a world Church in a fully official way.

. . . [T]heologically speaking, there are three great epochs in Church history, of which the third has only just begun and made itself observable officially at Vatican II. First, the short period of Jewish Christianity. Second, the period of the Church in a distinct cultural region, namely, that of Hellenism and of European culture and civilization. Third, the period in which the sphere of the Church's life is in fact the entire world. These three periods signify three essential and different basic situations for Christianity and its preaching.[59]

The difficult question remains: How is the old message to be proclaimed in a new era?

None of us can say exactly how, with what conceptuality, under what new aspects the old message of Christianity must in the future be proclaimed in Asia, in Africa, in the regions of Islam, perhaps also in South America if this message is really to be present everywhere in the world. The people in these other cultural situations must themselves gradually discover this—and here, of course, it cannot remain a question of formally declaring the necessity of such other proclamations, nor simply of deriving them from an inherently problematic analysis of the special character of these peoples.[60]

In closing this section, I think it pertinent and useful to illustrate the possibilities of inculturation from a concrete example. I am thinking of an Italian priest in the United States who revealed in striking fashion how to forge links between cultures in a religious context. Celebrating his own Italian heritage while appreciating the cultures of others was Charles A. Marciano, a diocesan priest assigned to a parish in the heart of the Latino crescent in southeast Pennsylvania. This region is defined *geographically* as Philadelphia and the area extending in a half-moon shape through Chester, Lancaster, Berks, Lehigh, and Northampton Counties and is defined *ethnically* as having one of the largest number of Hispanics—for example, Puerto Ricans, Cubans, and Dominicans, as well as Mexican migrant workers—on the east coast.

Father Marciano embraced his mission and parishioners with uncommon eagerness despite serving in a state that continues to have one of the largest numbers of organized hate groups in the United States.[61] In remarkably little time, he was celebrating Mass, preaching, and hearing confessions in English and Spanish and conversing in both languages in the homes and streets of Reading.

At a time when smaller ethnic parishes were closing for a lack of funds and "English only" was angrily chanted in schools and government buildings around the country, Father Marciano led his congregation to become *the largest parish* in the Diocese of Allentown. Throughout these nine years, this generous pastor urged his assistants at St. Peter's not only to become fluent in Spanish but also to learn and appreciate the similarities and differences among the various Spanish-speaking ethnic groups in the city.

Because the parish celebrates its diverse cultures through various feasts—especially through English, Spanish, *and* bilingual Masses— perhaps it should have surprised no one that Padre Marciano was invited to join the U.S. delegation to Cuba when Pope John Paul II visited the island nation in 1998.

In the summer of 2003, cancer took the life of Charles Marciano at age 59. The parish had two viewings to accommodate the far more than a thousand persons wanting to show their respect for this man who so fully embraced cultures not his own by birth. His Mass of the Resurrection was concelebrated by more than a hundred priests—an uncommon tribute to a parish pastor—and, yes, the Mass was celebrated partly in English and partly in Spanish.

In the United States we are experiencing change in the faces and voices comprising our church. Although "American bishops have projected that by the year 2050, Hispanics will constitute 24% of the population and over 50% of U.S. Catholics,"[62] Mario Vizcaino, priest and director of the South East Regional Office for Hispanic Affairs for the Archdiocese of Miami, predicts that by the year 2050, nearly 85 percent of all Catholics in this country will be Hispanic.[63] Priests with Marciano's vision and laity aware of their catholicity need to respond to this shift in culture.

Inculturation in a world church? Since Vatican II, there has indeed been a fresh beginning within Catholicism. Problems remain, will probably always remain: age-old antagonisms, cultural contradictions, different responses to the Church's invitations and demands. Still, a future high in hope. Despite a serious decline in vocations, more and more priests have the mentality of Marciano, yearn to bring their multicultured parishes to a greater appreciation of diversity. More and more laypersons, newly aware of their stature and power within the Church, are striving to live the second commandment of God's justice: Love every man, woman, and child as Jesus loves us, each an image of God whether friend or enemy, of whatever culture or color. In this context, we have every reason to hope for a church that is a single Body of Christ, wherein no one, absolutely no one, can say to any other, in the words of St. Paul, "I have no need of you" (1 Cor 12:21).

I V

JUSTICE GLOBALIZED

As I embarked on the globalization of justice in the summer of 2001, the media were awash with pertinent protests. A typical example was the July 23 issue of *Time* magazine featuring "Chaos Incorporated," when "150,000 anticapitalist-if-not-all-quite-anarchist demonstrators greeted George W. Bush and seven other leaders of the industrialized world in Genoa, Italy, that week."

> On the websites that summit-hopping protesters use to swap intelligence, the three days of action in Genoa are being hyped as the culmination of Europe's "summer of resistance," an antiglobalapalooza that included bust-ups in Göteborg, Barcelona and Salzburg. A convergence of events—Italy's election of metamogul Silvio Berlusconi as Prime Minister, the shooting of three demonstrators in Göteborg, the presence of Bush—will make Genoa, says Bernard Cassen, founder of the French antiglobalization group ATTAC, the "biggest demonstration against globalization ever."[1]

The anticipated rioting did indeed take place, with 50,000 demonstrators flowing through the streets of Genoa; protesters and riot police clashed; one demonstrator was fatally shot by an Italian policeman. Of particular interest to me were the broad interests represented by the protesters.

> The causes represented on the street today included environmental groups like the World Wildlife Fund, Roman Catholic social workers pushing an anti-poverty agenda, pacifists and myriad national groups calling for the liberation of Iran, the liberation of the Kurds in Iraq and greater democracy in Turkey. Labor unionists were in abundance and signs read "People

before profit" and "Stop the capitalist-profit circus." . . . A young Welsh protester . . . identified himself as a member of a group calling for more aggressive debt relief for the poorest nations. . . .[2]

It seems clear that globalization is a complex concept. The complexity calls for clarification; the involvement of cultures needs to be highlighted; and all this will lead to my central concern, the role of justice.

Globalization

How define globalization?[3] The term refers to an unprecedented intensification and acceleration of an ever more open flow of communication and movement of people, technologies, money, goods, images, and ideas across national borders. This cross-border interaction links individuals, organizations, countries, and cultures either actually or potentially. The interdependence resulting from such linkages, however, is frequently asymmetric.

In its fullest sense, globalization is a process that arises out of two interconnected historical developments. One is the advance in the technologies of communications, information, and transportation. The other is the implementation of liberalization policies and the opening up of local markets to international flows of goods, services, technology, and especially capital. These developments are multifaceted. They involve interlocking economic, ecological, sociocultural, and political activities that penetrate all areas of everyday life. Moreover, globalization is uneven both in the way it influences local cultures and in the way it is affected by its encounter with local cultures. It is uneven because developments in the individual countries take place at different speeds, and because the range and depth of its influence vary. It is affected in the sense that, while it has an impact on people, it is also shaped by them, whether their local response is resistant or receptive.

Economic globalization is driving the current process of globalization. We can understand the global economy best in its historical context. The recent wave of economic globalization is fundamentally different from the first wave (approximately 1870 to 1914). During the first period, reductions to barriers in international transactions led primarily to an increase of trade in goods. In this second and current period, beyond increases in trade, economic globalization is resulting in the progressive networking of national market economies. This networking occurs through the growth of foreign direct investments, an increase in the number of joint ventures, and an unprecedented integration of international financial markets. Along with the flow of information (electronic-commerce), these capital markets enjoy an openness that allows them to operate beyond national regulations. The increase of short-term capital in the overall flow of international capital creates the potential for economic and social instability (e.g., the Asian crisis).

The decision of government policy makers to open up their national and local markets is carried out through fiscal policies (budgetary, exchange-rate, and taxation policies). Historically, governments suffering from a critical shortage of financial capital have taken these steps because of the conditions that private, bilateral, and multilateral financial institutions have placed on their loans. These conditions (called for by "economic structural adjustment policies") have required governments to adopt fiscal policies associated with globalization. When structural adjustment policies are not accompanied by adequate social policies (poverty alleviation, healthcare, education), they often result in the exclusion of the poor from the benefits of economic growth as well as increased impoverishment.

Moreover, together with growing openness that permits the flow of goods and capital, we see contradictions in national policies of industrialized countries that promote globalization. For instance, the migration policies of many countries, which restrict cross-movement of peoples, run counter to the increasing liberalization of trade in finance capital, goods, and services. In addition, some national policies protect domestic employment through measures favoring products that are no longer internationally competitive.

Admittedly, this is heavy going, ever so much in so small a space. Perhaps a lighter fare, more easily digestible, might help. In 1999 a prominent American interpreter of world affairs, Thomas L. Friedman, declared, "The slow, fixed, divided Cold War system that had dominated international affairs since 1945 had been firmly replaced by a new, very greased, interconnected system called globalization. If we didn't fully understand that in 1989, when the Berlin Wall came down, we sure understood it a decade later." This he illustrated from full-page ads that Merrill Lynch ran in major newspapers throughout America on October 11, 1998, at the height of the global economic crisis, under the heading "The World Is Ten Years Old." The ads read:

It was born when the Wall fell in 1989. It's no surprise that the world's youngest economy—the global economy—is still finding its bearings. The intricate checks and balances that stabilize economies are only incorporated with time. Many world markets are only recently freed, governed for the first time by the emotions of the people rather than the fists of the state. From where we sit, none of this diminishes the promise offered a decade ago by the demise of the walled-off world. . . . The spread of free markets and democracy around the world is permitting more people everywhere to turn their aspirations into achievements. And technology, properly harnessed and liberally distributed, has the power to erase not only geographical borders but also human ones. It seems to us that, for a 10-year-old, the world continues to hold great promise. In the meantime, no one ever said growing up was easy.[4]

I have been especially enlightened by several pages in which Friedman explains what he means when he says that "globalization has replaced the Cold War as the defining international system with its own unique attributes."[5] Here my summary of most of the differences cannot do justice to the details.

First, whereas the Cold War system's overriding characterization was division, symbolized by the Berlin Wall, globalization's overarching feature is integration, symbolized by the World Wide Web. "In the Cold War we reached for the 'hotline,' which was a symbol that we were all divided but at least two people were in charge—the United States and the Soviet Union—and in the globalization system we reach for the Internet, which is a symbol that we are all increasingly connected and nobody is quite in charge."

Second, unlike the Cold War system, globalization "is not frozen, but a dynamic ongoing process." It is "the inexorable integration of markets, nation-states and technologies to a degree never witnessed before—in a way that is enabling individuals, corporations and nation-states to reach around the world farther, faster, deeper and cheaper than ever before, and in a way that is enabling the world to reach into individuals, corporations and nation-states farther, faster, deeper, cheaper than ever before." It is "also producing a powerful backlash from those brutalized or left behind by this new system." The driving idea behind globalization is free-market capitalism, spreading to virtually every country in the world, with its own set of economic rules revolving around opening, deregulating and privatizing your economy.

Third, globalization "has its own dominant culture, which is why it tends to be homogenizing to a certain degree. . . . Culturally speaking, globalization has tended to involve the spread (for better and for worse) of Americanization—from Big Macs to iMacs to Mickey Mouse."

Fourth, globalization "has its own defining technologies: computerization, miniaturization, digitization, satellite communications, fiber optics and the Internet, which reinforce its defining perspective of integration. Once a country makes the leap into the system of globalization, its elites begin to internalize this perspective of integration, and always try to locate themselves in a global context." The governor of Israel's Central Bank indicated to Friedman a reversal of perspective: "Let's not ask what markets we should export to, after having decided what to produce; rather let's first study the global framework within which we operate and then decide what to produce."

Fifth, while the defining Cold War measurement was weight, particularly the throw weight of missiles, "the defining measurement of the globalization system is speed—speed of commerce, travel, communication and innovation." The most frequent question? No longer "Whose side are you on?" but "To what extent are you connected to everyone?" The second most frequent question? No longer "How big is your missile?" but "How fast is your modem?" The defining document? No longer "The Treaty" but "The Deal."

Sixth, if the defining economists of the Cold War system were Marx and Keynes, each in his own way wanting to tame capitalism, the defining economists of globalization are Schumpeter and Grove, who prefer to unleash capitalism. In the latter view the essence of capitalism is creative destruction—"the perpetual cycle of destroying the old and less efficient product or service and replacing it with new, more efficient ones." Only the paranoid survive, "only those who are constantly looking over their shoulders to see who is creating something new that will destroy them and then staying just one step ahead of them." Only the countries "most willing to let capitalism quickly destroy inefficient companies . . . will thrive." "Innovation replaces tradition." If these systems were sports, the Cold War would be sumo wrestling; globalization, the 100-meter dash, over and over again.

Seventh, "If the defining anxiety of the Cold War was fear of annihilation from an enemy you knew all too well in a world struggle that was fixed and stable, the defining anxiety in globalization is fear of rapid change from an enemy you can't see, touch or feel—a sense that your job, community or workplace can be changed at any moment by anonymous economic and technological forces that are anything but stable."

Finally and most importantly, the defining structure of power. "The Cold War system was built exclusively around nation-states [and] . . . it was balanced at the center by two superstates," the United States and the Soviet Union. The globalization system "is built around three balances, which overlap and affect one another." (1) The traditional balance between nation-states. The U.S. is now the sole and dominant superpower. The balance of power between the U.S. and the other states still matters for the stability of the system. (2) The balance between nation-states and global markets. Millions of investors (Friedman's Electronic Herd) "mov[e] money around the world with the click of a mouse." This herd gathers in global financial centers (Friedman's Supermarkets), Wall Street, Hong Kong, London, and Frankfurt. Each can have a huge impact on nation-states, even triggering the downfall of governments. "[T]he United States can destroy you by dropping bombs and the Supermarkets can destroy you by downgrading your bonds." (3) The newest of all: the balance between nation-states and individuals (Friedman's Super-empowered individuals). Some are quite angry, some quite wonderful, all able to act directly on the world stage. To understand globalization, we have to see it as a complex interaction between all three actors (balances).

Since globalization is not easily grasped from a single author however impressive, I find it useful to add to the above the approach of Robert J. Schreiter, C.PP.S., in an address to the religious community of Sacred Heart Fathers and Brothers in Hales Corner, Wisconsin, August 18, 1999. Its title, "Pursuing Social Justice in an Age of Globalization," promises an added advantage: the relation of globalization to the primary concern of this book, justice.[6] Schreiter begins with an informative paragraph on "the dramatic shifts in the configuration of our world which have been occurring during the past decade."

There has been a powerful conjunction of three factors which have served to reshape our world. The first of these is the rapid change in communications technology. The advent of the personal computer in the 1980's, followed by the Internet in the 1990's, is producing changes in communication—and with it, the social relationships which different forms of communications make possible—the full extent of which we have yet to grasp. Secondly, the Cold War, the bipolar alignment of the world's nations, ended with the collapse of the Berlin Wall and the dissolution of the Soviet Union. It has challenged us to reimagine the geopolitical order: what constitutes peace and peacekeeping, how transnational issues such as ecology and human rights are to be understood, and how nations themselves are to relate to one another. Third, the collapse of state socialism in all but a few countries of the world has led to a global form of market capitalism—often called neo-liberal capitalism, since it resembles strongly the liberal capitalism of the late nineteenth century—which now envelopes all of the world's economies. Together, these three factors—communications technology, a new geopolitical arrangement, and neo-liberal capitalism—create what is becoming the name for the world order of our time: globalization.

At this point in history, Schreiter confesses, globalization is not yet susceptible of a clear definition, nor are we aware of its long-term consequences; for "it relies on a still-expanding technology of communications, a volatile form of market-driven economy, and a geopolitical arrangement which is still trying to find itself." In an earlier work, borrowing from an analysis by David Harvey, Schreiter defined globalization as "the simultaneous expansion and compression of time and space"—globalization as creating (1) a greater connection of elements in our environment (Marshall McLuhan's global village) and (2) an instantaneous reality where once there were great distances and time lags.[7] Now he finds more useful (if not more compact) a definition suggested by David Held and his colleagues: "a process (or set of processes) which embodies a transformation in the spatial organization of social relations and transactions—assessed in terms of their *extensity*, *intensity*, *velocity* and *impact*—generating transcontinental or interregional flows and networks of activity, interaction, and the exercise of power."[8]

Extensity concerns the way globalization stretches things across what had been their normal boundaries so as to have an influence in places where previously there was none. For example, the struggle over the price of bananas in Europe has devastated the Caribbean economy. *Intensity*, the increasing interconnectedness of everything, together with a greater sense of interdependence, means that everything affects everything else, from electrical power sources to bank accounting to airline performance. *Velocity* represents the speed with which information and images flow to us; we look for instantaneous contact with the entire world. Thanks to these three, distant events can have an *impact* beyond their locale—our knowledge of events in Rwanda and Kosovo, or the impact of the 9/11 terrorism in New York and Washington on the whole of the United States, even abroad.

With these four characteristics in mind, Schreiter has researched how globalization affects six of the major dimensions of human existence that make up our world.

1. *Communication* and the technologies which make it increasingly more comprehensive and more rapid are the driving forces in globalization. "Just as the printing press changed and speeded up communication a half millennium ago, and the advent of the telegraph and the telephone a little over a century ago, so now electronic communication has taken us all another step further." For that reason, the globalization of communication will demand close scrutiny when we address later what social justice will mean in so changed a world.

2. The *economy* is the dimension of our lives in which the impact of globalization is often most keenly felt. "The speed with which things can move in this economy, the fact that decisions having profound local impact may have been made thousands of miles away, and the disruptions that appear out of nowhere all combine to give the impression of an economical juggernaut that is *inescapable*, anonymous, and out of control." Here too questions of social justice will have to be addressed.

3. *Politics* is a dimension of contemporary life that finds it difficult to catch up with globalization. While the market economy seems to favor some form of democratic government, and democracy favors a greater attention to political human rights, the processes of democracy tend to move slowly. "The economics of market capitalism in its globalized form are changing the meaning and role of the nation-state, a political unit which has shaped Europe and subsequently the rest of the world the past 350 years. What new forms are going to be needed are still being born."

4. The *cultural* wares that signify globalization are consumption and entertainment. Consumption includes food (McDonald's and Coca-Cola) and clothing (T-shirts, sportswear, denim jeans). "Entertainment media create the environment in which these cultural images circulate. Films, television, popular music, and videos all create this world." Icons of this cultural flow: world figures such as Michael Jordan and Michael Jackson.

5. The *demographic* dimension of globalization cannot be overlooked; *people* as well as information, capital, and cultural images are

on the move. Intrastate conflicts have created increasing numbers of displaced persons and refugees. Other populations are created by people seeking better economic opportunities, "creating multicultural societies in places like Europe where such societies did not exist previously, or creating even more intensely multicultural societies in Australia, the United States, and Canada." A particular challenge is created by the speed with which such societies are being created and the intense relationships they generate.

6. Two significant dimensions of the *physical environment* call for mention. (1) "The pursuit of quicker and greater profit margins in the global economy is creating a dramatic increase in the scramble for natural resources that is stripping many poor countries of their wealth at an intensified rate. The energy requirements of market capitalism create what is increasingly recognized to be an unsustainable level of development." (2) Environmental pollution knows no national boundaries. "Rich countries cannot shield themselves from depletion of the ozone layer or from environmental disasters such as that of Chernobyl of some years ago."

Culture

Globalization by its very nature involves cultures. Hence a second adventure in clarification: What do we mean by culture? A now famous work from the mid-twentieth century by A. L. Kroeber and Clyde Kluckhohn listed 164 definitions of culture, categorizing them into six major groups and further subgroups.[9] From a vast field Jesuit scholar Michael Paul Gallagher has singled out three English-language approaches "because of their diversity from one another, and also because they highlight aspects partially neglected in the summary of Kroeber and Kluckhohn."[10]

For Clifford Geertz, culture "denotes an historically transmitted pattern of meanings embodied in symbols, a system of inherited conceptions expressed in symbolic forms by means of which men communicate, perpetuate, and develop their knowledge about and attitudes toward life."[11] To the crucial role of symbols as carriers of culture Geertz later added "common sense" as "an everywhere-found cultural form" of a less tightly integrated kind.[12] The omnipresence of this cultural system, the common sense of a society, Geertz sums up in a striking passage: "Religion rests its case on revelation, science on method, ideology on moral passion, but common sense rests its on the assertion that it is not a case at all, just life in a nutshell. The world is its authority."[13]

I cite Geertz explicitly not only because of his wide influence but more immediately because he leads me to the scholar on whom I shall largely depend in the following pages, Jesuit theologian Bernard Lonergan. For Lonergan has studied common sense as a gathering of incomplete insights that remain "within the familiar world of things"; the level of common sense "discourages the effort to understand," and this "in-built bias of common sense" can be an element of lived culture that undermines authentic culture.[14] On the other hand, Lonergan offers a definition of culture that goes beyond common sense, a definition I find powerfully persuasive, a definition that will prove useful when we introduce the question of justice.

The contemporary notion of culture is empirical. A culture is a *set of meanings and values informing a common way of life,* and there are as many cultures as there are distinct sets of such meanings and values. However, this manner of conceiving culture is relatively recent. It is the product of empirical human studies. Within less than one hundred years it has replaced an older, classical view that had flourished for over two millennia. On the older view culture was conceived not empirically but normatively. It was the opposite of barbarism. . . . It stressed not facts but values. It could not but claim to be universalist.[15]

Michael Paul Gallagher has probed Lonergan's thinking with several helpful insights.

With the term "informing," used in the sense of giving form to (rather than modern "information"), Lonergan bridges the inner world of philosophies and the outer world of shared patterns of life, and in his own way touches on practically all the six elements highlighted by Kroeber and Kluckhohn. For him, however, it is not enough to identify culture with what . . . Raymond Williams calls "a whole way of life"; Lonergan prefers to see culture as the communal expression of our self-understanding—through art, language and through the visions implicit in how we live and act. In his words, "culture is the meaning of a way of life" and thus he proposes a distinction between the social and the cultural, akin to the old relationship of body and soul.[16]

After indicating the multifaceted nature of culture, Gallagher finds a "rich synthesis" in a UNESCO definition produced at an international conference on "Cultural Policies" in Mexico in 1992. A rich synthesis because "it seeks to do justice both to the 'creative' or conscious culture exemplified by the imaginative, intellectual and spiritual dimensions of life and to the more 'lived' sense of culture associated with anthropology and sociology."

> Culture may now be said to be the whole complex of distinctive spiritual, material, intellectual and emotional features that characterize a society or social group. It includes not only the arts and letters, but also modes of life, the fundamental rights of the human being, value systems, traditions and beliefs. . . . It is culture that gives man the ability to reflect upon himself. It is culture that makes us specifically human, rational beings, endowed with a critical judgment and a sense of moral commitment. It is through culture that we discern values and make choices. It is through culture that man expresses himself, becomes aware of himself, recognizes his incompleteness, questions his own achievements, seeks untiringly for new meanings and creates works through which he transcends his limitations.[17]

Significant here are the shifts in the ways of human communication, as we have moved from oral cultures to the writing and printing revolutions and then to the electronic media of today. Gallagher has highlighted the work of Jesuit Walter J. Ong because he has studied these shifts for many years and views them from the perspectives of literary criticism and theology.

> [I]n each case the arrival of new technology had a major impact on culture itself. When, for instance, writing ousted the patterns of an older oral culture, it "transformed human consciousness," introducing "division and alienation," but also "highly interiorized stages of consciousness." Then a different phase of thinking arrived, when printing allowed knowledge to be localized in visual space, as distinct from the essentially communal and present-tense communication typical of "morality." The eye took over from the ear as the chief contact with reality. Thus writing and printing located knowledge in space, with the cold objectivity of words on a page. Oral cultures had trusted more in the

temporal world of speech and were therefore more naturally community-based.[18]

Important for our purposes here, these cultural developments presented challenges for the mediation of religious faith. Sound is "related to present actuality rather than to past or future" and is "a special sensory key to interiority."[19] Faith, says St. Paul, comes from hearing (Rom 10:17). The dominance of the visual caused a depersonalized culture and privatized religion. The "decay of dialogue," an indirect effect of the printing press, made for a radically different context for the communication of faith. Printing makes reality private and seemingly controllable, whereas "the spoken word moves from interior to interior" and genuine interpersonal encounter is "achieved largely through voice."[20] "Writing seals off its product from direct dialogue: the writer creates his text in isolation"; a certain lonely individualism results.[21]

What Ong calls "oral-aural" culture (because it involves both a speaking and a listening) is much more existentially real than the strange act of reading in silence. When he turns his attention to the twentieth century, Ong becomes enthusiastic about the potentials of a "secondary orality," caused by yet another technological development that again is having enormous impact on human consciousness: the world of electronic communications—especially radio and television—has retrieved the lost dimension of voice. This development is capable of healing some of the cultural imbalances caused by the impersonal world of print. . . . What printed visualization tended to neglect, this new orality makes possible again. Its relational quality not only leaves room for faith but fosters the human capacities for interpersonal hearing where the Word can enter. Thus as distinct from the "closed fields of systems" of print, now there is a fresh openness "connected with our new kind of orality, the secondary orality of our electronic age."[22]

Second Vatican Council

For the first time in the Church's history, and unexpectedly, an ecumenical council discussed culture at length and then devoted a substantial chapter to it. This section of Vatican II's Pastoral Constitution on the Church in the Modern World is unexpected because it was only after more than a year that the council moved away from sheerly internal issues and began to look beyond itself to the world outside its borders, started listening to the "signs of the times." *Gaudium et spes* "can be viewed as an essay in theological anthropology on contemporary culture."[23] Basic to chapter 2 is a description of culture.

> It is one of the properties of the human person that he or she can achieve true and complete humanity only through culture, that is, by cultivating natural gifts and values. Whenever, therefore, human life is involved, nature and culture are intimately connected.
>
> In its general sense, the word "culture" refers to all those things by which human beings refine and develop their various capacities of mind and body; strive to control the cosmos by knowledge and by work; humanize social life within the family and the civic community by improving customs and institutions; express by their works the great spiritual experiences and aspirations throughout the ages; communicate and preserve them to be an inspiration for the progress of many, even for the whole of humankind.[24]

In brief, what *Gaudium et spes* 53 does is to link "the older meaning of culture—as a field of human growth and of intellectual or aesthetic achievements—with the more empirical sense of culture (or cultures) as embodied in social structures and in historically diverse approaches to life."[25] The rest of the chapter has three subsections: the contemporary cultural context, principles of cultural development, and responsibilities of believers in the cultural field. From these packed paragraphs I select a small number of ideas that have proven influential on postconciliar Catholic thinking.

The council speaks of "a new age in human history" for the development of culture and its diffusion (54). Contributing factors: expansion of the natural and human sciences, progress in technology, advances in the means of communication. Results for culture: a highly critical judgment; deeper insights into human behavior; awareness of change and evolution; new mass cultures with new patterns of thinking, acting, and use of leisure; wider openness to the treasures of different cultures. Thus a more universal form of culture is gradually taking shape, whereby the unity of humankind is expressed in the measure that the particular features of each culture are preserved.

The council goes on to speak of "the birth of a new humanism"

(55) that involves a deeper awareness of "autonomy and responsibility." Men and women are increasingly conscious that they themselves are "the molders of their community's culture," with the duty of building a better world based on truth and justice. Human persons are primarily defined by responsibility to their brothers and sisters and to history.

Not to appear excessively optimistic, the council lists (56) in the form of questions certain contradictions in contemporary culture that call for resolution. How foster a new culture without losing fidelity to tradition? As specialization in knowledge continues its rapid increase, how preserve the power to contemplate and to wonder? Amid exchange between cultures, how prevent the loss of wisdom of ancestors and character proper to each people? How make all men and women share in cultural values "when the culture of the more sophisticated grows ever more refined and complex"? How recognize a legitimate independence in culture without promoting a merely earthbound humanism?

In harmony with its efforts to envision modern culture as a bearer of "positive values," the council declares that "cultural activities are central to the Christian calling" (57). Through technology and philosophy, through the arts and sciences, by participating in the life of social groups, the Christian "carries out the designs of God," can "elevate the human family to a more sublime understanding of truth, goodness, and beauty." Unjustified conclusions from the sciences "do not necessarily follow from today's culture."

On the links between the gospel and culture (58), the council notes that God through Christ "has spoken according to the culture proper to each age." While the Church transcends all cultures, purifying and transforming them, her mission [evangelization] is to embody the gospel in different cultures, enriching cultures and being enriched by them.

To safeguard certain ideal goals of culture (59)—defending the human person and serving the good of the community, fostering a sense of wonder and awareness on religious, moral, and social levels—a rightful autonomy has to be recognized: liberty of research, of expression, of information, and above all, "that culture be not diverted from its own purpose and made to serve political or economic interests."

Among a number of issues on the role of culture in Christian formation (62)—what Gallagher calls "something of a dustbin for ideas that did not fit in easily in other parts of the text"[26]—the council recommends, in pastoral care, appropriate use of the secular sciences, of literature and the arts; acknowledging new forms of art adapted to our age; efforts to close the gap between artists and the Church; openness to new vistas in contemporary thinking; interdisciplinary work in theology; and "for all the faithful, clerical and lay, a lawful freedom of inquiry, of thought, and of expression, tempered by humility and courage in whatever branch of study they have specialized."

Postconciliar Catholic Developments

Catholic concern with culture did not cease when Vatican II closed in 1965. In fact, many of the key issues opened up by the Pastoral Constitution on the Church in the Modern World were central to official Catholic approaches in the decades that followed. Here two popes, Paul VI and John Paul II, are of singular importance. A word on each.[27]

Paul VI's apostolic exhortation *Evangelii nuntiandi* (1975) is the papal text following upon the 1974 Synod of Bishops on evangelization; it deals in part with the "evangelization of culture." Paul calls evangelization "the essential mission of the Church" (14). The Church needs always to be "evangelized by constant conversion and renewal, in order to evangelize the world with credibility" (15). Evangelization means "bringing the Good News into all the strata of humanity and through its influence transforming humanity from within" (18). It means "affecting and as it were upsetting, through the power of the gospel, humankind's criteria of judgment, determining values, points of interest, lines of thought, sources of inspiration and models of life, which are in contrast with the Word of God" (19). Here Paul VI moves beyond the council. Vatican II seems, as Gallagher phrases it, "almost innocently optimistic" in its statements on culture, "due to a deliberate option . . . to avoid condemnations and to give a sympathetic pastoral reading of the modern situation."[28] Paul is aware that "the dominant criteria of common sense are often in silent conflict with the gospel," and so "evangelization has to include a new and ambitious goal—the Christian transformation of culture in its many senses."[29] In Paul's words, "The split between the gospel and culture is without doubt the drama of our time, just as it was of other times. Therefore every effort must be made to ensure a full evangelization of culture, or, more correctly, of cultures" (20).

John Paul II's interest in culture did not begin with his elevation to the papacy. As theologian (now Cardinal) Avery Dulles noted a decade ago, "Culture has been a major concern of John Paul II from his early days, when he developed his talents for music, poetry and drama. Between 1977 and 1980 he published several important papers on the philosophy of culture."[30] On December 16, 1983, he told a meeting of European intellectuals: "You are aware that the theme of culture as such, and even more so the relation between faith and culture, is one that I have pondered much, in the light of my different experiences as a scholar, a Christian, a priest, a bishop, and now as pope."

From the pope's many speeches on culture Gallagher has distinguished three somewhat different meanings for the term: "creative or humanizing culture, sociological or lived culture, and particular or local cultures."[31] He finds these illustrated in the pope's visits to various countries: There are his meetings with "people of culture," that is, artists, intellectuals, educators, the mass media. There are the discourses in which he focuses on lifestyles, lived assumptions that can easily become an "anticulture"—the negative connotation in "dominant culture." And there are his sessions with representatives of indigenous or traditional cultures, where he praises the locally inherited wisdom, a sense of the sacred, a reverence for the family, while acknowledging potentially ambiguous elements and recognizing the sin that marks all human creations.

Perhaps the most significant expression of John Paul's vision of a creative or humanistic culture is a speech he delivered in Paris to the members of UNESCO on June 2, 1980. Gallagher has called this address "a cornerstone of his thinking."

Even though this UNESCO discourse builds on the treatment of culture in *Gaudium et Spes* (without ever citing it), it is much more ambitious in its intellectual range. When the Council spoke of humanity being the "author of culture" (No. 55), it was referring to a new sense of responsibility for history in modern times. When John Paul speaks of the human person being the subject or architect of culture, he is not thinking of a contemporary sensibility but of something in the very constitution of humanity. More penetratingly than Vatican II, he wants to ground the nature of culture in a reading of human nature as self-transcending. Frequently John Paul offers variations on this metaphysical anthropology of culture, insisting that "culture is of humanity, by humanity, and for humanity."[32]

A fascinating development: As the years of his papacy moved on, John Paul gave more and more attention to the lived culture, the pastoral side of culture. This is strikingly evident in a 1982 letter founding the Pontifical Council for Culture. Claiming that human destiny is at stake in the field of culture, he asserted:

> Hence the importance for the Church, whose concern it is, of a careful and far-sighted pastoral activity with regard to culture, and in a particular way with regard to what is called living culture, that is, the whole of the principles and values which make up the ethos of a people: "The synthesis between culture and faith is not just a demand of culture, but also of faith. . . . A faith which does not become culture is a faith which has not been fully received, not thoroughly thought through, not fully lived out."[33]

Finally, an indication of the pope's awareness of the positive and the negative in cultures—this on October 8, 1995, in the United States: "Sometimes witnessing to Christ will mean drawing out of a culture the full meaning of its noblest intentions. . . . At other times witnessing to Christ means challenging that culture, especially when the truth about the human person is under assault."[34]

Globalization and Justice

With the above as background, we are more adequately prepared to address the heart of our concern: How does globalization affect justice? Human justice: giving every man, woman, and child what they deserve, what they can claim as a right simply because they are human. Biblical justice: fidelity to relationships that stem from a covenant—relationships to God, to people, to the earth. I shall begin with questions of principle: What is required, what is indispensable, from a Catholic Christian perspective if globalization is to meet the demands of justice? Then I shall present four specific approaches to globalization and justice that seem to me to represent the four most significant attitudes toward the relationship in question. In a final segment I shall attempt an appraisal, tentative indeed at this early stage of a complex problem, but perhaps useful as a framework for further discussion.

Requirements of Principle

An address at Boston College on April 18, 2002, by moral theologian Kenneth Himes, O.F.M., has served to focus my approach to matters of principle. Entitling his address "Globalization and Inequality: Perspectives from Catholic Social Teaching," Himes laid out two Catholic claims that center on inequality, opened up the new context called globalization, and concluded with a Catholic response to globalization and inequality.[35] Two characteristics of the human person have always been part and parcel of Catholic social teaching. In each person there is an innate dignity based not on personal achievement but on creation in God's image. And there is the actual realization of this dignity in community, in sociality: "We cannot be truly human apart from being in relationship. After all, the God in whose image we are created is Trinitarian."

Catholic social teaching is an effort to draw out the political, economic, social, and cultural implications of these two claims. It involves a growth in understanding. What conditions do we now see as needed if people are to experience human sociality? Equality of opportunity to participate in community. Borrowing from Douglas Hicks's *Inequality and Christian Ethics*, Himes proposes "a broader set of indices than gross domestic product for measuring developmental progress"—specifically, "using the statistical spans in per capital [*sic*] income, years in school enrollment and age at death for assessing whether a person has been reasonably equipped to capably function in a society. . . . This way of thinking requires not only absolute standards above destitution and oppression, but also relative standards which permit capable functioning relative to others within one's society." How describe "the human good"? Certain socioeconomic goods directly affect human well-being. Dramatic inequalities preventing participation must be opposed as dehumanizing.

A new context for thinking about inequality is globalization. It "has become the catch-all term for the multiple developments which impact our economic, political, cultural, social and religious experiences." As industrialization broke down many traditional communities and traditions, so now globalization will likely be as disruptive for social, cultural, and religious experiences. Globalization means at least two things: "1) The world is smaller, we can reach around it faster and deeper than ever before; and 2) the world is a frame of reference for my thinking; I see myself in a global context."

Himes recognizes two responses thus far to this phenomenon: the hyperglobalizers and the antiglobalizers. The hyperglobalizers are "champions of free trade and ever more instant communication, who often assume a cosmopolitan view of things and assume that the world will simply get smaller, quicker-paced and more competitive in almost all ways. Their self-defined task is to overcome whatever obstacles to globalization exist: political nationalism, economic protectionism, religious fundamentalism, cultural parochialism." The antiglobalizers, who often protest on behalf of the poor and marginal, oppose some of what the marginal and poor want to see happen— "economic expansion, more and cheaper consumer goods, wider access to the middle-class affluence which many Americans experience."

In Catholic political theory the purpose of the state is to promote the common good of society. "Here is a void in the structure of globalization: There is no agency or organization at the international level comparable to the state at the domestic level. For this reason Catholic social teaching is supportive of various regimes and treaties which bring a measure of governance to the developing global order. In this the church's teaching will be at odds with those who equate globalization with an unfettered market system of economics. . . . Only negotiated, enforceable, minimum standards can protect workers, the environment and the vulnerable in a free-market society." The effort to humanize globalization calls for a better integration of moral concerns with economic and political systems. "Catholic social teaching identifies four essential components of a code of ethics for the present globalization: the preferential option for the poor, solidarity, participation and basic human rights." The demand on Catholics for involvement was proclaimed in strong language by Vatican II when it declared that "the promotion of human unity belongs to the innermost nature of the Church, because she is, by her relationship with Christ, both a sacramental sign and an instrument of intimate union with God and of the unity of all humankind."[36]

All of this may serve as background—and not simply for Roman Catholics—to my four representatives of the globalization-and-justice issue.

Approach/Analysis 1:
Globalism Almost Irreversible

I begin my four approaches with Thomas Friedman, if only because his understanding of the globalist system that is transforming our world is difficult to match. In a delightfully humorous chapter of his *The Lexus and the Olive Tree*, he presents "The Golden Arches Theory of Conflict Prevention." Through a highly factual investigation, the theory stipulated "that when a country reached the level of economic development where it had a middle class big enough to support a McDonald's network, it became a McDonald's country. And people in McDonald's countries didn't like to fight wars anymore, they preferred to wait in line for burgers." The sole exception as he wrote was "the nineteen McDonald's-laden NATO countries" that "undertook air strikes against Yugoslavia, which also had McDonald's."[37] Friedman then transferred this insight to today's globalization.

> The simple point I am making . . . is that today's globalization system significantly raises the costs of countries using war as a means to pursue honor, react to fears or advance their interests. . . . Today's version of globalization—with its economic integration, digital integration, its ever-widening connectivity of individuals and nations, its spreading of capitalist values and networks to the remotest corners of the world and its growing dependence on the Golden Straitjacket and the Electronic Herd —makes for a much stronger web of constraints on the foreign policy behavior of those nations which are plugged into the system. It increases the incentives for not making war and increases the costs of going to war in more ways than in any previous era in modern history.
>
> [This] does not guarantee that there will be no more wars. There will always be leaders and nations who, for good reasons and bad reasons, will resort to war, and some nations, such as North Korea, Iraq or Iran, will choose to live outside the constraints of the system. Still, the bottom line is this: If in the previous era of globalization nations in the system thought twice before trying to solve problems through warfare, in this era of globalization they will think about it three times.[38]

This way in which the Golden Arches Theory affects geopolitics— by greatly raising the cost of warfare through economic integration— is, for Friedman, only one of many ways. "For instance, it creates new sources of power, beyond the classic military measures of tanks, planes and missiles, and it creates new sources of pressure on countries to change how they organize themselves, pressures that come not from classic military incursions of one state into another, but rather by more invisible invasions of Supermarkets and Super-empowered individuals."[39]

Friedman is aware that as yet not everyone sees the world through the globalist prism. Genuine causes for worry are the nation-states divided from us: Iraq, Iran, North Korea. Of increasing concern are threats coming from those to whom we are connected: over the Internet, through markets, and from Super-empowered individuals—not always clearly visible but with enormous potential to destabilize or impact the behavior of states. From what has been said above, it is not surprising that recent years have witnessed a backlash against the system of globalization. To this backlash Friedman devotes a whole chapter of *The Lexus and the Olive Tree* (pp. 325-47). This is not to deny positive effects: an unprecedented flowering of wealth and technological innovation. "But this sort of rapid change . . . has challenged traditional business practices, social structures, cultural mores and environments. . . . This is not surprising. Markets generate both capital and chaos; the more powerful markets become as a result of globalization, the more widespread and diverse their disruptions."[40] In a useful paragraph Friedman has ventured beyond this general sense of disruption and dislocation.

> [Some] opponents of globalization resent it because they feel that as their countries have plugged into the globalization system they have been forced into a Golden Straitjacket that is one-size-fits-all. Some don't like the straitjacket because they feel economically pinched by it. Some worry that they don't have the knowledge, skills or resources to enlarge the straitjacket and ever really get the gold out of it. Some don't like it because they resent the widening income gaps that the straitjacket produces or the way it squeezes jobs from higher-wage countries to lower-wage ones. Some don't like it because it opens them to all sorts of global cultural forces and influences that leave their kids feeling alienated from their own traditional olive trees. Some don't like it because it seems to put a higher priority on laws to promote free trade than it does on laws to protect turtles and dolphins, water and trees. Some don't like it because they feel they have no say in its design. . . .[41]

An emotionally charged example experienced by Friedman in Brazil was the problem created by Conservation International, which had built an ecopark in the Atlantic Rain Forest in co-operation with people from the nearby town of Una, to help them develop a tourist industry providing enough jobs for them to quit logging. The mayor of Una, a lumberjack who knew each tree species by its Brazilian name, explained that intellectually he understood that logging was no longer sustainable; but he also knew that his little town was not prepared for life without logging. His question to Friedman: "Do we have any future?" The question hit Friedman like a fist in the stomach, almost brought tears to his eyes; for he knew what lay behind it: His villagers could no longer live off the forest and were not equipped to live off computers. "My father and grandfather made a living off logs and my grandchildren might make a living off the Internet. But what are all the rest of us in between supposed to do?" More than that, when he gets to his office each morning, two hundred people are waiting for him, asking for jobs, housing, and food—not to mention out-of-work loggers threatening his life. If he cannot provide jobs, housing, and food, "they will eat the rain forest—whether that's sustainable or not."[42]

The mayor of Una is not an isolated case; he represents a whole generation of people around the world threatened by globalization. Friedman calls them "the turtles"; they are not equipped to run fast.

> The turtles are all those people who got sucked into the Fast World when the walls came down, and for one reason or another now feel economically threatened or spurned by it. It is not because they all don't have jobs. It is because the jobs they have are being rapidly transformed, downsized, streamlined or made obsolete by globalization. And because this global competition is also forcing their governments to downsize and streamline at the same time, many of these turtles have no safety net to fall into.[43]

Saddening to me, and frightening, is Friedman's conviction that we are not likely to see a new coherent, universal ideological reaction to globalization, because he does not "believe there is an ideology or program that can remove all of the brutality and destructiveness of capitalism and still produce steadily rising standards of living."[44] And still the backlash is not to be despised. The poorest of the poor in developing countries, those left utterly behind by globalization, simply take what they need—ransack stores, invade supermarkets, rob banks, sell weapons to Iraq, log the rest of the rain forest—potentially dangerous because the reaction arises from the depths of their being and from their pocketbooks.

In some countries, however, the strongest backlash stems not just from the poorest but from the middle and lower-middle classes, whose security rested largely in the protected communist, socialist, and welfare systems. With the walls of this protection collapsing, and their safety net shrinking, these groups are not only unhappy; they have the political clout to organize against globalization. Example: the AFL-CIO labor union federation, which "has become probably the most powerful political force against globalization in the United States. Labor unions covertly funded a lot of the advertising on behalf of the demonstrations in Seattle to encourage grass-roots opposition to free trade."[45]

A third backlash group—Friedman's "wounded gazelles"—"comprises people who feel they have tried globalization, who have gotten hammered by the system, and who, instead of getting up, dusting themselves off and doing whatever it takes to get back into the Fast World are now trying artificially to shut it out or get the rules of the whole system changed."[46] A strategy of retreat, however, is not possible, "will not produce growth over the long run." Even slowing it down is out of the question. As Friedman said to the editor of an Egyptian journal, "I wish we could slow this globalization train down . . . [but] there's no one at the controls."[47]

A fourth backlash stems from fundamentalists, all those millions who despise the way globalization homogenizes people, erases the distinctiveness of cultures, uproots the olive trees that anchor one in his or her own world. It is a backlash that becomes most politically destabilizing when it is wed to one of the other backlashes. Friedman finds that

Benjamin Netanyahu's election to Prime Minister of Israel in 1990 was partly a political backlash against the problems of the Oslo peace accords, but it was also a cultural backlash against the globalization and integration implicit in Israel's peacemaking with the Arabs. Israeli religious scholar Moshe Halbertal once remarked to me that Shimon Peres's vision that his grandchildren and Yasser Arafat's grandchildren "would all make microchips together" was something fundamentally threatening to many religious Jews in Israel. They feared that if the ghetto walls fell around Israel and Israel assimilated into the Middle East—the same way American Jews assimilated into America—it would not be good for Judaism. They worried at some level that "Peace Now" and "Jewish Now" could not really coexist—particularly when peace seemed to mean more globalization, more integration, more Blockbuster Video, more smut-ridden cable stations and Pizza Huts. . . .[48]

Friedman recognizes that the attempt to anchor your society on a foundation of religious and traditional values is not wrong in itself. The problem arises when this fundamentalism is motivated not by genuine spirituality but by a backlash against globalization. Then "it often lapses into sectarianism, violence and exclusivity. And the more noninclusive you become, the less networked you are, the more you will fall behind, and the more you fall behind, the more you will want to retreat and reject the outside world with more exclusivity."[49]

A word, necessarily brief, on the backlash against the backlash, what Friedman calls a "groundswell propelled by millions of workers who have been knocked around by globalization, but who nonetheless get up, dust themselves off and knock again on globalization's door, demanding to get into the system. . . . They want to get a piece of the system, not to destroy it."[50] Here Friedman makes an important but uncommon claim: "while the gap between rich and poor is getting wider—as the winners in today's globalization system really take off and separate themselves from everyone else—the floor under the poor has been rising steadily in many parts of the world. In other words, while relative poverty may be growing in many countries, absolute poverty is actually falling in many countries. . . . Since 1960, infant mortality rates, malnutrition and illiteracy are all significantly down, while access to safe water is way up."[51]

Friedman asks whether there is anything about globalization and the rise of the Internet and other modern technologies that can make a difference "for those at the bottom of the barrel—the 1.3 billion people still living on one dollar a day." He refines the question: "Is there something about globalization that can both enhance freedom and contribute to the alleviation of poverty in ways that previous systemic changes and technological leaps have not?" Yes, on both counts. Story after story convinces him that "while globalization can produce a profound sense of alienation, as power keeps moving up to more and more abstract levels that are difficult to touch, affect or even see, it can also do the opposite. It can push down to the local level and to the weakest individuals more power, opportunities and resources to become shapers than ever before."[52]

A problem here. As globalization increases and new technologies improve productivity in a factory, workers will lose their jobs. Why?

Because the robot can do the job more efficiently than the assembly-line worker. A simple, widespread example: The voice-mail chip in a phone does the job better than an operator. As my sense of justice protests, Friedman is ready with a statistical response. "Alan Greenspan once pointed out that in mid-1999 roughly 300,000 jobs were getting destroyed by new technologies in America every week. But 300,000 new jobs were also being created by these new technologies each week, which is why America's aggregate unemployment rate was holding steady at a low level."[53] Still, a gnawing question will not leave me: What of the assembly-line workers who have lost their jobs but cannot be trained for positions requiring greater skills? A serious question for America, a unique superpower that excels not only in the traditional sources of power (e.g., military might, nuclear weapons) but in all the new measures of power in the era of globalization. For all his exuberance over America's power, Friedman has to admit that America "is globalizing the best of America and the worst of America."[54] In the context of America's gas stations, "whose only purpose is to provide the most gas at the cheapest price," he remarks: "If that can be done with no employees at all—well, all the better. A flexible labor market will find them work somewhere else. Too cruel, you say? Maybe so. But ready or not, this is the model that the rest of the world is increasingly being pressured to emulate."[55] This measure of realism, a kind of shrug of the shoulder, I find less than acceptable. Here Lady Justice raises her arms in protest.

Another justice problem arises when globalization is combined with Americanization. "What bothers so many people about America today is not that we send our troops everywhere, but that we send our culture, values, economics, technologies and lifestyles everywhere—whether or not we want to or others want them."[56] Here we are touching the heart of justice/injustice globalized. Touching it in unique fashion. Not by military might but by soft power: the unmatchable pile of chips we hold. On this all-important level all other powers together—Europe, China, Japan, Russia—cannot form an effective alliance against the United States. And, warns Friedman, "In the near term it is only going to get worse, because the economic power gap between the United States and the rest of the world is going to widen more before it narrows."[57]

How assess Friedman's approach to justice? Not an easy task. For one thing, in a rather detailed double-column index of 11 pages, there is no entry for "justice." And after a close reading I do not recall seeing the word in the text. Moreover, as indicated above, I found his reaction to unemployment caused by globalization somewhat casual, unconcerned; that's the way it is with globalism. On the other hand, he does not approve of its negatives; and the negatives have to do ultimately with people. And when explaining why globalization is "almost irreversible," he writes: "It could happen because the biggest threat to globalism today is globalism." That is, "the system contains within it the potential for its own destruction. It contains within it traits and tendencies that, if allowed to run riot, could become so oppressive that large majorities in a large number of countries would start to feel like losers, and therefore rebel against the system or try to erect new walls."[58] "How will people start to react if they find this system just too damn hard and too damn fast for too damn long . . . just too connected . . . just too intrusive . . . just too unfair for too many people . . . just too dehumanizing?"[59] There is justice language here.

Friedman is convinced that the only way to counter effectively the resentment and rage of those who feel steamrolled by Americanization-globalization is to isolate the hard core, the Super-empowered angry, from the much larger society around them. "The only way to do that is by making sure that as much of that society as possible has a stake in the globalization system."[60] How one does that is a feature of Friedman's final chapter, "There Is a Way Forward."

That chapter begins with a quotation from John F. Kennedy: "If a free society cannot help the many who are poor, it cannot save the few who are rich." Briefly, Friedman's "way forward" demands (1) that we educate the public about the real nature of today's world and demystify globalization, and (2) fashion a set of Integrationist Social-Safety Net policies for dealing with that world, a right balance of policies, specifically a new social bargain between workers, financiers, and governments that will make for sustainable globalization.

We Integrationist Social-Safety Netters believe that you dare not be a globalizer in this world—an advocate of free and unfettered trade, open borders, deregulation and Internet for all—without also being a social democrat. Because if you are not willing to spend what it takes to equip the have-nots, know-nots and turtles in your society to survive in this new system, they will eventually produce a backlash that will choke off your country from the world. You will not be able to maintain the political consensus you need for openness. At the same time, you believe you dare not be a social democrat, or safety-netter, today without being a globalizer, because without integration with the world you will never generate the incomes you need to keep standards of living rising and to take care of the left-behinds.[61]

In summary, I find Friedman a highly knowledgeable, enthusiastic supporter of today's system of globalization, while acutely aware of its need for significant reforms. With that, I see a genuine concern for the left-behinds, an issue he faces in his final chapter, where he suggests ways to achieve "the appropriate equilibrium between integrationism and social safety nets." This concern for the left-behinds he does not explicitly denominate justice, but it is clearly an ethical issue for him—the failure to provide millions of men and women with what they can claim as strict rights. It is a negative that in Friedman's analysis might well be classed among the worst features of globalism.

Worth noting here are two paragraphs from Geoffrey Wheatcroft's largely favorable review of Friedman's more recent *Longitudes and Attitudes: Exploring the World after September 11*[62] in the *New York Times Book Review*:

> . . . like many well-meaning Americans, Friedman doesn't quite see that his country has a very distinctive take on "the spread of commerce." The business of America is business, and what American business has always believed in isn't free trade but free investment, a very different thing. In any case, and quite apart from the fact that there seems some time to go before the whole House of Islam is converted to consumerism and the American way, it isn't necessarily true that the expansion of American markets must always bring sweetness and light.[63]

Approach/Analysis 2:
Globalism Reformed

If Friedman is difficult to match for detailed analysis, Tina Rosenberg, free-lance journalist and 1996 Pulitzer Prize winner, offers a stirring counterview in nine pages titled "The Free-Trade Fix."[64] No summary can do justice to her closely packed information and argument; I shall report enough to present a coherent reproduction of her chain of thought.

When first setting out to see for herself whether globalization has been for better or worse, Rosenberg was perplexed: sympathy for some issues raised by the protesters, but surely "the masters of the universe" must know what they are doing. But that was before she had studied the agreements that regulate global trade—including the August 2002 new law granting President Bush a free hand to negotiate trade agreements, and before she had looked at globalization up close in Chile and Mexico, which have embraced globalization with special ardor. Since then she no longer believes the masters of the universe know what they are doing.

The architects of globalization are right that international economic integration is not only good for the poor; it is essential. To embrace self-sufficiency or to deride growth, as some protesters do, is to glamorize poverty. No nation has ever developed over the long term without trade. Asia is the most recent example. Since the mid-1970's, Japan, Korea, Taiwan, China and their neighbors have lifted 300 million people out of poverty, chiefly through trade.

But the protesters are also right—no nation has ever developed over the long term under the rules being imposed today on third-world countries by the institutions controlling globalization. The United States, Germany, France and Japan all became wealthy and powerful nations behind the barriers of protectionism. East Asia built its export industry by protecting its markets and banks from foreign competition and requiring investors to buy local products and build local know-how. These are all practices discouraged or made illegal by the rules of trade today.[65]

Rosenberg points out that the World Trade Organization, designed as a meeting place where willing nations could in equality negotiate rules of trade for their mutual advantage, has become an unbalanced institution largely controlled by the United States and the nations of Europe. The International Monetary Fund (IMF), created to help prevent the Great Depressions by lending money to countries in recession and pressing them to adopt expansionary policies (e.g., deficit spending), has become a long-term manager of the economies of developing countries, a champion of market supremacy in all situations, more interested in getting wealthy creditors repaid than in serving the poor.[66]

Globalization, Rosenberg declares, is neither unstoppable nor irreversible; a previous wave was stopped dead by World War I. Today's globalization is more likely to be sabotaged by its own inequities, as nations withdraw from a system they find indifferent or injurious to the poor. The rules have been drawn up by, and written to benefit, powerful nations and interests. To work, the system needs serious reform, rules rewritten to spread the benefits to the ordinary citizens of wealthy countries and give the poor a stake in the process. Hence Rosenberg's nine new rules for the global economy, to save the system from itself—rules I abbreviate with reluctance, aware that only the complete text can do justice to the author's powerful presentation of data and arguments.

Rule 1: Make the state a partner. Rosenberg focuses on Chile, because between 1987 and 1998 Chile cut poverty by more than half. How? By growing its economy—admittedly the most important thing a nation can do for its poor, if they have governments that actively make it happen. In the 1980s the Washington Consensus held that government was in the way. Globalizers' tasks? Privatization, deregulation, fiscal austerity, financial liberalization. The state was considered the devil. The fact is, "when the economy opens, you need *more* control mechanisms from the state, not fewer."[67]

Rule 2: Import know-how along with the assembly line. To simplify a section compacted of closely knit factual material, I believe it best to conflate two segments of Rosenberg's text.

> Volkswagen Mexico is the epitome of the strategy Mexico has chosen for globalization—assembly of imported parts. It is a strategy that makes perfect sense given Mexico's proximity to the world's largest market, and it has given rise to the maquila industry, which uses Mexican labor to assemble foreign parts and then re-export the finished products. . . . [But] Mexico has never required companies to transfer technology to locals, and indeed, under the rules of the North American Free Trade Agreement, it cannot. "We should have included a technical component in Nafta," says Luis de la Calle, one of the treaty's negotiators and later Mexico's under secretary of economy for foreign trade. "We should be getting a significant transfer of technology from the United States, and we didn't really try."[68]

Rule 3: Sweat the sweatshops—but sweat other problems more. In many of the factories in Mexico, Central America, and Asia that produce American-brand goods (e.g., clothes, sneakers) exploitation is the norm. Young women workers endure starvation wages, forced overtime, and dangerous working conditions. In some ways victims of globalization, but some are beneficiaries. To Rosenberg, "The losers are those who get laid off when companies move to low-wage countries, or those forced off their land when imports undercut their crop prices, or those who can no longer afford life-saving medicine—people whose choices in life *diminish* because of global trade."[69]

Rule 4: Get rid of the lobbyists. In the Third World, controlled economics theoretically allow governments to help the poor, but rarely in practice. Those who prosper are people who can organize, strike, lobby, and contribute money. A system that would take corruption and undue political influence out of economic decision making would indeed help the poor, but that system has not yet been invented, and it is not the current system of globalization, which is soiled with special-interest groups. "Lobbyists have learned that they can often quietly slip provisions that pay big dividends into complex trade deals. None have been more successful at getting what they want than those from America."[70]

Rule 5: No dumping. After a lengthy exposition of the unfair competition and economic reforms that have forced half a million Mexican corn farmers to leave their land and move to Mexican cities or to America, and the government subsidies that provide such large incomes to European and American farmers, Rosenberg concludes:

> Wealthy nations justify pressure on small nations to open markets by arguing that these countries cannot grow rice and corn efficiently—that American crops are cheap food for the world's hungry. But with subsidies this large, it takes chutzpah to question other nations' efficiency. In fact, the poor suffer when America is the supermarket to the world, even at bargain prices. There is plenty of food in the world, and even many countries with severe malnutrition are food exporters. The problem is that poor people cannot afford it. The poor are the small farmers. Three-quarters of the world's poor are rural. If they are forced off their land by subsidized grain imports, they starve.[71]

Rule 6: Help countries break the coffee habit. In the latter half of the twentieth century, the architects of import substitution could not imagine that anything but commodities could be exported. Poor East Asia showed in the 1980s and 1990s that it can be done. But the rules of global trade now prohibit countries from using the strategies successfully employed in East Asia. But the rules rich nations have set— for example, on technology transfer, local content, and government aid to their infant industries—are destroying the abilities of poor nations to move beyond commodities. And the commodities that poor nations are left to export are more of a dead end today than in the 1950s.

Rule 7: Let the people go. Here Rosenberg recommends, as probably the single most important change for the developing world, to legalize the export of people—specifically a scheme of legal short-term migration. If rich nations opened three percent of their work forces to temporary migrants, argues economist Dani Rodrik, it would generate $200 billion annually in wages—and technology transfer.

Rule 8: Free the IMF. "Formal influence in the I.M.F. depends on a nation's financial contribution, and America is the only country with enough shares to have a veto."[72] Many economists consider the IMF part of the "Wall Street-Treasury complex." Various authorities see the fund serving the interests of global finance, listening to the voice of the markets, a front for the U.S. government. The voices of the IMF argue that their advice is completely equitable; but Rosenberg is clearly not convinced.

Rule 9: Let the poor get rich the way the rich have. Under this final rule Rosenberg devotes much space to the pros and cons of the IMF. For my purposes here, I believe that her final paragraph is a moving close to a stimulating article:

> China, Chile and other nations show that under the right conditions, globalization can lift the poor out of misery. Hundreds of millions of poor people will never be helped by globalization, but hundreds of millions more could be benefiting now, if the rules had not been rigged to help the rich and follow abstract orthodoxies. Globalization can begin to work for the vast majority of the world's population only if it ceases to be viewed as an end in itself, and instead is treated as a tool in service of development: a way to provide food, health, housing and education to the wretched of the earth.[73]

As with Friedman, so with Rosenberg, I do not find the word "justice" in her vocabulary. But even more often and more centrally than he, she is dealing with the reality. Whereas Friedman focuses on the positive aspects of the system without overlooking the negative, Rosenberg concentrates on the negative, to reveal how reforms in nine areas could increase globalization's service to the poor and disadvantaged. They complement each other. Having both before me has enriched my understanding of justice globalized as neither could have done in isolation.

Approach/Analysis 3:
Globalism Rejected

Another movement has been growing "alongside global capitalism and terrorism."[74] Andrew Hartman begins his short article entitled "The Globalization of a Movement" with a paragraph in bold that leaves no doubt about his intentions.

To terrorists and their sympathizers world-wide, the World Trade Center symbolized the global nature of corporate money and power—a seemingly never-ending expansion of capitalism, siphoning funds and resources from people everywhere and fostering gaps in wealth the likes of which the world has never before seen. The Pentagon symbolizes the U.S. military's protection and enforcement of this global system. Because much of the resulting poverty and suffering exist in the Muslim world, Osama bin Laden has had less difficulty recruiting his minions. The resultant widespread discontent fuels terrorism—a reality brought home to the developed world on September 11, 2001.[75]

What Hartman calls "the anti-global-capitalist movement" he sees awakened in Seattle in November 1999. Not a violent movement like terrorism, it does not threaten the majority of the global village. It "should be welcomed and encouraged. For the ultimate threat to humanity is economic globalism."[76]

Hartman is not afraid of globalism; the protest is itself a global phenomenon. What he and untold others fear is "globalism as designated according to the imperialistic goals of a few rich people. The aim of the growing unrest . . . is to shift the focus of globalism to benefit all of humanity." For, as he sees it, economic globalism "has bullied and seeped its way into every nook of humanity, and the results are scary: loss of democracy, human rights violations, rapid environmental degradation, expanding inequality."[77] Hartman claims that the Old World Order, colonialism, has given way to the New World Order, but the greed that drove the Old never left us.

Hartman's four-page brief makes five points. First, "Don't believe the elite." Concretely, the mainstream media and our elected leaders. The media experts, "representing the ultra-elite five corporations that own the national media in the United States, have yet to generate critical analysis of the movement surrounding these huge protests." Thomas Friedman is quoted as an example: "To be against globalism is to be against so many things . . . that it connotes nothing." And the "wisdom" of our elected American presidents at every meeting of world leaders: "To be against free trade is to be against poor people."[78]

Second, the so-called Washington Consensus, the name for the undue influence of the sole superpower in the world on the global village's economic and political aspirations. "The United States government primarily works for corporate interests."[79]

Third, the World Trade Organization (WTO), "democracy's nightmare," the arm of the Washington Consensus. Created to allow trade to exist without artificial barriers, the WTO "ensures that 'free trade' will benefit corporate interests." Hartman's examples are a WTO decision against the labeling of genetically modified foods in the United States and the European Union; its ruling against legalizing the generic reproduction of expensive drugs to fight AIDS in South Africa; its effort to overturn a Massachusetts law forbidding any corporation using labor or resources from the brutal military dictatorship of Burma to sell its goods in the state; its ruling against the United States' Clean Air Act; and a ruling against the Endangered Species Act in favor of fishing interests.[80]

Fourth, the International Monetary Fund and the World Bank "have two major functions: create a risk-free environment for predatory, speculative financing and open world markets to investors. . . . Now it is estimated that 95 percent of capital is speculative, which results in quick returns for the investors and dangerous instability for markets worldwide. . . . The huge amounts of money that are lost by lending institutions are then subsidized," resulting in poor people of the poor countries bearing the brunt of repaying IMF and World Bank loans.[81]

Fifth, "Austerity measures are how the Washington Consensus ensures that the domestic policy of other countries measures up to the needs of foreign investors. Social programs, such as health care and public education, are dismantled so taxes can be funneled into repaying the debt. The indebted countries are then forced to privatize their public resources."[82] Another austerity measure: forcing indebted countries to get rid of troubling labor laws. This allows sweatshops to exist, and "companies such as Nike and the Gap search for factory locations where they can pay the least possible wages and where unions aren't allowed to exist. In the process the manufacturing base in the United States is destroyed."[83]

Toward the end of his essay Hartman offers an important pointed observation:

> Rather than measure the success of an economy according to gross domestic product (which includes, among other anti-human measurements, the cost of weapons building and pollution cleanup exercises), quality-of-life indicators measure an economy by how well the people are doing. These take into account infant mortality rates, hunger rates, literacy rates, and the like. Redefining the world according to people, not profit, is the ultimate objective.[84]

How assess Hartman's approach? Not an easy task. Although the word "justice" is not in his vocabulary, the reality that is ethical justice pervades the article: giving people, all the people, but especially those in greater need, what they can claim as human rights. Admirable indeed. But is this overkill? Is economic globalization totally corrupt, unjust on all counts? Moreover, I would have appreciated a global program, spelled out in detail, that would replace the system currently in control.

Approach/Analysis 4:
Globalization in a Catholic Perspective

Here I return to Robert Schreiter, whose understanding of globalization was summarized earlier in this section.[85] In his August 1999 address in Hales Corners, Wisconsin, he recognized that, since globalization is a relatively recent phenomenon, we are at an early point in grasping what effective pursuit of social justice might mean, what it might look like, in this new context, in this new world. Catholic social teaching is indeed a treasure surpassing what is available elsewhere within the Christian Church. In a number of places the teachings of the last century continue to serve us well. In other areas—just war, for example—traditional teaching is under some strain. How address so young, so vast, so intricate an issue as globalization?

In the course of his address Schreiter noted briefly the positive and the negative dimensions of globalization—useful background for an effort to evaluate the system from a justice perspective.

The *positive* dimension of globalization is the possibility of communion, interconnectedness, and solidarity which it could give the planet. It could be the way we recognize our interdependence and realize our concern for mutual well-being. It can give us the sense of being part of something far greater than ourselves.

The *negative* dimension of globalization is its power to exclude and diminish large parts of the population. To speak of the wonders of global communication means little to a citizen of the African state of Chad, for example, where there is but one telephone per thousand people (as compared, for example, with over seven hundred telephones per thousand people in North America). To see one's resources leeched away by powerful, distant corporations leaves one with a sense of anger, loss, and even helplessness. To see one's children depart in the hopes of finding a better life leaves a hollow ache in one's heart. The negative dimensions of globalization have caught the imagination of those concerned for social justice in many parts of the world, especially in poor countries. Analysis and alternative proposals, however, often do not keep pace with the passion of denunciation. For us to be effective and faithful in the pursuit of social justice, it seems to me that we must find ways to combine both analysis and action, proposals and passion.

Schreiter notes that within very recent years documents at the papal and Vatican level have begun to take up issues of globalization. What have they emphasized? The importance of solidarity with the poor and the excluded, and the "second generation" of human rights: nutrition, health, housing, education, and employment.

Since Catholics must examine their tradition of social teaching in light of a changing world, Schreiter suggests three pertinent areas. First, closer attention to contexts and causes. By contexts he means special attention to local, regional, and global settings. What we see as local issues—for example, racism or the recent outbreaks of violence in secondary schools—are the causes possibly more than local? And will a local response address the problems or only the symptoms? "Engaging local passion is important for regaining some sense of control over our lives, but if there can be little effective resolution, it will soon end in frustration."

Emerging as important for social justice is "a rebuilding of regional structures and a reassertion of what can be done regionally." Local structures are often too limited, global structures too vast to be effective. Only much attention can bring about regional structures. "Yet it is precisely at the regional level that the limitations of the local can be overcome and the global can be challenged." Then an insight I find profound: At the level of the worldwide Church, if we have only the local church and the centralized structures of the Vatican, we can only impose in religious terms the kinds of hegemony which globalization can impose. A crucial observation at a time when high-level Roman authority (Cardinal Joseph Ratzinger, prefect of the Congregation for the Doctrine of the Faith, and Pope John Paul II himself in his motu proprio *Apostolos suos*) insist that national conferences of bishops may not impose doctrine on all their faithful unless their vote is unanimous or with a two-thirds majority has been granted a *recognitio* by the Holy See.[86]

While looking at the contexts of the issues at all three levels, we must look more analytically at their causes. "Thus, to see current market capitalism as the same pattern of exploitation that marked earlier forms of capitalism may miss the mark about what is really going on."

Second pertinent area: Following upon earlier analysis of the means of production, contemporary analysis must look into the means of reproduction, that is, the ways in which society replicates itself. "Communications technologies open up the possibilities of new forms of relationships that can be constructed to address injustice in society." Three examples. (1) Communications technologies make it more and more impossible to restrict information and to keep secrets. Recall Beijing's Tiananmen Square in 1989 and the faxes from the United States that kept the students aware of similar movements. Information is a form of power. (2) Communications technologies can be used to mobilize public opinion in ways that effect genuine change. Recall the opposition to land mines organized on the Internet that led to a treaty endorsed by most nations. (3) Public opinion to effect political change is heavily affected by news media, which in turn are dependent on the news they can gather. Recall the networks of missionaries providing information on the Sierra Leone conflict to policy makers in Washington.

Third pertinent area: new institutions and approaches. There are the nongovernmental organizations (NGOs) such as the Franciscan NGO at the United Nations to pursue peace and ecological issues. New approaches include three stances suggested by David Held in terms of globalization: (1) The liberal-international project, seeing the world moving toward greater democratization, emphasizes the reform of current structures to make them more amenable to liberal and international ideals. (2) The radical republican project, more skeptical about globalization's reformability, seeks alternatives to current structures "from the bottom up." (3) The cosmopolitan project develops a network of overlapping loyalties and commitments to overcome partisanship for the sake of a genuine transnational civil society as the basis for a truly just world order.

My assessment? I am impressed, and influenced, by Schreiter's insistence that we are at an early stage of contemporary globalization. It keeps him from the swift and facile answer to profound problems. Recognizing the positive and the negative, he realizes that reform is required but will take time, thoughtful analysis, open and intense discussion from differing points of view. His awareness of contexts and causes opens the way to realistic appraisals of just where we are and how we got here—a needful basis for moving ahead intelligently. He is not afraid to suggest ideas and approaches where the insights of others complement his own, even perhaps have compelled him to revisit and revise his way of proceeding. Importantly, the Catholic tradition of justice is never far from his thinking on globalization; and he is aware that this tradition itself demands reconsideration, updating, to meet needs that are new. The process of globalization and justice has much to learn from him.

Before presuming to present final reactions of my own on globalization and justice, I believe it helpful to discuss several issues that touch directly on the United States in those twin areas.

Failures in Capitalism:
From America to England

Within the economic effects of globalization, a current example of the need for an agency or organization at the international level comparable to the state at the domestic level is provided by the United States and England. The issue here has been so succinctly expressed by an editorial in the London *Tablet* that I do best to reproduce it word for word.

The unmasking of shady accounting practices in the United States has led to a series of company scandals and a severe downturn in the New York Stock Exchange. This has pulled London share prices down with it. As a result property owning has become a much better investment, with likely capital gains lying between ten and 20 percent a year. This in turn is one of the factors putting house-buying beyond the means of an increasing number of first-time buyers, including families with children—a grave social disorder.

So the globalization of capitalism links the crisis in affordable housing in Britain with the failure of American companies like Enron, WorldCom and Xerox. Nor is the damage confined to housing. Millions of people are seeing the value of their pension assets fall as share prices sink lower. There is not a suburban street in Britain that is unaffected by the crisis of confidence that has hit American big business.

But this is very much a manmade crisis, a failure within capitalism itself. Capitalism is part of the American way of life and unquestioning faith in it includes the belief that most of its problems are self-correcting. This is almost a fourth "truth" that America holds to be self-evident, alongside the three enshrined in the Declaration of Independence whose 226th anniversary came round this week. Adam Smith wrote in *Wealth of Nations*, published the same year, that if a man "intends only his own gains", he is nevertheless "led by an invisible hand" to promote the public interest, though that was no part of his intention. Laissez-faire (or "leave it alone and all will work out well in the end") is still the central creed of free market economics.

But Smith's stern Scottish ethic did not countenance a business climate devoid of integrity and trust, which is what appears to be developing on both sides of the Atlantic. It is significant that the crisis in American business starts with the very people who are supposed to oversee its conduct, namely the accountants. Their job it is to audit the books and speak up if they find anything wrong. Instead, they too have just been maximizing their profits, while showing their clients how to hide losses and hence how to maintain their share price, to which directors' remunerations are linked.

President Bush has belatedly promised reforms in regulatory regimes, though as a puppet of big business himself, his heart is unlikely to be in it. In Britain the regulatory authorities have been insisting that they are ahead of the Americans in this respect. Nevertheless, the dangerous fiction that capitalism is a self-righting system and that selfishness always serves the common good, as suggested by Adam Smith, still prevails in the City. As Pope John Paul II said in his 1991 encyclical *Centesimus Annus*, this faith in laissez-faire economics "carries the risk of idolatry of the market". It ignores the fact that market forces can just as easily do more harm than good. They have to be carefully regulated to ensure they serve the interests of the community— and in the case of accountants employed as company auditors, the regulators have to be regulated too.[87]

Clearly the collapse of Enron and the conviction of its accounting firm, Arthur Anderson, showed the world that the interests of communities had not been served but replaced by underhandedness that ultimately led to the loss of billions of dollars and caused thousands of persons to lose their jobs. A mere two years later, Richard Grasso's exodus from his seat as Chairman and Chief Executive of the New York Stock Exchange with $140 million in his pockets evidenced that the supposed protection of investors had again been sacrificed to greed. The little man wanting to realize his share of the American dream became the symbol of a global nightmare in which the rich get richer and the poor get poorer. The poor man may not have his own stock portfolio but he too suffers because he no longer gets paid to cut the grass of the woman whose stocks became worth no more than paper in the investment debacles of the 1990s. With similar impact, the man whose retirement monies dwindle to nothing no longer travels and even the poor woman cleaning hotels in Europe becomes affected by U.S. capitalism at its worst.

Financing for Development: U.N. International Conference, Monterrey

In the effort to link globalization and justice, worth attention is the Report of the United Nations International Conference on Financing for Development (FfD).[88] It begins with a summary statement of the ends the conference had in view:

We the heads of State and Government, gathered in Monterrey, Mexico, on 21 and 22 March 2002, have resolved to address the challenges of financing for development around the world, particularly in developing countries. Our goal is to eradicate poverty, achieve sustained economic growth and promote sustainable development as we advance to a fully inclusive and equitable global economic system.[89]

It involves a turning point for the involvement of the U.N. in shaping the global economic system. The first step in achieving internationally agreed development goals, including those in the United Nations Millennium Declaration, is to mobilize and increase "the effective use of financial resources . . . to eliminate poverty, improve social conditions and raise living standards, and protect our environment. . . ."[90]

A summary of so lengthy and complex a document is well-nigh impossible. At the risk of seeming unfair, I shall approach FfD from the succinct critique of Aldo Caliari, a legal researcher with the Human Rights Project at the Center of Concern in Washington, D.C.[91] Nine brief points.

1. FfD recognizes, at least in principle, that national development must be supported by an enabling international economic environment. It declares that "globalization should be fully inclusive and equitable" and closes with a commitment to promoting "national and global economic systems based on the principles of justice, equity, democracy, participation, transparency, accountability and inclusion."

2. The detailed prescriptions on the mobilization of domestic resources, mostly needless for an international conference, "often resemble those demanded by multilateral financial institutions as loan conditionalities, prescriptions widely criticized as inimical to poverty reduction and growth in the borrowing countries."

3. The section on mobilization of international financial resources stresses the need to achieve higher levels of private capital as a way of boosting development efforts. "However, key concerns for developing countries and civil society have been sidelined."

4. The section on trade, carefully drafted to avoid conflicts with the WTO, could still "have addressed a crucial issue for developing countries: the sharp fall in the prices for their export commodities." There are no new commitments to remedying the concerns of developing countries about the current world trading system.

5. On Overseas Development Assistance (ODA), FfD makes no commitments, sets no time frames "for developed countries to achieve the 0.7% of GDP target agreed to at previous U.N. conferences. . . . Though individual countries, including the U.S., announced at Monterrey that they would increase their levels of ODA, the promised increases . . . fall far short of what is needed to achieve the agreed upon [U.N.] Millennium goals."

6. FfD "barely addresses the critical issue of debt sustainability assessments. . . . The assessments have been criticized for not ensuring that countries are able to fulfill the basic needs of their people before repaying their debts." Not adequately considered is a debt arbitration mechanism.

7. Among a number of systemic issues, all too weak is the call for increased participation of developing countries in fora that design international economic policies and financial standards. "However, threatened many times by the unwillingness of developed countries to discuss systemic issues, the mere presence of this section in the final document must be seen as a major accomplishment of civil society and developing countries."

8. A final chapter on follow-up mechanisms: (a) a new format that will include, for example, participation of the WTO and a dialogue segment with civil society and the business sector; (b) a reconstituted biannual dialogue on international co-operation at the U.N. General Assembly; (c) a conference to review implementation of FfD.

9. "The failure of the 'Monterrey consensus' must be acknowledged. Still, FFD has brought to the forefront of the international agenda the need for a comprehensive and holistic approach to development that links financial debt and trade policies with social, gender, and environmental issues. The discussion of economic policies that took place at the U.N. throughout the FFD process is the first one in decades."

World Summit on Sustainable Development, Johannesburg

From August 26 to September 4, 2002, Johannesburg in South Africa hosted the World Summit on Sustainable Development (WSSD). The conference, ten years after the Rio de Janeiro gathering, attracted about 60,000 delegates representing different civic, religious, and environmental bodies from all over the world. "Many of the agreements made at Rio on the ozone layer and conserving the world's resources later foundered over the costs of implementing them."[92]

That WSSD did make some progress has been argued, for example, by John Gummer, the United Kingdom's longest-serving Secretary of State for the Environment, who attended as chairman of the Marine Stewardship Council.

The commitment to clean water and sewerage for half of those who lack it today was a real breakthrough. The fact that the promise had a target and a date made it credible. So too with the agreement on the better preservation of the oceans and the world's fish stocks. It was essential to insist that the most powerful international body—the World Trade Organization—should in future give environmental protection a central place in its decision-making. It was important too that we should reassert the primacy of the Kyoto Protocol on climate change and specifically deny the American attempt to write in their own ineffective and self-serving alternative.[93]

Despite such concessions, Gummer argues that the text finally agreed "is pathetically weak."

The world's governments had no chance of anything better. They were negotiating, not with the United States but with Exxon, the giant American company which, with its acolytes and fortified by its merger with Mobil, now directs American energy policy. These are the companies that welcomed President Bush's nose-thumbing rebuff to the international community in refusing to come to Johannesburg. They made it clear that they would oppose even the easiest targets and timetables in the energy field. . . . We were not able to agree, therefore, on increasing our use of renewable energy, even though the huge expansion in the use of fossil fuel is changing our climate and that change will hit the poorest hardest.[94]

In brief, Gummer believes that "the summit was not all bad." Disappointing, yes, for so much remains to be done. Yet, if Europe can seize the initiative it has begun, it is possible that Johannesburg "will be the beginning of something quite new—a world where we see that it is in our own interest to live together as children of one God."[95]

Jesuit Jim Hug, president of the Center of Concern in Washington, D.C., was less sanguine in his brief initial evaluation of WSSD.[96] First, Hug takes issue with the position of the Bush administration that trade liberalization is the best and only strategy for sustainable development, a position summed up by Secretary of State Colin Powell in a speech of July 2002: "Countries that have opened their economies have done better than those who have remained closed. It's as simple as that." Not really, Hug responds. The single World Bank study justifying this position has been discredited for "intellectual sloppiness," and more plentiful evidence shows that "trade liberalization enriches a few people at the top of liberalizing societies while increasing inequality, poverty and marginalization within and among countries." Hug also argues that the United States does not practice what it preaches. "While it uses its power at the World Bank and IMF to demand open markets in poor nations, the Bush Administration is rapidly compiling a protectionist record at home with the recent Farm Bill, subsidies for energy, tariffs on steel, soft lumber and textiles." Despite so indefensible a position, this was the most fundamental division among delegates going into the conference.

Second, Hug finds it ironic that a results-oriented U.S. administration mentality actively opposed formal commitments, specific targets, and timetables. How else evaluate the success or failure of different strategies? How else shape a world where, as Powell phrased it, "children can grow up free from hunger, disease, and illiteracy; a world where men and women can reach their human potential, free from racial or gender discrimination, and a world where all people can enjoy the richness of a diverse and healthy planet"? The Bush administration should have taken the lead in tough, realistic planning.

Third, the United States has been resisting "good governance" on the international level. Strangely, it supports a crackdown on corporate malfeasance at home but resists effective structures for accountability at the global level—"a clear, just and enforceable governing framework."

Constructive U.S. participation was crucial for the success of WSSD. Did it happen?

Jim Hug's comments call to mind that the Society of Jesus (Jesuits) has committed itself to the pursuit of justice and peace as a constituent element of the gospel.[97] Present at the Summit was Michael Czerny, S.J., director for ten years of the Jesuits' Social Justice Secretariat in Rome, who led a team of Jesuits and laypeople to cover the conference. After he returned from Johannesburg, Czerny expressed some of his reactions to the conference in an interview with Robert Blair Kaiser, Rome's correspondent for the London *Tablet*.[98]

"It was," said Czerny, "a complicated affair, with action going on simultaneously in four different arenas. It took all of our combined energies to gather the facts. I am not even sure how well we did that." Actually it was, he declared, "an honest and true summit." But democracy was bypassed. "Those few who wrote the Political Declaration and the Plan of Implementation did so in secret. None of us, no members of the press, none of the non-governmental organizations could attend meetings of the inner circle, much less have any influence on the plan. The plan was written, in effect, by the world's business conglomerates." And these are "centred in the United States."[99]

Czerny seemed reluctant to call Johannesburg a failure. "We have to mine," he said, "what was honest and true in Johannesburg and move ahead from there—on behalf of the poor. We can't let Johannesburg be a failure. The poor can't afford a failure."[100]

Far more detailed is an initial evaluation from the Jesuit-led group as a whole: 22 Jesuits and seven laypeople from 17 countries.[101] Only brief excerpts are possible here.

> The US won on energy, the EU won on water, sanitation, and Kyoto. The G77 (the association of developing countries) displayed its internal divisions, occasionally found an ally in the EU, but remained largely sidelined. Big corporate interests made their presence very felt, and the WTO emerged as the dominant international organization. . . .
>
> The larger, better-known NGOs . . . produced excellent analyses. Some of them set up broad alliances which brought environmental and developmental groups together under the same umbrella. . . . But they were unable to provide the social movements and Third World NGOs with organizational guidance and so failed, as did the South African NGO leadership to bring us together into the process. . . .
>
> The UN set the stage, leading everyone to expect the process to be democratic, but the UN didn't really direct the play. The original themes of poverty, social injustice, and environmental degradation . . . were downgraded in favour of market globalization. . . . The Johannesburg Plan of Action still repeats humanitarian, social, and environmental language, but reflects the increased corporate sway and the dominance of trade over practically all other considerations. The real battle is over governance—between the WTO (and big business) and the UN. . . .
>
> "Success" and "failure" are the wrong terms [for passing judgment on Johannesburg]. Rather, these were seventeen days of an abundant and scattered Expo on sustainable development representing the planet's majority, and ten days of opaque and frustrating official Summit, reflecting rich and powerful interests. The two events together . . . represent the world of 2002.

Johannesburg was an honest and true summit, no more failed or successful than our world—scarred as it is with gaping divisions like those separating upscale Sandton from degraded Alexandria and alienated Soweto. . . .

Development Assistance: United States

Here I continue to be concerned with role of the United States in global development. One of the best resources I found on development assistance and the U.S. was published by the United States Conference of Catholic Bishops in February 2002. The statement is pellucid in detail, strong in its insistence on Christian responsibility. Because I cannot add to its clarity, I reproduce the statement in its entirety:

Issue
Poverty and disease that plague the poorest countries of the world and impede economic growth, development, and international stability. The United States is the wealthiest country in the world, but its foreign assistance is lower, as a percentage of its wealth, than that of any other major donor country. Moreover, less than 20% of U.S. foreign aid is allocated to development assistance and health programs that could help the poorest countries.

Background
Nearly half the world's population of six billion people lives in poverty, on less than $2 a day. In sub-Saharan Africa, more people live in poverty than the entire population of the United States. For the poorest countries, the situation is worsening, not improving. The gap between the richest and the poorest has been steadily increasing over the past decade. In the year 2000, the richest 10% of the U.S. population (around 25 million people) had a combined income greater than that of the poorest 43% of the *world's* people (around two billion people).

Eight million people die every year from hunger. But the symptoms of poverty are not just starving families and children, but also lack of education, lack of economic infrastructure, lack of proper healthcare and access to clean water, and environmental degradation. The burden of heavy debt payments diminishes the already limited resources for addressing these problems.

A significant international investment is needed to bring hope and possibilities to the poorest and most vulnerable of our world. For global health alone, estimates are in the range of $10 billion to $15 billion each year. However, investments to address health crises will not succeed if they are not part of a comprehensive development strategy that addresses some of the root causes of disease. At least an additional $4 billion per year is needed from the international community just to halve hunger by the year 2015.

The United States Investment
The U.S. investment in foreign assistance is scandalously low. For the past three years, the United States contributed just 0.01% of gross national product, lower than any other major donor country. This figure represents a 45% drop in U.S. official aid as a percentage of GNP since 1990-94 (average 0.18% of GNP).

Over the past two years, the U.S. investment in global health has grown about $200 million each year, with these funds dedicated to fighting infectious diseases such as HIV/AIDS, malaria, and tuberculosis. While these increases are helpful, they are far from the magnitude needed to address the devastation of the population inflicted by these diseases in the poorest nations of the world. Apart from the global health increases, the U.S. investment in development assistance and health programs has remained relatively constant over the past three years. Meanwhile, foreign military assistance is proposed to increase by half a billion dollars in FY 2003.

Legislators often reject claims that U.S. aid is scandalously low by observing that the country is second highest among major donor countries in terms of the total volume of official development assistance. While true, this ranking is a dubious distinction, since it compares U.S. aid with that of much smaller countries with lower per capita income [see graph on Bishops' Web site]. The European Union, with a slightly lower combined GNP than the United States, gives 2-1/2 times as much aid by volume, and Germany, France, and Italy, with only half of U.S. GNP, together give the same volume of aid as the United States.

USCCB Position
Pertinent here is the position taken by the United States Catholic Conference of Bishops (USCCB). The Catholic Church in the United States supports:

- a significant increase in U.S. foreign aid for sustainable development;
- Senate Resolution 182, which would combat global poverty by tripling U.S. foreign assistance by the year 2007, through 25% increases in each of the next five years;
- continued attention to debt relief, by limiting debt payment to no more than 10% of government revenues or, if the country is suffering a severe health crisis, to no more than 5% of government revenues.

Our country has a moral obligation to provide effective and appropriate aid in solidarity with our poorest brothers and sisters. The nation faces many demands upon its budgetary resources in the aftermath of the September 11 attacks, including the critical need to remain engaged in the rebuilding effort in Afghanistan [and now Iraq, too]. But the response to these challenges should not be at the expense of addressing the harsh realities of global poverty. It is shortsighted and counterproductive to consider only the military aspects of national security without providing adequate funding for sustainable development essential to international stability and peace.

What You Can Do
- Help educate the American public about the low levels of U.S. foreign assistance and about the urgent needs of the poorest countries.
- Encourage constituents to contact legislators to convey strong support for a significant increase in U.S. foreign assistance, incorporating a comprehensive development agenda for the poor, to satisfy the nation's moral responsibility and to help build a safer, more secure, and more peaceful world.[102]

In this context, on February 25, 2002, at the Annual Social Ministry Gathering in Washington, D.C., John Carr, director of the USCCB Secretariat for Social Responsibility and World Peace, delivered an informative, encouraging, motivating address entitled "Where Are We Now?"[103] He was aware that "times are tough": the aftermath of the terrorist attacks on the World Trade Center and the Pentagon, a recession, budget deficits, a church burdened with sexual abuse and scandal. Still, he insisted, September 11 did not change our common Catholic mission and message. The way to build a nation of greater unity is by caring for those left behind, a new sense of solidarity, a serious and sustained commitment to deal with the roots of terrorism, building a world of more development and less debt, aware of Paul VI's words, "If you want peace, work for justice." Before detailing what we can do for the poor and vulnerable in our midst, Carr spoke eloquently of the difference we can make beyond our shores and our intramural interests.

We *can* make a difference. We've done it in the past by working with others to persuade our nation to forgive its bilateral debt and to invest hundreds of millions of dollars in multilateral debt relief for the poorest nations. But much more is needed; we're halfway home. So your voices are needed now to advocate for greater debt relief and more development assistance, for new efforts to confront the global health crises of HIV/AIDS and other diseases in Africa and elsewhere. The President's commitment to increase foreign aid by $5 billion is a step.

Carr went on to cite other examples of what we have done in the past: We have worked with others to build a global citizens' movement to ban antipersonnel land mines; our nation has committed itself to stopping the production, sale, and use of land mines (except for those now in place in Korea). But more is needed. "We must urge our government to do everything it can to insist that violence, occupation, and terror give way to new negotiations to bring about a secure state for Israelis, a viable state for Palestinians, and a peace based on equality and dignity for all the people of the Middle East." (In spring 2002, the Bush administration began to insert itself into the conflict, with demands on both parties.) With the U.S. bishops, Carr asserts that "Israeli aggressive military acts and occupation cannot be sustained morally or militarily," that "Palestinian attacks on innocent civilians are morally indefensible. . . . Our voices must be heard for a just peace in the Middle East—in communication with our leaders, and in dialogue with Jewish and Islamic communities."

Conclusions

After these several years of research, summarized in the pages preceding, I think it pertinent to indicate where I myself stand on justice and injustice in the context of globalization. I do so because with

Friedman I see today's globalization as "almost irreversible." I mean that the system in its main components, especially the economic, is not likely to break up soon, is here to stay a significant number of years. Assuming that as fact, I find it imperative to attempt a fairly brief critical look at justice in the system. By "justice" I mean (1) ethical or philosophical justice, giving to every man, woman, and child what they can claim as a right, not because they are wealthy or powerful, but because they are human; (2) legal justice, giving to each what just, fair, and impartial laws require; and (3) biblical justice, fidelity to relationships that stem from a covenant with God: relationships to God, to our sisters and brothers, and to the earth. (These areas of justice I have explained at some length in the first section of this book.) An important critique, because it involves the way we humans live, or should live, or have a right to live on planet Earth. Important because globalization is about relationships—relationships that are changing in space and time.

Within globalization the possibilities for good, for justice, are enormous; I dare say unprecedented. In a special way, opportunity for interconnectedness. Here I submit some evidence that does not make the headlines but is touchingly real. I mean the housebound, the untold millions confined to home or hospice through age or illness, men and women till now condemned to a life of loneliness, but through e-mail and the Internet now make contacts across the world, communicate constantly, share their experience of living with lupus or histoplasmosis, develop fascinating friendships that make it possible to help one another to come alive or stay alive, to discover that there are others who care.

With the new forms of communication distance disappears. Not entirely, not for everyone, for problems abide: languages, cultures, animosities. But the mechanisms, the techniques, the systems are there—globally.

Given interconnectedness, the possibilities of solidarity are increased immeasurably. Pope John Paul II made it clear that solidarity is more than the famous struggle of Polish workers against communist repression. Solidarity "helps us to see the other—whether a person, people, or nation—not just as some kind of instrument, with a work capacity and physical strength to be exploited at low cost and then discarded when no longer useful, but as our 'neighbor,' a 'helper' (cf. Gen 2:18-20), to be made a sharer, on a par with ourselves, in the banquet of life to which all are equally invited by God."[104] After indi-

cating how solidarity excludes the exploitation, oppression, and annihilation of others, the pope continues:

> In this way, the solidarity which we propose is the path to peace
> and at the same time to development. For world peace is incon-
> ceivable unless the world's leaders come to recognize that inter-
> dependence in itself demands the abandonment of the politics of
> blocs, the sacrifice of all forms of economic, military or political
> imperialism, and the transformation of mutual distrust into col-
> laboration. This is precisely the act proper to solidarity among
> individuals and nations. . . .
>   In the light of faith, solidarity seeks to go beyond itself, to take
> on the specifically Christian dimensions of total gratuity, for-
> giveness, and reconciliation. One's neighbor is then not only a
> human being with his or her own rights and a fundamental
> equality with everyone else, but becomes the living image of God
> the Father, redeemed by the blood of Jesus Christ and placed
> under the permanent action of the Holy Spirit. One's neighbor
> must therefore be loved, even if an enemy, with the same love
> with which the Lord loved him or her, and for that person's sake
> one must be ready for sacrifice, even the ultimate one: to lay
> down one's life for the brethren (cf. 1 Jn 3:16).[105]

I realize that what John Paul II was commending has two levels: a
solidarity motivated by reason, by sheer intellectual recognition of the
interdependence necessary for world peace; and a solidarity inspired
by Christian faith, by gifts of grace that enable a sinful, self-centered
humanity to extend its love to a Saddam Hussein, to a terrorist like
Osama bin Laden, to the untold millions who dislike or even abomi-
nate us and so much that America unfortunately represents. Unreal?
Only if we are yoked to a secularism that excludes the religious factor from public life.

Granted that globalization makes "one world" more and more
realizable, what of the negatives? I have spoken at length of globalism's backlash; it is not insignificant. Critics such as Hartman demand
globalism's destruction. Others, more numerous, recognize that Friedman's "almost irreversible" does not mean globalization is unchange-
able. In the interests of justice, they call for reform. And reform there
must be. Here I resonate to words uttered on August 26, 2002, in
Johannesburg during the first plenary session of the World Summit on

Sustainable Development, by South African President Thabo Mbeki (elected president of the Summit): "There is every need for us to demonstrate to the billions of people we lead that we are committed to the vision and practice of human solidarity, that we do not accept that human society should be constructed on the basis of a savage principle of the survival of the fittest."[106] Human solidarity, a prime component of social justice. It reflects a vision of globalization concisely expressed in 1999 by U.N. Secretary-General Kofi Annan, and since then by score of others: "Globalization with a human face."

Globalization with a human face. Schreiter estimates that while a small segment of the world's population has been unbelievably enriched by globalism, a huge proportion, perhaps 80 percent, is made poorer, even plunged into misery. How? Recall the acute observation of Tina Rosenberg: Whereas "a previous wave [of globalization] was stopped dead by World War I, today's globalization is more likely to be sabotaged by its own inequities." In what areas are these inequities to be found?

I would focus on free trade.[107] Essentially, free trade is about making trade easier by allowing the market to balance needs—supply and demand. In theory, unfettered free trade can be a positive force for development. The disturbing question, however, is whether the current system of free trade in its reality is the free trade described by the theorists. For example, Joseph Stiglitz, former chief economist of the World Bank and Nobel Prize winner, has argued that many of the complaints voiced by protesters in recent years—that IMF structural adjustment programs have caused widespread suffering, that free-trade agreements mainly benefit the rich, that privatization has proven disastrous in many countries—have a solid basis in fact. He warns that, unless the rules of global capitalism are radically altered, the gap between the world's rich and poor, and therefore the social conditions that have forced instability in places like Pakistan, will not go away anytime soon. Asked once what developing countries should do with the annual report the IMF prepares on member nations, Stiglitz recommended "picking it up, saying 'thank you very much' and dropping it straight in the garbage can."

A number of other criticisms are worth pondering. (1) At times influential decision making is taken away from publicly elected governments and given to privately owned corporations. Some even call large transnational corporations and their drive to open up markets around the world a modern form of colonialism. (2) In an address at the U.N., former Chilean President Patricio Aylwin claimed, "Only poverty has been truly globalized in our age. . . . The overpraised neoliberalism and the omnipotent market is a mistaken vision and it is the root cause of some of the most serious problems that afflict us." (3) Most developing countries complain that the Western nations themselves are very protectionist but want the developing countries to completely remove barriers to free trade, which would cause an imbalance in favor of the industrialized countries. (4) The argument that globalization should move the world further toward interdependence would have merit if there were a truly fair free-trade system. But the current global system appears to be more mercantilist. Furthermore, given the current international institutions in place (WTO, IMF, World Bank, et al.), it is the large multinational corporations and their governments that would benefit from the interdependence within the framework of the current form of globalization. The governments of more influential and powerful nations can impose certain types of interdependence and easily force dependence in their favor through economic or military pressure. (5) "In order for 'free markets' to be 'free,' the exchange of labour, land, currency, and consumer goods must not be encumbered by elements of psychological integration such as clan loyalties, village responsibilities, guild or union rights, charity, family obligations, social roles, or religious values. Cultural values 'distort' the free play of the laws of supply and demand, and thus must be suppressed" (Noam Chomsky in 1994, but still relevant today). (6) As the affluent members of society face some controls, they and the institutions they own will increase the pressure on their government to remove or reduce these controls, increase liberalization in industries other than their own, open the economy to access a larger variety of goods. Often this occurs prematurely; the majority often lose out; large debts are incurred; measures made to repay them affect the poor even further.[108]

Postscript: A Teilhardian Vision

Not to end on a negative note, I shall sketch a unique global vision propounded as early as World War I by a Jesuit priest and paleontologist, Pierre Teilhard de Chardin. It has been accurately, if broadly, titled "Globalization and the Soul."[109] Thomas King, gifted interpreter of Teilhard, has recognized Teilhard's influence on several extraordinary minds, themselves men of considerable influence: communications expert Marshall McLuhan, economist Kenneth Boulding, and arguably the leading practitioner of globalization Michel Candessus, who called for developing a sense of the universal "at the deepest level of consciousness."

It was while studying fossil history at the University of Paris in 1914 that Teilhard began to wonder whether the human species had completed its evolution. As King points out, "His answer would come not from the fossils but from the battlefields of World War I."[110] A stretcher bearer to the trenches outside Paris, he told of discovering Humanity. In the spring of 1916 he wrote to tell Christians "they could have a communion with God through their communion with the Earth; by their 'passionate' work they might build the great body of Christ."[111]

In the heat of battle, with death all around him (two of his brothers died in the war), Teilhard felt free of his day-to-day burdens, found his own life more precious than ever, and yet would have abandoned it without regret. Like the mystics he had studied, he had found a higher Self.

At the front Teilhard found "an extremely vivid feeling of Presence," a "new and superhuman Soul which takes over from our own," "a Soul greater than my own," the everyday man effaced by "a Personality of another order." This Presence, higher Soul, Personality of another order, was summoning him to return to the Front. . . . Mystics [have] told of the divine visitation in moments of solitude when the world and its clamor were stilled. But Teilhard told of the Visitation as troops poured over trenches and terrain loaded with rations, flares, and hand grenades. Shells were exploding overhead as "the Soul of the Front was being reborn." Teilhard would claim that World War I was the first time the globe as a whole was engaged in a common action. Globalization had begun! It began in war, but Teilhard envisioned a globalization of peace that might follow. (His term was *planetization*.) The World War as a totalizing action in which humanity was coming together, and together they might build a New Jerusalem.[112]

Teilhard was aware that, once war ended, the former melancholy and trivialities would return. With demobilization and the old routines, he felt almost of another species. He was seeking what others did not see: the "All" he had seen at the front. In the midst of war he had discovered a power of union, a common feeling, a capacity for sacrifice that for a moment swept away all differences. The experience seemed to answer his question in Paris: Would the human species continue to evolve? In their bonding on the battlefield, the soldiers seemed to unite in a higher Soul. The friendships, the energy, the exaltation Teilhard saw as a revelation of a future when all people would share a common global life. It convinced him that an extraordinary revolutionary change was occurring. "He looked forward to the day when 'the consciousness of all (would be) working together in a task as great as the world itself.'"[113]

Teilhard believed we were entering a new phase in evolution when human individuals would come together to form some sort of global union.

St. Paul spoke of Christians forming the Body of Christ, a Body to be built up in love. In this tradition Teilhard argued that the Body of Christ involves education, the environment, industry, international cooperation, and, above all, scientific research; on the new and unifying earth God would bestow his Soul. This was the spiritual meaning Teilhard found in globalization. He wrote of it in the language of the mystics, and the ardor of his words resonated with others.[114]

For Teilhard, radio and television provided the nervous system for the global Body. His enthusiasm for secular aspects of the process—travel, international business, peace, and environmental restrictions—worried a businessman taken by his vision. Teilhard's response:

Since everything in the world follows the road to unification, the spiritual success of the universe is bound up with the correct functioning of every zone of the universe. . . . Because your enterprise (which I take to be legitimate) is going well, a little more health is being spread in the human mass, and in consequence a little more liberty to act, to think, and to love.[115]

The last end would be the Pleroma, the "All" of which St. Paul spoke, when the Body of Christ would include all things.

Thomas King has observed that St. Ignatius of Loyola, founder of the Society of Jesus, the religious order to which Teilhard belonged, had a recurring vision of a luminous golden globe—interpreted by psychiatrist Carl Jung as an ancient symbol of unity.

> In 1522 Magellan was the first to circle the globe, and this was the very year Ignatius . . . had his religious awakening. . . . At the time of Ignatius the world was seen for the first time as a "whole." Ignatius accordingly developed a global mission, sending Jesuits to India, Indonesia, Africa, Japan, and Brazil. . . . In his *Spiritual Exercises,* Ignatius tells of the Trinity looking at the earth in its entirety ("the whole extent of the earth filled with human beings"), and [tells] the one making the Exercises . . . to do the same, that is, to see "in imagination the great extent and space of the world where dwell so many different nations and peoples"—some at war and some at peace, some weeping and some laughing. For Ignatius and his followers, every action should be animated by this sense of the Whole: *Quo universalius, eo divinius*—the more universal, the more divine the action. As a Jesuit, Teilhard meditated on the texts of Ignatius every year. He worked with the same vision of the globe that Ignatius had known; the Whole was the earth itself evoking a response in the soul.[116]

Teilhard's role in globalization today, almost a half century after his death? King has issued a sobering challenge: Unless we take Teilhard's vision seriously, the emerging world is not likely to be shaped in harmony with the hungers of the soul. In that case "we will have created a soulless monster that will consume us."[117]

V

JUSTICE COMMUNICATED

Why a section on communication? Because, as should be evident from the preceding section, communication is an essential feature of globalization, is at once its cause and effect. It is communication that brings people together, not only individuals but nations as well. It brings together those who have never been in touch at all, but also makes it possible for enemies to be reconciled or at least to understand why they disagree. That is why *Merriam-Webster's Collegiate Dictionary* (10th ed., 1997) can define "communicate" as "to convey knowledge of or information about," "to reveal by clear signs," "to transmit information, thought, or feeling so that it is satisfactorily received or understood."

For most of my priestly and scholarly life, until quite recently, my methods of communication were almost exclusively word of mouth, pen on paper, or fingers on typewriter. For my field of specialization was patristic theology, the Fathers of the Church, the early theologians down to St. John Damascene in the eighth century (some would close the patristic age, begin the early Middle Ages, with St. Gregory the Great in the fifth century). I taught "the Fathers" to young Jesuits at storied Woodstock College in Maryland, to a broader audience at Union Theological Seminary in New York City, and to (mostly) seminarians in a master's program at The Catholic University of America in Washington, D.C. My outline for each class was neatly typed, my lectures a model of oral delivery, calculated to have the last sentence end as the bell rang for dismissal. Similarly with preaching, an apostolate especially precious to me since ordination to priesthood in 1941. In that capacity my method moved from mind to typewriter to a living audience I could see—save for rare radio and TV appearances.

All of this was highly satisfactory, profoundly satisfying—until my late introduction to the electronic age. Not only has it changed my methods of research, my approach to spirituality, my involvement with people. It has also transfigured my work for justice, my method of communicating the just word—and so thoroughly that I must close this volume with an extensive presentation of today's miracle of communication, the computer. I realize that the computer has already played a significant role in my discussion of globalization. Still, a more comprehensive treatment, centering on justice, is demanded if workers for justice are to appreciate and utilize the remarkable resources literally at their fingertips.

I shall begin with the computer, expending extensive attention on the Internet, the World Wide Web, and e-mail, as background for the substantive issue: the indispensable link that binds the Internet to effective action for justice. Internet experts may well turn the early pages briskly. I make bold to hope that my effort to extract from this technical information important resources for practitioners of justice may prove as helpful to them as it has been for me.

Computer

Without a doubt, the most useful new tool in my own research and publication during the past decade has been the computer. Like everyone else I know who uses a computer regularly, I delight in no longer enduring messy attempts to correct a mistake not only on an original page but on multiple carbon copies as well. An inkjet seems several generations ahead of carbon paper and the ease of using a computer printer makes memories of photocopiers seem as archaic as mimeograph machines did 20 years ago.

Internet

Beyond the obvious facility of a word processing program for typing my homilies and manuscripts, I find the Internet and World Wide Web to be indispensable tools in my research. The terms Internet, the World Wide Web, and e-mail often are used synonymously but in fact are three distinct, though related, entities.

The development of computers—first large mainframes and then smaller personal computers—gave people hope that communication would become easier. Soon, however, it became evident there were not even standards for hardware, much less for software.[1]

Despite the incalculably immense challenges of many people developing computers and computer programs essentially in isolation from one another, through "synergy, serendipity, and coincidence," the

Internet became a massive network of networks, a networking infrastructure in less than half a century.[2] This mega-network now connects globally millions of computers and allows any computer to communicate with any other computer as long as both are connected to the Internet.

Perhaps the most intriguing aspect of the Internet is the relative speed with which it came into wide use. As late as the early 1970s there was no consistency in the ways information was exchanged between persons via computers. Think, "tower of babbling technology." Much time and intensive energy were expended again and again in the competition to establish even basic consistency in the transfer of information. Results have been giant in stride. What began as a military communication system designed to survive a nuclear war, the Internet is now supported almost entirely from commercial sources and connects people and services in myriad ways with instant gratification and without geographic boundaries.[3]

World Wide Web

The World Wide Web, often referred to simply as "the Web," is a way of accessing information through the network we now call the Internet. The Web leads me to more information in a matter of seconds than I could possibly find in the hours it would take me to put on my coat, travel to a library, flip through a card catalog, collect appropriate books and periodicals from the shelves, find the actual information I am seeking, and take notes.

In June 1993 there were only 130 Web sites available through the World Wide Web.[4] In early 2003, while preparing this manuscript, I used the search engine Google to find Web sites about justice. In less than a fifth of a second, Google searched 3,083,324,652 Web pages and found 13,900,000 Web sites—yes, nearly 14 million Web sites—related to issues of justice. Such growth of the availability of information in less than a decade is staggering to my psyche; the speed necessary to read more than three billion Web pages in less than half a second actually exceeds my comprehension.

E-mail

Speed has also prompted mammoth growth in the use of e-mail on the Internet. Although these numbers include unwanted messages commonly called "spam," it is nonetheless impressive that "the number of e-mail messages transmitted daily across the Internet is expected to exceed 60 billion worldwide by 2006, up from 31 billion in 2002."[5] Despite my personal joy when receiving a letter evidencing the care and concern of a friend who has taken significant time and effort to correspond with me in his or her own handwriting, I must confess consolation in being able to type e-mail messages as my own hands grow more arthritic by the year. And, yes, there is remarkable delight in being able to communicate with a friend overseas in a matter of seconds rather than the two weeks or more it used to take to get a letter across the ocean and then the additional wait for a response. The Internet is bringing people around the world closer.

E-mail and the Internet merge in powerful ways. One is with educational opportunities afforded to persons around the world to take classes either online or via e-mail. Noncredit classes can be found online in hundreds of arenas, e.g., literature, genealogy, health, foreign languages, journalism, local history, global archeology, environmental justice, communications. Tutorials and full-term classes in almost any subject one might want to explore are available nearly every hour of the day or night. Well-respected colleges and universities, such as Columbia[6] and Stanford,[7] have joined the ranks of nontraditional providers of education, such as Barnes & Noble bookstores[8] and the BBC in the United Kingdom,[9] to provide courses online. Both degree and nondegree programs are available and vary in cost from free to what many would consider expensive.

Some courses are totally solitary experiences, with the students downloading the curriculum and studying at their own pace. Other classes have a teacher who prepares curricula and also moderates open fora through instant messaging. People with work schedules that vary greatly from one day to the next often prefer the first option. The second option is sometimes chosen eagerly by persons desiring to interact with persons in other parts of the world without ever leaving home.

Another combined use of e-mail and the Internet burgeoned in the weeks prior to the start of the war in Iraq. That marriage of communication brought forth hundreds of petitions around the world calling on the United Nations or Tony Blair or Saddam Hussein or George W. Bush or the leaders of the Republic of Turkey or the Congress of the United States and other groups and individuals to stop the war before a bomb was ever dropped. These protests were carried out with computers not banners, with peace not belligerence. In "Beyond Regime Change Dissent: Antiwar and Postwar, Too? You Bet," Robert Kuttner describes "[the] antiwar movement [is] actually two rather different movements that partly overlap. One movement is in the streets and on the Internet—often led by radicals, sometimes joined uneasily by liberals. The other is pragmatic and mainstream. Both were non-plused, but only temporarily, by the outbreak of war, and neither has gone away."[10]

One of the largest and best known antiwar groups is MoveOn, which builds electronic advocacy groups when there is a "disconnect between broad public opinion and legislative action."[11] With a nationwide base of 600,000 online activists, MoveOn is striving to bring back into politics ordinary citizens who have grown weary of, and feel isolated in, an arena dominated by big money and big media. Persons are given opportunities to sign (or not) online petitions or petitions sent via e-mail and then to forward them (or not) to others for their consideration.

An editorial in the *National Catholic Reporter*, "The Peace Enterprise Goes Global," declared: "If Vietnam was the first television war and the Gulf War made CNN a media power, the attack on Iraq seems likely to be the first war of the Internet. . . . If the Internet has changed the way we live, then part of that change has involved the birth of new and creative peace actions that cross national, ethnic, and religious lines."[12]

Another remarkable effort, EarthFuture, is largely the work of one person, Guy Dauncey in Victoria, British Columbia, Canada. In addition to his efforts toward global sustainable economy, he pulled together myriad links and created a Web page entitled "101 Ways To Stop the War on Iraq." Ten of those ways addressed how to stop the war with e-mail.[13] Electronic mail could be sent to every member of the U.N. at one time or to every member of the U.S. Senate, a virtual march so to speak. Petitions could try to persuade the U.S. House of Representatives to impeach President George W. Bush, a serious move proposed by former Attorney General Ramsey Clark.[14] E-mail could also be a way for women, whose gender has suffered all too much violence, to plead with government officials to stop a war that would cause many other women to experience violence.[15]

Dauncey's EarthFuture Web site includes insightful words from Pierre Teilhard de Chardin: "Today, something is happening to the whole structure of human consciousness. A fresh kind of life is starting."[16] "Driven by the forces of love, the fragments of the world are seeking each other, so that the world may come into being."[17] Nowhere is this insight more visible than on the Internet and through the billions of e-mail messages sent across the globe each day.

Instant Messaging
    If two or more people are available at the same time, they do not have to send e-mail and wait for a response from the other(s). They can chat through instant messaging—silent conversations in which people write back and forth in real time just as they might talk to one another on the telephone, but without long-distance charges. This popular mode of communication is developing its own system of abbreviations and use of icons, which themselves facilitate global communication. Ah yes, another change: The word "icon" now prompts thoughts of a tiny printer on my tool bar or of a "smiley face," sometimes called an emoticon, much more often than the word triggers thoughts of Greek religious imagery.

Games
    Games provide other venues to connect people through the Internet. I can play Scrabble at my desk with a woman in the Philippines, a man in India, and a student in England. "Come to the (cyber) table" invitations extend beyond my room, my city, my country. Half a century ago who among us could have envisioned that a game designed for four players (the trademark for Scrabble was registered in 1948) could one day be played simultaneously by people in four different countries in real time? These persons also can "chat" with one another while playing the game. No doubt these cyber encounters are going to strengthen global connections between individuals, making them less likely to join in the name-calling of government officials eager to justify violence against others.

Accessories and Other Tools
    To aid persons in utilizing the wonders of the Internet, accessories such as built-in magnifiers enlarge text or visual images. Also there are various translation programs available online which, despite their ofttimes rudimentary results, do provide enough basic translation of materials from one language to another to enable the computer user to know in what direction to search next for additional information.

Access
    Despite these advances with the Internet and the World Wide Web, access is not available to everyone. Individuals must have either their own Internet access or the availability of libraries or cybercafes that have computers linked to the Web. Of course, finances can limit access to the World Wide Web. Often cybercafes and even many

libraries charge for the time one spends surfing the Web or checking his or her Web mail. Someone with a computer at home needs money for an Internet connection, be that a dial-up access or one of the new, faster modes of access—DSL (digital subscriber line) or cable. One who needs to visit a library or other facility may need transportation money in addition to whatever fees the facility may charge for Internet access. Disparity of finances clearly helps determine how often, if at all, one can use a computer.

Obvious factors, too, are geography and weather. Although in this country the number of households with computers is growing significantly, there are many places in the world where there are few computers and those computers are far from the rural areas in which a large proportion of a population lives. Limited transportation makes those distances seem even farther. Add to the distance either soaring hot temperatures or ice-covered roads, and access to computers shrinks even more.

The Internet and Justice

Peace Fellowships

Perhaps no other call to justice more fully combines the necessity for fidelity in relationships to God, to people, and to the earth than our calling to be peacemakers. The Web is home to North American peace fellowships, several of which have links to peace fellowships in other parts of the world. Though international in scope, these groups are sometimes mistaken for community-based organizations because their monetary assets do not afford them the dazzle and glitz of Web sites belonging to larger, more financially endowed groups. In consequence, links are especially important for these small groups, not only to educate visitors to the Web sites but also to empower individuals committed to working for justice with others around the globe.

Baptist Peace Fellowship

"The purpose of the Baptist Peace Fellowship of North America (BaFP) is to unite Christians and enable them to effect peace with justice in a warring world. We are called by God to the gospel of peace. This calling is rooted in our faith in Jesus Christ, who is our Peace, in whom God is reconciling the world and through whom God calls us to the ministry of peacemaking. Peace is not only our goal; it is our means. The foundation of peace is justice. The force of peace is love."[18]

The BaPF also acknowledges that our present criminal justice system is not working and because "retribution can only push people farther apart, increasing the harm done to victims, their families, the community, and the offender," the fellowship works for restorative justice. This Web site has a remarkable section on the distinction between restorative justice and retributive justice. Not provided simply as a source of information, this Web site is designed to urge readers to take action for peace and justice.[19]

Raised and nurtured in the Baptist Church, President Jimmy Carter unequivocally answered the call to be a peacemaker. Not only his efforts in negotiating peace in the Middle East but also his many substantial global efforts were recognized when he was granted the 2002 Nobel Peace Prize. The home page of the Carter Center Web site clearly states the work of Jimmy, his wife and full partner Rosalynn, and their staff: "Waging peace, fighting disease, building hope."[20] From their work with Habitat for Humanity here in the United States to their medical initiatives in many countries, Rosalynn and Jimmy Carter show us they comprehend "that bridging the unacceptable gap between the rich and the poor of our world is the greatest challenge of our time . . . and [that they view] global development not only to be a moral concern, but also imperative to achieving world peace."[21]

In April 2002, the Baptist Peace Fellowship and the Muslim Peace Fellowship led a three-day conference in Dearborn, Michigan: "Muslims & Christians To Explore Conflict Transformation Together."[22] Participants aimed to learn skills for conflict transformation and cross-community bridge building; explore the Qur'anic and biblical roots of peacemaking; develop meaningful relationships across religious lines; and gain new perspectives for analyzing global and community events and issues.

Buddhist Peace Fellowship

Founded in 1978, the Buddhist Peace Fellowship (BuPF) "aim[s] to help beings liberate themselves from the suffering that manifests in individuals, relationships, institutions, and social systems."[23] A poster carried at the 1999 World Trade Organization protest in Seattle summarized the message of the BuPF: "The end of suffering comes about locally through global solidarity."[24]

The BuPF Web site indicates that the group's practice of contemplation and social action is guided by [its] intentions to "recognize the interdependence of all beings to meet suffering directly and with compassion; appreciate the importance of not clinging to views and outcomes; work with Buddhists from all traditions; connect individual and social transformation; practice nonviolence; use participatory decision-making techniques; protect and extend human rights; support gender and racial equality, and challenge all forms of unjust discrimination; work for economic justice and the end of poverty; work for a sustainable environment."[25]

This Web site has an uncommonly comprehensive links section for the "socially engaged" Buddhist from the "Vote to Impeach Bush" campaign, to addiction treatment, to "Free Burma," to the Zen Environmental Studies Center, to gay and lesbian concerns, to prison projects, to Tibetan women refugees, to the interfaith peace Fellowship of Reconciliation.[26]

Catholic Peace Fellowship

In 1964, the Catholic Peace Fellowship (CPF) was founded by Jim Forest and Tom Cornell "to support Catholic conscientious objectors, draft resisters, anti-war activists, and all Catholics committed to peacemaking in accord with the teaching and example of Jesus."[27] It is no surprise that Jesuit priest and activist Daniel Berrigan was pivotal in keeping this fellowship alive for nearly 20 years.

Even prior to September 11, the Catholic Peace Fellowship was being resurrected by original founders Forest and Cornell. Their foci were to speak and act, as well as to encourage others to speak and act, in the name of Christ's peace in providing counseling and legal advice to military conscientious objectors—those who, after enlisting, undergo a change of conscience that forbids them to engage in combat or service in the military; reminding military chaplains of their obligation to inform Catholics and others in the armed forces about their right to conscientious objection as set forth in military regulations; challenging the free access to Catholic high schools enjoyed by military recruiters; and challenging Catholic high school students to consider the profound moral issues military service entails; addressing all issues arising from the participation in Catholic colleges, universities, and high schools in Reserve Officers Training Corps (ROTC) programs; and informing all young Catholics about laws on draft registration and the process by which a civilian may obtain legal recognition as a conscientious objector should Selective Service resume the draft.[28]

Like other peace fellowships, the revived Catholic Peace Fellowship headquartered at the University of Notre Dame in Indiana works with other peace groups in their justice efforts. The World Wide Web becomes not merely a network of computer Internet sites but also a "meeting place" for an ever-growing network of persons working for justice.

Often working for the same goals, the CPF and Pax Christi USA are two distinct groups. The latter group is affiliated with Pax Christi International, which began in France at the end of World War II. Both the international and the U.S. Pax Christi groups "work in all areas of peace but have specific focus on demilitarization, security and arms trade, development and human rights, and ecology."[29]

Included on this Web site are links to readings on the spirituality of nonviolence and peacemaking; human rights and global restoration; disarmament, demilitarization, and reconciliation with justice; and economic and interracial justice in the United States.[30]

Disciples Peace Fellowship

In 1935, at the Convention of the Christian Church (Disciples of Christ), the Disciples Peace Fellowship (DPF) was formed. Of all the peace fellowships, DPF is the oldest. Welcoming all persons regardless of race, gender, ethnicity, or sexual orientation, reiterates the fellowship's call for "peace with justice for all."[31]

At present, there are four central issues of the DPF: demilitarization and the nuclear threat; abolishing the death penalty; seeking justice in maquiladora plants along the U.S.–Mexico border; corporate responsibility for financial investments by the Church and individuals.[32]

Working to abolish war and to create the conditions of peace and justice among all people and nations were issues of the original covenant of the Disciples Peace Fellowship. The Web sites of this and other peace fellowships emphasize in a variety of significant ways that peace is not merely the absence of war. Peace and justice always go hand in hand; it is not possible to have one without the other, to work for one is to work for both. This observation was made both by Pope Paul VI and also by members of the Disciples Peace Fellowship—people who I suspect never met each other. In different times and locations, Mahatma Gandhi, Martin Luther King Jr., Mother Teresa, Dorothy Day, and Jimmy Carter have all shown through their actions as well as their words that they, too, embrace this reality as an inescapable truth. If we want peace, we *will* work for justice.

Episcopal Peace Fellowship

On Armistice Day, four years after the establishment of the Disciples Peace Fellowship, the Episcopal Peace Fellowship (EPF) began as the Episcopal Pacifist Fellowship.[33] Members were required to sign a commitment: "In loyalty to the Person, Spirit and teachings of Jesus Christ, my conscience commits me to His way of redemptive love and compels me to refuse to participate in or give moral support to any war."[34] Efforts to get resolutions passed by the triennial General Convention and the "once a decade" Lambeth Conference—a meeting of all Anglican bishops from around the world—met with little success. In 1930, however, the Lambeth Conference had passed the statement, "War as a means of settling international disputes is incompatible with the teaching and principle of our Saviour Jesus Christ." This statement has been reiterated every ten years since 1948.[35]

The work of the fellowship kept alive many issues surrounding peace. Areas needing attention changed and eventually so did the name of the fellowship. On the eve of the Vietnam War in 1966, the name was changed to Episcopal Peace Fellowship. Today the group continues

to aid and encourage all Episcopalians to strive for justice and peace among all people and to bear nonviolent witness to Christ's call to peace. As a community we are dedicated to discovering and practicing the biblical concept of peace. This Shalom/Salaam includes a commitment to renounce, so far as possible, participation in war and other forms of violence. The EPF recognizes that there can be no peace without a commitment to justice, and no justice without reconciliation.[36]

Jewish Peace Fellowship

Established in 1941 to acknowledge the right of Jews to be recognized as conscientious objectors, the Jewish Peace Fellowship (JPF) maintains that respect for the dignity of everything created in God's image, especially the poor, the weak, and the vulnerable, will bring about true, positive peace among family, neighborhoods, and nations.[37] Paul Wellstone, the remarkable Minnesota senator killed in an airplane crash in 2002, was a frequent speaker at JPF events and lived out that understanding of social justice in uniquely effective ways.

Committed to "active nonviolence as means of resolving conflict," the JPF draws on "Jewish traditional sources within the Torah, the Talmud, and contemporary peacemaking sages such as Martin Buber, Judah Magnes, and Abraham Joshua Heschel."[38] Heschel's sense of worship and wonder has had significant influence on my own preaching.[39]

One of the many links listed on the JPF Web site is to "Jews for a Just Peace," founded in Vancouver over a decade ago. Its purpose is "to build support for a fair and just solution to the Israeli-Palestinian conflict."[40] Accompanying a tribute to Governor George Ryan of Illinois for his courage and wisdom in commuting to life imprisonment without parole the death sentences of all those in his state on death row, the JPF Web site has a link to the Web site for "The Justice Project: Campaign for Criminal Justice Reform." That Web site profiles more than a dozen of the 100 people in the United States sentenced to die since 1973 and later exonerated.[41]

Following links on the World Wide Web reminds me of the hypothesis "six degrees of separation." Just as it appears that there are no more than six people separating me from any other person on earth, sometimes it requires no more than six links from any Web page to another page one wants to explore on the Web.[42]

Lutheran Peace Fellowship

The poignantly God-centered Web site belonging to the Lutheran Peace Fellowship (LPF) reminds us that not only are we called to be peacemakers but also we *are* empowered by the grace of a compassionate and loving God. In March 2002 the LPF board issued a statement, "We are called to be peacemakers," which emphasized that with this empowerment we can act. How?

> [By] admit[ting] our vulnerability and turning to God; open[ing] ourselves to discover the creativity and discipline taught by Jesus, Gandhi, King, Day, and open[ing] ourselves to the power to interrupt the spiral of violence; giv[ing] ourselves to God [so that we are able] to address the roots of violence—oppression, discrimination, poverty, hunger, powerlessness; plac[ing] our trust in God, [we] find the courage to examine our complicity as citizens and as a nation in the violence all around us.

The board concluded: "We oppose violence in all its forms." The LPF board specifically stated how "we can renounce violence and domination in our personal lives, in our churches and communities, and in our nation and [also] affirm the love of God for all people."[43]

The LPF Web site contains several links to Web pages dealing with statistics on violence. It is alarming to read that of all 15-24-year-old young persons in this country, one in four will die from a firearm wound and that here 270,000 guns go to school *each day*. These realities are even more chilling to comprehend when looking at numbers from other countries. In 1999 the number of deaths from firearms was 381 in Germany, 255 in France, 165 in Canada, 68 in the United Kingdom, 65 in Australia, 39 in Japan, but 11,127 in the United States.[44]

Muslim Peace Fellowship

Founded in 1994, the Muslim Peace Fellowship (MPF) is dedicated to evidencing the beauty of Islam through efforts of justice-oriented Muslims of all backgrounds. The group's Web site lists specific ways to work for peace. Highlighted are those elucidated by Giasuddin Ahmed, the executive director of Sampreeti—the Society for Peace in Development. The first way is "to promote the basic foundational qualities for peacemaking: (a) faith (there is no god but One God); (b) holy knowledge and remembrance of the Creator; (c) prayer (obligatory and optional); (d) realization of the will of the Almighty, complete obedience to Him, commitment, pleasing Him and serving His purposes; (e) sublime character; (f) love and fraternity; (g) endeavor to help others build their character."

Ahmed's five other ways to become a Muslim peacebuilder are to encourage family meetings, organize the good people of the society, give to the poor, advocate kindness to others and the approach of love, and teach people religion.[45] In harmony with Muslim Scripture, give food out of love for Him (Allah) to the poor and the orphan and the captive: "We only feed you for Allah's sake; we desire from you neither reward nor thanks" (Koran 76.8-9).[46]

Although currently there are not as many electronic versions of the Koran/Qurʾan as there are of the Bible, there are many more online sites of both holy books than I had expected to find. No doubt, one of the best ways to grow in understanding of other persons is to read their sacred books. Sometimes such effort is actually made with others, as was the case at the Christian/Muslim conference in Michigan mentioned earlier in the discussion of the Baptist Peace Fellowship. At other times one studies alone and the Internet facilitates this effort greatly.

Equally poignant as working for justice is coming to grips with the reality that justice *is* work. I am blessed to be living when the Internet is growing exponentially and facilitating my work in ways I could not have imagined a decade ago.

Orthodox Peace Fellowship

The Orthodox Peace Fellowship of the Protection of the Mother of God (OPF) is an association of Orthodox believers "trying to apply the principals [*sic*] of the Gospel to situations of division and conflict, whether in the home, the parish, the community [where] we live, the work place, within our particular nation, and between nations. We work for the conservation of God's creation and especially of human life."[47]

Repeatedly I come back to biblical justice—fidelity to relationships: to God, to others, to the earth. With that focus, I was drawn to the section of the OPF's Web site that centers on the earth itself as well as its inhabitants: "Aware that we are in need of conversion not only in the way we relate to other people but to the world God has put into our care, we will try to change our lives in order to live as priests of God's world, asking continuously for the Holy Spirit to descend and transfigure the earth."[48]

> [Because the Orthodox Church seeks] reconciliation of enemies [rather than victory over them], a conversion which grows from striving to be faithful to the Gospel, the Orthodox Church has *never* regarded any war as just or good, and fighting an elusive enemy by means which cause the death of innocent people can be regarded only as murder. Individual murderers are treated by psychiatrists and priests and [are] isolated from society. But who heals the national psyche, the wounded soul of a nation, when it is untroubled by the slaughter of non-combatant civilians?[49]

Other Church-Related Initiatives

By now it should be clear that this book cannot possibly discuss every Web site that addresses issues of justice. These Web pages exist by the millions and would require not merely a book but a series of books that would be outdated before they even left the publisher. One of the strengths of the World Wide Web is information being added every minute. This reality is wonderful for Web surfers but nightmarish for authors writing about Internet resources. Readers, note please, although all URLs (Uniform Resource Locators sometimes called Universal Resource Locators) were active when this book went to press, it is not possible to guarantee all will be accessible indefinitely.

When I write a homily, I am not content with data published ten years ago; I want the most current information available. For instance, on a Web site of the Canadian Red Cross, I recently discovered that at the turn of *this* century, war dominated life in more than 80 countries around the world. A report released in October 2002 from the World Health Organization indicated that about 35 people are killed every hour as a direct result of armed conflict. From 1890 to 2000, one and a half million children were slaughtered, between 4 or 5 million injured or permanently disabled, and 20 million left homeless because of conflict. Between 1945 and 2000, 280 major wars took place, killing 24 million people. In today's wars an estimated 10 civilians die for every one soldier or fighter killed in battle. An estimated 300,000 children engage in combat each year.[50]

Early in March 2003, a new study was released by the Robert Woods Johnson Foundation indicating that at some time in the past two years nearly a third of all nonelderly individuals in the United States (about 75,000,000 persons) were without health insurance. At least two-thirds of these persons were uninsured for at least six months. A fourth had no health insurance at all during those two years. And four out of five were, in fact, in the work force.[51]

When I learn of these dire realities, where do I go to learn who is trying to remedy these injustices? Fortunately, for all their importance, the peace fellowships are not the only church-related organizations to which I turn for resources about these and other critical areas. Pressed by space, I list only five of the more important.

Pontifical Council for Justice and Peace

Not surprisingly, my own background prompts me to begin my search within the Church, this time with the Vatican's official Web site. The Second Vatican Council proposed creating a body "to stimulate the Catholic community to foster progress in needy regions and social justice on the international scene."[52] Three stages reflect the development of this initiative. In 1967, Pope Paul VI established the Pontifical Commission Justitia et Pax. A decade later, the same pontiff gave the commission definitive status—motu proprio *Justitiam et Pacem*. More recently, Pope John Paul II changed its name from Commission to Pontifical Council and reconfirmed its general work.[53]

The Vatican's Web site discusses the origin, objectives and mandate, structure, activities (justice, peace, and human rights), and publications of this commission.

[Special] mention must be made of various links with secular organizations working for the promotion of justice, peace and the respect for human dignity. Over the years, relations with international organizations have increased considerably. Because of the interest of the Holy See in the work of the United Nations, the Pontifical Council, in collaboration with the Secretariat of State, has frequent contacts with the United Nations and its specialized agencies, especially at the time of the major international conferences that deal with such questions as development, population, environment, international trade, or human rights. Equal importance is given to regional organizations, among which [are] the Council of Europe and the European Union. The Pontifical Council also welcomes exchanges with non-governmental organizations that share its aims and are working in the field of peace, justice and human rights.[54]

Working with other organizations is highlighted also in the objectives and mandate of the council: The council will promote justice and peace in the world, in the light of the gospel and of the social teaching of the Church.

§1. It will deepen the social doctrine of the Church and attempt to make it widely known and applied, both by individuals and communities, especially as regards relations between workers and employers. These relations must be increasingly marked by the spirit of the gospel.

§2. It will assemble and evaluate various types of information and the results of research on justice and peace, the development of peoples and the violations of human rights. When appropriate, it will inform episcopal bodies of the conclusions drawn. It will foster relations with international Catholic organizations and with other bodies, be they Catholic or not, that are sincerely committed to the promotion of the values of justice and peace in the world.

§3. It will heighten awareness of the need to promote peace, above all, on the occasion of the World Day of Peace [January 1] each year.[55]

On World Peace Day 2003, Pope John Paul II echoed words from Pope John XXIII's encyclical letter *Pacem in terris*. Described are the "four pillars of peace":

Truth will build peace if every individual sincerely acknowledges not only his rights, but also his own duties towards others. *Jus-*

tice will build peace if in practice everyone respects the rights of others and actually fulfils his duties towards them. *Love* will build peace if people feel the needs of others as their own and share what they have with others, especially the values of mind and spirit which they possess. *Freedom* will build peace and make it thrive if, in the choice of the means to that end, people act according to reason and assume responsibility for their own actions.[56]

The Vatican Web site also addresses the work of other councils, including the Health Pastoral Care and the Pastoral Care of Migrant and Itinerant People. The section for each council has links to major papers, homilies, other speeches, and activities relative to each. For instance, the Health Pastoral Care section[57] has numerous talks given each February 11, World Day of the Sick. Most texts are translated into English, French, and Italian, and sometimes also into Spanish, German, and Portuguese. Also listed are links to Catholic Associations of Health Care Workers.

Similarly, the section on Migrants and Itinerant People[58] has links to speeches and homilies given each June 20, the day annually set aside by the United Nations as International Refugee Day. Also in this section are addresses given by members of the Holy See delegation at the United Nations concerning the perils of racism, xenophobia, and other intolerance.

A national group with obvious ties to the Vatican and which, like Rome, addresses issues of global importance is the United States Conference of Catholic Bishops.[59] Several of their letters and statements I cited earlier in this book. This Web site not only has an archive of past publications but also announces conferences coming up in future months, offers resources for dioceses and parishes on "the way to peace," and even a section on employment opportunities with the conference.

International Jesuit Network for Development

Beyond the walls of the Vatican, another initiative striving for global justice is the International Jesuit Network for Development (IJND). In 1997 in Naples, Italy, Jesuit social action directors from around the world came together. From a concept of a co-ordinated international Jesuit response to the growing injustice of the global social and economic system, they created the Jesuits for Debt Relief and Development. That initiative evolved into a network of more than 350 partners and members in five regions who share data, analyses, and ethical/theological reflection on "facilitating the voices of the voiceless and supporting the power of the oppressed around the world."[60]

The 2003 board comprises Jesuits and non-Jesuits from 11 countries: Brazil, Colombia, the Democratic Republic of the Congo, Ecuador, India, Ireland, the Philippines, Spain, the United States, Venezuela, and Zambia. Only a few days after the bombing began in Iraq (March 19, 2003), the IJND issued this statement:

> The International Jesuit Network for Development is saddened, angered, and deeply concerned by the launch of war by the United States in Iraq. In choosing the path of violent aggression over available nonviolent means, against a non-imminent threat, the United States has acted in clear violation of the principles of a Just War. In acting without the support of the United Nations Security Council, the United States has shown a disturbing disregard for international law.
>
> One casualty of this war is trust, and the consequence could be the further polarization of the powerful and the weak, the Muslim and the Christian, and the poor and the rich. Because of this, the call for international solidarity becomes all the more pressing and crucial. The family of nations should act quickly to mitigate these divisions and prevent their worsening. Countries involved in this war must be made responsible for the damages inflicted on the environment and the loss of lives. More importantly, the members of international organizations, especially the United Nations, and civil society should continue to denounce this war, and immediately begin the work of reconstruction and reconciliation.
>
> Our thoughts and prayers at this time are with all those who are caught up in this conflict and who will suffer from its consequences.[61]

Every day the Internet brings to my fingertips new information. Never before have the earth's inhabitants—in times of peace *and* in times of war—had such immediate access to statements coming from every part of the globe in reference to any one incident. Web sites display not only their own information but also links to others that share visions and hopes, concerns and fears.

In addition to information about its own work and writings, the IJND Web site displays in its entirety a letter to the (Jesuit) Provincial Co-ordinators of the Social Apostolate from Fernando Franco, S.J., Secretary of the Social Justice Secretariat, centered in Rome with the General Curia of the Society of Jesus. This letter begins with the words of John Paul II, "War is not always inevitable, it is always a defeat for humanity."[62] Later in the letter Franco lists reasons for efforts on behalf of peace:

1. The "doctrine" of a pre-emptive war is neither in accordance with UN doctrine and law, nor morally defensible. The application of this doctrine would open the door to an infinite war, a "war without end."

2. Rather than bringing a stable peace in the region (Middle East), a war against Iraq would heighten the tensions between Muslims and Christians. The seeds of dialogue between them so patiently sown would be trampled in a spiral of violence and intolerance.

3. The willingness to incur massive military expenditure that destroys life seems to stand in sharp contrast with the unwillingness to promote, with the same determination, the sustainable development of all. In a world of growing inequalities, where the majority lack basic necessities; in a world where trade and financial structures benefit the rich rather than the poor countries, many continue to question with increasing discomfort whether the true motives of war against Iraq have to do more with economic than security reasons.

4. In the new emerging world political order, vital decisions on global security affecting the lives of people across continents are proposed to be taken unilaterally by the leaders of a few industrialized countries outside the control of the UN, and disregarding their obligation to build a broader consensus through legitimate democratic processes.

5. Experience has shown us that the poor are always the main victims of violence and war. As Jesuits we are "friends in the Lord," and this "means *being friends with the poor*, and we cannot turn aside when our friends are in need." In a situation of generalized violence, and when war is projected as inevitable, we cannot turn our gaze away from our professed friends, the poor, especially women and children.[63]

World Council of Churches

Representing more than 300 million Christians, the World Council of Churches (WCC) is a fellowship of churches committed to ecumenism. In 2003 the WCC included more than 340 churches from nearly all Christian traditions in over 120 countries.[64] Although the Roman Catholic Church is not a member, it works co-operatively with the WCC. Efforts to initiate the formation of a world council had begun in the 1930s; however, war intervened and slowed those efforts for more than a decade. The mid-1940s saw meetings of a provisional committee both in Europe and in the United States. By 1947, members of this committee were aware that the tragedy of the war had strengthened their resolve to evidence reconciliation to the world, and invitations were issued to churches to join a world council. In 1948 in Amsterdam, Netherlands, the WCC was inaugurated with 147 churches in 44 countries.[65]

A powerful initiative of the WCC is "The Decade To Overcome Violence (2001-2010)." This effort calls persons "to empower those oppressed by violence, and to act in solidarity with those struggling for justice, peace and the integrity of creation. It calls us to repent for our complicity in violence, and to engage in theological reflection to overcome the spirit, logic and practice of violence."[66]

Four foci have been identified for study and reflection during the decade: the spirit and logic of violence; the use, abuse, and misuse of power; the issues of justice; religious identity and plurality.

Another strength of the Internet is the vast amount of material that is often found on individual Web pages. Study notes for "The Decade To Overcome Violence" initiative are available on the council's Web site.[67] These notes can be downloaded, adapted for local context, and used freely. For persons wanting "ready-to-use materials," this Web site also provides a form for ordering notes already printed.

Church World Service

Similar in name to the World Council of Churches but different in scope is the Church World Service (CWS), a ministry founded in 1946 to provide relief, development, and refugee assistance by helping meet basic needs of people, advocating for justice, human rights, and the dignity of all, educating for peace and reconciliation, and promoting the integrity of the environment.[68] Though probably best known for sponsoring Crop Walks to raise money for hunger-fighting agencies, this United States effort of 36 Protestant, Orthodox, and Anglican denominations works together with indigenous organizations in more than 80 countries. No doubt, the Internet and e-mail have facilitated the work of these volunteers coordinating efforts across the globe.

The service's home page advises, "More people will die of AIDS in Africa over the next decade than [died in] all the world's wars of the 20th century." Attempts to answer that cry will surely require the efforts of people in many countries. One such effort is the African AIDS Jesuit Network, which starkly reminds us on its home page that "HIV-AIDS is the biggest threat to Africa since the slave trade."[69]

A joint effort of the Church World Service and the Mennonite Central Committee, Jubilees Partners, the National Council of Churches, and Sojourners is the global campaign "All Our Children," an expansion of the CWS initiative "Iraq Humanitarian Crisis Appeal." Aimed at raising one million dollars to provide health assistance for the children of Iraq, "All Our Children" is endorsed by Jimmy and Rosalynn Carter, who continue to proclaim by word and by deed that they "believe . . . God intends us always to seek ways to alleviate suffering and to settle differences so that the innocent are not harmed."[70] Although estimates vary on the number of children in Iraq who died in the last 20 years, a half million children is the *lowest* estimate I found and that number was published by the CWS *prior to* the 2003 war on Iraq.

In March 2003 a delegation from Liberia, the Gambia, Sierra Leone, Guinea, and Ghana told both the United Nations and the United States government that there can be no sustainable development in West Africa without *immediate* end to hostilities and without durable peace. The delegation was sponsored by the Church World Service, which arranged for the African church and grassroots leaders to meet with American church representatives, NGOs, and public audiences to appeal for greater international support for the critical needs of West Africa's Mano River subregion.[71] Churches in Africa play a vital role in empowering civil society and promoting peace and justice. The support to indigenous groups by international collaborations, such as those led by the Church World Service, is incalculable.

Catholic Worker

The Catholic Worker (CW), founded by Dorothy Day and Peter Maurin in 1933, now comprises 185 communities "grounded in a firm belief in the God-given dignity of every human person. . . . [These communities] remain committed to nonviolence, voluntary poverty, prayer, and hospitality for the homeless, exiled, hungry, and forsaken.

Catholic Workers continue to protest injustice, war, racism, and violence of all forms."[72]

Often our thoughts of the Catholic Worker movement go to Dorothy Day serving food to and praying with men in New York City's Bowery section. But there are more, many more, images, because now the communities extend from one end of the United States to the other. One of these communities is the Casa Juan Diego (CJD) in Houston, Texas. Founded in 1980, CJD serves immigrants and refugees and has grown from one to 15 houses. Its Web site contains a powerful article written by Patrick McColloster, a physician who volunteers at the CJD. This horrific saga tells of an undocumented alien with an inborn defect that slowly scarred her liver. This mother of four U.S.-born children waited tables at a cantina after her husband was deported. After becoming too weak to work, she resorted to begging on the street. Soon it was apparent that without a liver transplant this woman would die.

When Dr. McColloster tried to get Medicaid to cover the fee, he was advised that she was ineligible for complete benefits. Several times this woman had to be admitted to a hospital for treatment of esophageal bleeding. The doctor then approached a hospital that was initially receptive to the woman applying for an organ, but then rejected her application after realizing she was an undocumented alien. The chief surgeon told Dr. McColloster government guidelines limit foreign recipients to five percent of the transplanted organs in any given year. This particular hospital had already exceeded that figure, as had the hospital he next consulted.

Wanting to confirm this guideline, Dr. McColloster contacted the United Network for Organ Sharing (UNOS), where he was advised that hospitals could surpass that limit. If they did, however, they would be subject to detailed case reviews. This mandate was the result of some institutions having given too many livers to affluent patients from abroad.

Most startling were the surprising demographics that UNOS provided on Texas transplants. "For every 16 Hispanic undocumented alien livers harvested, *only one* was transplanted in another undocumented alien. The remainder went to US citizens and wealthy foreign nationals."[73]

Although an agreement was made with a hospital in New Orleans for this woman to receive a liver, she bled to death before she could be transported. "Her outcome reveals a flaw in our society. Organs of undocumented aliens are harvested with minimal likelihood of demographic reciprocity. We exploit them at work—and in death."[74]

The Catholic Worker Web site has a collection of essays by cofounder Peter Maurin as well as more contemporary essays. Tom Cornell's "From the Cradle of Civilization–to the Grave?" ends with a chill: "We need prayers even more than the Iraqis. It is no sin to die. It is a sin to murder."[75]

Political Sites

Beyond useful links to the United States Senate,[76] the House of Representatives,[77] and the White House,[78] the World Wide Web has numerous links to both other governmental and nongovernmental organizations. In these days of not just rumors but the reality of war, unprecedented secret arrests, and a shrinking number of freedoms in this country and abroad, it is good to visit the Web site of the United Nations and reread the 1948 "Universal Declaration of Human Rights" and remind ourselves that "recognition of the inherent dignity and of the equal and inalienable rights of all members of the human family is the foundation of freedom, justice and peace in the world."[79]

This segment will highlight Web sites both for government agencies and for nongovernmental organizations (NGOs). The World Bank defines NGOs as "private organizations that pursue activities to relieve suffering, promote the interest of the poor, protect the environment, provide basic social services, or undertake community development. In wider usage, the term NGO can be applied to any nonprofit organization which is independent from government."[80]

United Nations

A highly impressive Web site on the World Wide Web is that of the United Nations.[81] From major areas of peace and security, economic and social development, human rights, humanitarian affairs, and international law to a section on publication, stamps, and databases, this Web site is a remarkable cyber experience. Multilingual; vibrantly colored; radio and TV airings available both in real time and from archived broadcasts. Zoom with incredible speed (even from a 56k dial-up modem) from briefing transcripts to a tribute to detained, abducted, or missing staff, to more information on the Iraqi war than can fill a single Web page.[82]

The CyberSchoolBus is a magnificently innovative Web experience. The curricula include indigenous peoples, briefing papers, peace education, poverty, cities, "schools demining schools," human rights, women's rights, health, school kits about the United Nations, saving tomorrow's world, cleaner oceans, U.N. in space, and links to U.N. related teaching materials and to other U.N. educational sites. Primarily the CyberSchoolBus "hauls" middle and high school students not only through the various curricula but also through quizzes, games, and an array of options for activities one can do to contribute both to one's local community and to world peace.

For the student needing statistics for a school paper or the homilist eager for current statistics, InfoNation is a remarkable tool of global teaching. One can select up to five different countries and get comparisons of their populations in the year 2001, population density, surface area, and the largest urban agglomeration (biggest city in population, not in physical size, including areas of contiguous build-up).[83] From that screen one can opt to see an overview of each country with information such as its capital, currency, and admission date to the United Nations. Even more detailed information is only a click away from the overview screen. Details span *health* data including percentage of population undernourished, infant mortality rate, percentage of the population under the age of 15, and the total fertility rate; *environmental* data including energy consumption and water resources per capita, carbon monoxide emissions, average amount of precipitation, cropland per capita, and threatened species; *economy* data including gross domestic product, GDP per capita, number of tourists arriving, poverty rate, and government education expenditure (gross national product percentage); and *technology* data including number of motor vehicles per 1,000 inhabitants, telephone lines per 100 inhabitants, estimated number of Internet users per 1,000 inhabitants, television receivers per 1,000 inhabitants, and newspaper circulation per 1,000 inhabitants.

My mind raced as I surfed from page to page on this vast Web site. Only once did I stumble. The site index alphabetizes people by first name. "Kurt Waldheim" under K confused me momentarily. But I will concede a new way to alphabetize in exchange for the speed in which I learned that the number of Internet users in Slovenia soared from 8 per 1,000 inhabitants in the year 1990 to 250 users per 1,000 inhabitants in the year 2000. This nearly paralleled the growth in Iran but was remarkably higher than in the Bahamas, where the estimated number of Internet users climbed from 3 per 1,000 inhabitants in the year 1990 to only 13 per 1,000 in the year 2000. Never would I have imagined greater Internet use in Iran than in the Bahamas.

Amnesty International

Despite incredibly effective initiatives made by the United Nations to achieve global justice, injustices still exist. Since 1961 Amnesty International (AI) has been a worldwide movement campaigning to promote internationally recognized human rights. Like the United Nations, Amnesty International's vision of the world is one in which every person enjoys all of the human rights enshrined in the "Universal Declaration of Human Rights." AI's mission is "to undertake research and action focused on preventing and ending grave abuses of the rights to physical and mental integrity, freedom of conscience and expression, and freedom from discrimination, within the context of our work to promote all human rights."[84] With more than a million members and supporters in over 140 countries and territories, AI works to mobilize public opinion to put pressure on governments and others with influence to stop human-rights abuses.

Initiatives of Amnesty International range from working to stamp out torture of women, children, ethnic minorities, lesbians, gays, bisexual and transgendered persons, to working for particular individuals, campaigning for suspension of electro-shock weapons, and working with other NGOs to campaign successfully for controls on the international diamond trade, because profits from the diamond trade are often used to purchase weapons which contribute to human-rights abuses.[85]

Available in English, French, Spanish, and Arabic, the Amnesty International Web site contains more than 20,000 files and each day receives more than 10,000 visitors from all over the world. Online are Amnesty International's annual reports for the years 1993-2003, detailing human-rights violations for each *previous* year. Records for 2001 show confirmed or possible extrajudicial executions in 47 countries; people "disappeared" or remained "disappeared" from previous years in 35 countries; people reportedly tortured or ill-treated by security forces, police, or other state authorities in 111 countries; confirmed or possible prisoners of conscience in 56 countries; people arbitrarily arrested and detained, or in detention without charge or trial in 54 countries. Records for 2002 show human right abuses in 151 countries but also show the success of establishing an International Criminal Court at The Hague in the Netherlands to prosecute persons accused of genocide, crimes against humanity, and war crimes. Even with this important development, AI stresses that although "[g]overnments have spent billions to strengthen national security and the 'war on terror,' . . . for millions of people, the real sources of insecurity are corruption, repression, discrimination, extreme poverty and preventable diseases."[86]

Regional summaries are also available. The links section to other sites addressing human rights is perhaps the most comprehensive on the World Wide Web. That said, one should not understate the wealth of information presented and hope generated on the site itself, which tells of the breadth of work being conducted through Amnesty International. In a dynamic speech, "Globalize This! Respect for Human Rights," Paul Hoffman, chair of AI in 2002, made three points on the human-rights framework struggling to build another world:

> *First,* the human rights framework provides a moral compass for the road ahead—reminding us of why global inequities matter and why we must mobilize globally to counter these inequities; *second,* human rights law offers comprehensive standards based on fundamental, widely shared values for the new world we aim to build; and *third,* the human rights framework identifies the targets of our human rights activism in a way that helps us focus our activism and make it more effective.[87]

Hoffman then reiterated that Amnesty International believes that "citizens of one country, no matter how powerful, cannot buy their security if the price is insecurity for people elsewhere, and also that freedoms for one minority group will be illusory if they lead to greater repression for other groups."[88]

It was at the Third World Social Forum in Porto Alegre, Brazil, in January 2002, that Hoffman gave this speech. A bit more than a year later, with the Iraqi war dominating the airwaves, it was good to be reminded that peace is not merely the absence of war. Rather, peace and justice come from the realization of the comprehensive vision of life in freedom and dignity cited in his speech:

> Protection of life, liberty and security, rights to free speech, to political participation, to protection of privacy, family rights, and due process of law but *equally, and I mean equally*, rights to education, health, social security, to work and the basic right to an adequate standard of living—to housing, clean water, and to food [together constitute freedom and dignity]. . . .
>
> We need now to convince the world that extreme poverty creates its own kinds of prisons, that arbitrariness in the way the law operates affects livelihoods no less than lives, and that the

insecurity that comes from waking each morning hungry, without a home or job, can be as terrifying as that instilled by a repressive police force. . . .[89]

International Center for Justice and Reconciliation

Another astonishingly comprehensive Web site belongs to the International Center for Justice and Reconciliation (ICJR). The purpose of its online resources is to be a credible, nonpartisan source of information on restorative justice (RJ).[90] The Web site has several key sections including: an *introduction* with basic definitions in English, Spanish, and French in addition to slide shows on some of the important issues of restorative justice, including victim–offender mediation, victim assistance, ex-offender assistance, restitution, and community service; a *resource section* with an online searchable, annotated bibliography on restorative justice as well as links to other RJ sites and also to documents of governments around the world, the United Nations, and the Council of Europe; an *action section* filled with tutorials on RJ theory and practice; and a *chapel section* with materials out of the Judeo-Christian tradition.

In various ways this Web site explores three principles that form the foundation of restorative justice. (1) Justice requires that we work to restore those who have been injured. (2) Those most directly involved and affected by crime should have the opportunity to participate fully in the response if they wish. (3) Government's role is to preserve a just public order; the community's role is to build and maintain a just peace.[91]

Another area of this site, "Web Tour," has short descriptions of numerous restorative justice Web sites and provides links to these sites from Australia to Minnesota, from South Africa to Canada.[92] The strength of this Center's Web site is that it is uncommonly user-friendly and is comprehensive in practical application.

Families against Mandatory Minimums

Mandatory minimum what? Mandatory minimum sentences. One of the attempts in the 1980s to keep drug dealers off the streets in the United States was the introduction of mandatory minimum sentences. Unfortunately, these sentences have "handcuffed" judges by not allowing them to shorten sentences and have kept wives, lovers, mothers, grandmothers, and sisters in jail long after drug dealers have left prison. How is this possible? A just question.

Police arrest a drug dealer and perhaps some of his or her accomplices. They are offered deals of lesser sentences if they co-operate and name others in their operation. If these dealers were under surveillance, the police know where the dealers live and with whom they live. In attempts to diminish drug trafficking, the police also bring in the persons with whom the dealer lived, and ask for their co-operation. Here the problem begins to manifest itself in ugly ways. Although the dealer may go home to sleep at night, most often he or she does not involve a spouse, parent, or sibling in the "street work." So while the dealer can co-operate and give names to the police, other people in the house cannot always co-operate. "Can not" is not the same as "will not." Obviously, one cannot give up names one does not know. Thus the dealer becomes the "good guy," the one who co-operates. The others in the house are viewed as blocking "justice" by seemingly refusing to give names. Ignorance of a crime becomes refusal to co-operate and that immediately jacks up the minimum sentence. While the dealer may be back on the street in two or three years, those around him or her who were not accomplices may spend 24.5 years in prison. Yes, more than 24 years in a federal prison without chance of parole for a crime one did not commit.

This system favors the "big fish" that have much to reveal, while the "prisoners of love"[93] spend years away from their children. There are persons convicted of murder who spend far less than 24 years incarcerated. The NAACP has determined that the number of women in prisons has tripled in the last 15 years. This is a direct result of mandatory minimum sentencing.[94] CourtTV's *Guilt by Association*[95] is a feature film about a widow, mother of three, who fell in love with a man who was good to her and her children. Once she came to grips with his drug use and that of his friends, she left him but not soon enough. Like the women in the film *Prisoners of Love*, this woman was picked up by the police, and while her lover and his drug-trafficking buddies received short prison terms, she received the mandatory minimum sentence for not co-operating with police. In the film she talks about meeting in prison the mother, a grandmother, and a sister of a drug dealer. He was back on the street. All three women were serving mandatory sentences without chance of parole.

Enter Families against Mandatory Minimums (FAMM), a national nonprofit organization founded in 1991 to challenge the excessive penalties required by mandatory sentencing laws. The group's Web site has two primary objectives: to educate people about unjust mandatory sentences and to mobilize a powerful sentencing reform movement.[96] The goals of the organization are to restore judicial discretion so that the punishment fits the crime and to replace mandatory sentencing laws with flexible sentencing guidelines.[97] These goals will only be realized when we return sentencing to the discretion of judges rather than forcing judges to give fixed prison terms set by the U.S. Congress and many state legislatures.

On President Bill Clinton's last day in office, he granted clemency to 21 persons serving time for drug crimes, one of them the woman whose story was told in *Guilt by Association*. Her case had been brought to the attention of the Clinton administration by FAMM. However, many more persons are still serving mandatory minimum sentences. Fortunately, the work of FAMM is growing and being recognized as a significant contribution to our society. In October 2002, Julie Stewart—founder and president of FAMM—was one of 20 recipients, out of 1400 nominations, of the Ford Foundation's "Leadership for a Changing World" award. She received $100,000 to advance the work of FAMM and an additional $30,000 for supporting activities.[98]

One state that realized these mandatory minimum sentences have not deterred people from using or selling drugs is Michigan. Beginning in March 2003, new laws in Michigan eliminated most of the state's mandatory minimum sentences for drug offenses and replaced them with sentencing guidelines. Additionally, lifetime probation for lowest-level drug offenders was replaced with a standard five-year probationary period. It is estimated that in the first year alone Michigan taxpayers would save 41 million dollars.

These changes came with bipartisan support from lawmakers and groups as varied as the Prosecuting Attorneys Association of Michigan, the NAACP, the Michigan Catholic Conference, and the Citizens' Alliance on Prisons and Public Safety.[99]

Since the announcement of this change in Michigan, FAMM has received calls from across the country as state legislators, governors' offices, and advocates for change grapple with the high cost and unintended consequences of mandatory minimum sentencing.

FAMM's Web site offers fact sheets addressing some of the most disturbing facets of the U.S. prison population, including women and mandatory sentencing (the number of women in state and federal prisons increased over 500 percent between 1980 and 1998) and children of prisoners (1.5 million children in the United States have a parent in prison; more than 60 percent of those parents are incarcerated more than 100 miles from home; African-American children are nearly nine times more likely and Latino children are three times more likely than white children to have an incarcerated parent). FAMM is additionally concerned about race and mandatory sentencing (when sentenced for drug offenses in state courts, whites serve an average of 27 months and blacks serve an average of 46 months). Some critics of mandatory minimum sentencing refer to the racial disparity in arrests in the war on drugs as the "New Jim Crow." The best-known example of inequality is the disparity between the minimum sentences given for the sale of crack cocaine and powder cocaine. Although crack and powder cocaine have the same active ingredient, crack is sold in less expensive quantities and in lower-income communities of color. A five-gram sale of crack cocaine receives a five-year federal mandatory minimum sentence but one must sell 500 grams of powder cocaine to get the same sentence. "In 1986, before the enactment of federal mandatory minimum sentencing for crack cocaine offense, the average federal drug sentence for African Americans was 11 percent higher than for whites. Four years later, the average federal drug sentence for African Americans was 49 percent higher."[100]

Even more devastating in some ways than mandatory minimum sentences is the reality that 1.4 *million* African-American men (i.e., 13 percent of the *entire* black adult population in the United States and 36 percent of the total disenfranchised population) have permanently lost their right to vote because of a felony conviction. Yes, permanently. Even after these persons have served their sentences, they are barred from voting, barred from participating in the process of democracy, barred from really being able to leave one's past in the past.

Aware that disenfranchisement laws are vestiges of medieval times when criminals were banished and suffered "civil death," the Sentencing Project reminds us poignantly:

The expansion of suffrage to all sectors of the population is one of the United States' most important political triumphs. Once the privilege of wealthy white men, the vote is now a basic right held as well by the poor and working classes, racial minorities, women and young adults. Today, all mentally competent adults have the right to vote with only one exception: convicted criminal offenders. In forty-six states and the District of Columbia, criminal disenfranchisement laws deny the vote to all convicted adults in prison. Thirty-two states also disenfranchise felons on parole; twenty-nine disenfranchise those on probation. And, due to laws that may be unique in the world, in fourteen states even ex-offenders who have fully served their sentences remain barred for life from voting.

While felony disenfranchisement laws should be of concern in any democracy, the scale of their impact in the United States is unparalleled: an estimated 3.9 million U.S. citizens are disenfranchised, *including over one million who have fully completed their sentences.* . . .

In the late twentieth century, the laws have no discernible legitimate purpose. Deprivation of the right to vote is not an inherent or necessary aspect of criminal punishment nor does it promote the reintegration of offenders into lawful society. Indeed, defenders of these laws have been hard pressed to justify them: they most frequently cite the patently inadequate goal of protecting against voter fraud or the anachronistic and politically untenable objective of preserving the "purity of the ballot box" by excluding voters lacking in virtue.[101]

Given the instances in recent years in which the "purity of the ballot box" has been tainted, this objection hardly seems viable these days. Our country appears to be in violation of its own democratic principles and also in violation of international human-rights law. Neither in actual numbers nor in proportion does *any other* democratic country deny as many citizens the right to vote as we do. Such injustice is even more detestable because it exists within a presumed system of justice. This is a prime example of "justice" as purely punitive.

Electronic Iraq

One of the most unusual Web sites addressing issues of the war in Iraq has been "electronic Iraq" (eIraq), a joint venture of "Voices in the Wilderness," a U.S./U.K. campaign demanding that the U.N. Security Council and the U.S. government end the economic sanctions against Iraq; and "The Electronic Intifada"—an online independent, educational gateway to information about the Israeli–Palestinian conflict. In February 2003, the eIraq project was launched to provide online e-zines, news and analyses, OpEd pieces, Iraq diaries, fact sheets, and reflections on international law, aid, and development.[102] The diaries provide eyewitness reports from Iraq, which the Web site published during the hostility as counterpoint to the reports of more traditional media. The Web site also contains reports from other organizations, such as Amnesty International, responding to the reality of the war. In addition to the ravages of war itself, the photographs on the Web site also focus on the plight of ill persons in Iraq whose medicine was blocked from entering the country during the years of economic sanctions. In words, images, and links, the overriding message of eIraq is clear: "war is our common enemy."

When the bombing ceased in Iraq, the eIraq Web site continued to explore issues of concern. What will happen to injured and traumatized children? Where will the art work surface that was looted from museums? Will the communist party in Iraq resurrect itself and try to wrestle control of the country? What calamities await Iraqis whose water will contain untreated raw sewage once dwindling supplies of chlorine vanish completely?

Environmental Justice and Public Health

Woes in abundance. Global warming. Oil spills. Bhopal. Chernobyl. NIMBY ("Not in my backyard"). Lawmakers. Asthma. Starvation. Flooding. Droughts. Urban sprawl. Rural isolation. Economic migrants. Soil erosion. All these factors impact the environment and public health, two realities that impact us 24 hours a day, every day that we live.

Add to this litany of woes the damage done to the environment and to public health by well-meaning persons undertaking efforts to improve one or both of these realities, and the resulting problems seem beyond our ability to resolve. For more than a decade, students of medical geography have studied how irrigation projects have disrupted environmental habitats in Africa, resulting in remarkable increases in the incidence of schistosomiasis, sometimes called "snail fever." Slow-moving water in irrigation canals is the ideal environment for the snail which is the vector of the schistosomiasis organism. Increasing development of waterways has triggered greater morbidity and mortality from this disease. In Ghana the incidence of schistosomiasis tripled in the 1950s and 1960s, when a large number of agricultural projects were initiated; even now, schistosomiasis is the cause of 18 percent of all deaths in Kenya.[103] The World Resource Institute reported that more than 30 diseases have been linked to irrigation. Despite the Carter Center's significant strides in eradicating schistosomiasis, this parasitic illness remains second only to malaria in its devastation on rural economies and public health.[104]

Another example of well-intentioned but inadequately researched efforts occurred in Nepal, where the government began a reforestation project promoting eucalyptus. In a world plagued by the injustices wrought by deforestation, imagine the horror of discovering that this particular reforestation was wreaking devastating effects. People realized too late that eucalyptus leaves were "useless as fodder, did not make good animal bedding material, reduced the undergrowth and consequently the groundwater recharge capacity, and increased soil erosion."[105] Now and in future decades, persons developing new projects will have vast resources available at their fingertips through the World Wide Web. Good intentions augmented by broader research will, I hope, culminate in better quality of life for those affected by change.

Environmental justice is transboundary in nature: what is just in one place is not just in another. The same is true of public health. What bodes well for persons in one spot can be literally deadly for people in another spot. All too often in the past, decision making about matters home and abroad was centralized; there was little regard for local citizens who would be impacted by decisions made by others. The Internet now affords us ample opportunities to define and redefine environmental justice in its varied forms; resources on how to set environmental standards; examples of incentives to enact and enforce laws relative to developing and sustaining the environment; hints on educating persons "on top and below" about environmental and public health issues; mandates pertaining to the surveillance of public health; insights about deficiencies already assessed in the public-health system; and reports of professionals who have responded sufficiently, if not superbly, to global public health needs.

The Internet enabled me to add here to my earlier discussion in Section II about the environment. Beginning with a modern-day David overcoming both governmental and big-business Goliaths, I will explore five examples selected from myriad online references of initiatives striving for environmental justice and enhanced public health.

Center for Health, Environment and Justice

"Love" is an uncomfortable word when it precedes "Canal." Named for William Love, who in the last decade of the nineteenth century began digging a canal between Lake Ontario and Lake Erie, the area around this canal has become synonymous with living in a toxic world. The Love Canal has also become synonymous with environmental justice. Largely through the efforts of one woman, Lois Gibbs, and a handful of local activists, the Love Canal (a neighborhood in Niagara Falls, New York) gained the attention of local, state, and national government officials, especially after citizens were so perturbed by the lack of government action to relocate families that they held hostage for several hours two employees of the Environmental Protection Agency. What brought ordinary residents to such a bold move?

A brief history of the area. Love's attempts to dig a canal were gnashed during the Depression. He abandoned his project, leaving behind a partially dug section about 60 feet wide and 3,000 feet long. In 1920 the land was sold at public auction and for more than the next three decades the land was used as a dumping site. Although both the City of Niagara and the United States Army dumped garbage and chemical warfare material into the canal, the principal "dumper" was the Hooker Chemical Company. After covering the area with dirt in 1953, Hooker sold the canal to the local school district for one dollar. The papers of the sale disclosed that chemical waste was buried on the site and transferred all responsibility for same to the school district, thereby absolving Hooker from all future liability. The following year the school district began construction of an elementary school for 400 students.

During this same year, construction of a hundred homes began, attracting baby-boomers who delighted in moving near the school their children would attend. Potential buyers were not alerted to the 20,000 tons of chemicals buried beneath the houses and the school. For the next 20 years (during which time dwellings swelled to 800 houses and 240 apartments), people complained of stench in the air and liquid oozing up into basements and backyards. The city responded by sending workers to cover up the ground.

Although three children suffered chemical burns in 1958, no one took serious notice of the problem until the winter of 1975-76, when an unusually heavy blizzard resulted in drums surfacing and muddy puddles of chemicals forming. Finally the city and county hired a consulting firm to investigate complaints. After finding toxic chemical residue both in the air and in sump pumps in a large percentage of homes, and also finding high levels of PCBs in the sewer system, the firm recommended that "the canal be covered with clay, home sump pumps be sealed off, and a tile drainage system be installed to control the migration of wastes. Nothing was done by the city, however, except for placing window fans in a few homes found to contain high levels of chemical residues."[106]

Early in 1978 several actions began a collision course. A local newspaper reporter wrote a series of articles on the problems of hazardous waste in the Niagara Falls area, including the Love Canal; the New York State Department of Health, in response to concerns raised by residents who had read the newspaper articles, (1) conducted air and soil tests, (2) collected health data on persons living around the canal, and (3) revealed findings of an increase in reproductive problems among women and high levels of chemical contaminants in soil and air. Lois Gibbs founded the Love Canal Parents Movement.

The actions and tenacity of Gibbs are reminders of the powerful strength of a mother's love. She had known nothing of the chemical dumping ground until she read the newspaper articles and began wondering about the link between the dumping ground and ailments in her child. With notes from two physicians recommending the transfer of her child to another public school, Gibbs approached the school board. "But the Board refused to transfer her child, stating that if it was unsafe for her son, then it would be unsafe for all children and they were not going to close the school because of one concerned mother with a sickly child."[107] The board's response was the impetus for Gibbs to rally other parents to canvass the area with petitions for the school to be closed.

For two years activities escalated. First, in August 1978, the state health department recommended that the school be closed, that pregnant women and children under the age of two be evacuated, that people not eat food from their gardens, and that they spend as little time as possible in their basements. Within days the state opted to buy the 239 houses closest to the canal. Finding those recommendations incomplete, the parents' group immediately changed its name to the Love Canal Homeowners Association, elected officers, and came up with goals.

While the state insisted the problems were confined (surely there was no problem outside the fence around the 239 houses the government was buying), the Homeowners Association had conducted its own health survey and knew that the placement of the fence had no relationship whatsoever to the morbidity of the area. Worried mothers and angry fathers took to the streets, held prayer vigils, and even took symbolic coffins to Albany in attempts to get the state to address the problem adequately. Throughout the long, cold winter of Niagara

Falls, these parents protested every day. The state made a few concessions, but not nearly enough for parents whose children were ill.

A scientist hired by the group and paid by the state conducted yet
another study. This study revealed increases in miscarriages, stillbirths, crib deaths, nervous breakdowns, hyperactivity, epilepsy, and
a 300 percent increase in urinary tract disorders in persons living well
beyond that fenced-in area of 239 houses. In nine (56 percent) of the
16 children born between 1974 and 1978, birth defects were docu-
mented: three ears, two rows of teeth, and mental retardation. The
reality worsened in the next two years, when out of 22 pregnancies
there were only four babies born without problems. The other 18
pregnancies ended in miscarriages, stillbirths, or babies with birth
defects. The Homeowners Association presented its data to officials at
the state health department, who "quickly dismissed the study calling
it 'useless housewife data,' saying residents' illnesses were all in their
heads, the birth defects were genetic, and the urinary disease the result
of sexual activity (in a five-year-old boy??)."[108] The parents were not
deterred. They continued to protest; finally, in February 1979, the
state health department confirmed the findings of the Homeowners
Association's study and ordered a second evacuation of pregnant
women and children under the age of two. In October 1980 President
Jimmy Carter ordered a complete evacuation of the Love Canal area
and advised 900 families that they could sell their houses to the government for fair-market value.

Relocation was not the end of the quest for justice for these families. They had been affected so horribly by chemicals and learned
through their own struggles that there was no local, state, or national
organization providing communities with advice, guidance, training,
and technical assistance concerning appropriate disposal of dangerous
waste materials. Wanting to respond to the large number of phone
calls from persons around the country who were facing similar problems, Lois Gibbs in 1981 formed the Citizens Clearinghouse for Hazardous Waste, now known as the Center for Health, Environment and
Justice (CHEJ). A small sampling of this group's accomplishments
includes the creation of a federal superfund to clean up waste sites; the
Superfund Technical Assistance Project, which provides $50,000 fed-
eral grants to local communities to hire technical assistance consul-
tants to evaluate cleanup options and to conduct site-specific studies
of environment and public health; the Right-To-Know Project, which
gives people access to information on chemicals being stored, dis-

posed of, and released in their communities; the Toxic Merry-Go-Round Campaign to develop strategies and regulations to prohibit taking waste from one community and dumping it into another; and the McToxics campaign, which lobbied McDonalds to stop using styrofoam in packaging its products and then urged McDonalds to be the leader in an effort to get restaurants, schools, and various public and private institutions to stop using styrofoam.

CHEJ's Web site offers not only a history of the Love Canal but also practical advice about organizing grassroots initiatives addressing environmental issues, a list of publications and other resources, specific instruction on how to ask for assistance from CHEJ, and updates on environmental science and public health.

Why so much space on the work of CHEJ? In a time when many persons feel weary and impotent, convinced they cannot make a difference in local, state, or federal government, when they sense that justice is an elusive concept with little hope of becoming reality, it makes good sense to explore efforts of people who organized themselves and through their own initiatives discovered that justice is actually achievable. Then instead of resting, these same persons continue to work with others for justice in the environment and in the public health of other communities around the country. The CHEJ Web site says of this work: "Our experience has shown that the most effective way to win environmental justice is from the bottom up through community organizing and empowerment. When local citizens come together and take an organized, unified stand, they can hold industry and government accountable and work towards a healthy, environmentally sustainable future."[109]

Panos Institute

In 1986 the Panos Institute was founded with a decentralized structure having autonomous offices in London, Paris, Washington, Kathmandu, Kampala, Lusaka, Dakar, Addis Ababa, and Haiti. The Institute's mission is to work with media and other disseminators of information to enable people in developing countries to shape and communicate their own development agendas through informed public debate. Panos focuses in particular on amplifying the voices of the poor and the marginalized, which all too often are unheard.

Recently the environment has been the focus of much attention, resulting in debate and activism around the globe. Exploring the efforts of Panos South Asia provides insights into environmental issues as well as hints on how to create independent spaces for informed public debate and how to strengthen the talents of those having a personal stake in a particular locale.

Like everywhere else, poverty and environmental problems are inextricably linked in South Asia, home to a large percentage of the world's poor. As in many other places, urban slums are becoming a part of the landscape. Living in unhealthy environments, the poor drink impure water and eat contaminated food. Not surprisingly, when they fall ill, they cannot afford basic healthcare evaluation, much less treatment even if it is available. When their illnesses stretch on, the poor cannot work, their poverty becomes even more entrenched, and entire families suffer, not just the person who is ill. As in all too many other places on earth, the poor in South Asia have not felt able to raise their voices against injustice and are ill-equipped to take remedial action. Consequently they get less than their fair share of resources and receive far more than their share of the blame for environmental problems. Panos South Asia's environmental justice program aims to take environmental debate beyond protection and conservation to include the concepts of environmental accountability and justice, so that all persons are better informed about their rights and responsibilities relative to a safe, productive, healthy environment.[110]

In September 2002 Panos initiated efforts to meet these aims with a three-day workshop in Kathmandu entitled "Justice for All—Promoting Environmental Justice in South Asia." Thirty journalists from India, Pakistan, Bangladesh, Sri Lanka, and Nepal were given the Panos report on promoting environmental justice as a background document. The objective of the workshop was to explore questions of equity, responsibility, and accountability linked to the environment and environmental resources.

> The workshop [introduced] the concept of environmental justice and the need to define it for South Asia because, unlike the West where the concept was mooted, the majority of people in South Asia are directly dependent on their immediate environment. The [workshop underscored] the need for media in the region to sensitize the public to justice issues because the success of all environmental programs and, as a result, sustainable development hinges on addressing the imbalances, not so much in resource distribution but in the allocation of accountability. Jus-

tice for those lower down the pecking order can be guaranteed only if fair allocation of accountability is made and fair compensation for the consequences takes place.[111]

At the 1992 Earth Summit in Rio de Janeiro, world leaders agreed on a comprehensive strategy for "sustainable development," emphasizing that while meeting our own needs, we must take measures to leave a healthy and viable world for future generations. One of the key agreements adopted to reach this goal was the Convention on Biological Diversity, a pact among the majority of the world's governments agreeing to maintain the world's diverse ecological base while pursuing economic development. The main goals are the conservation of biological diversity, sustainable use of its components, and fair and equitable sharing of the benefits from the use of genetic resources.[112]

Because governments around the world have often neglected rural areas, many basic resources are now available only in cities. This has caused a shift in populations from rural areas to cities, causing a flock of "economic migrants" to crowded urban areas. Unfortunately these same poor are grateful to find employment of any kind in large cities and often end up breathing air that is toxic from industrial pollution. In many spots around the world, cars are still powered by leaded gasoline that further contaminates the air. Economic migrants likely work for low wages and without health benefits. When men migrate to cities in search of employment, the farm work they used to do is left to women. These mothers, subsisting on nutrition far below standards set by nearly every health organization around the world, find their energy soon depleted while tending to home and children after tackling work in the field. For both a husband in the city and a wife on the farm, water is increasingly a significant issue. "With increasing population, there are few regions that can escape water problems—of both quality and quantity—in the near future. Environmentalists urge people to reduce per capita water consumption by 10% by the year 2025. . . . There are many facets to the water problem in the region [of Southeast Asia]: too little, too much, too early, too late, too polluted, too expensive."[113]

If we add to these dilemmas the particular needs raised by indigenous persons, injustice manifests itself through efforts developed around inadequate information, knowledge, or research. Irrigation projects in Africa and the reforestation initiative in Nepal, cited in the introduction to this section, are prime examples of too little information, knowledge, and research negatively impacting both the environment and public health.

World Health Organization

"Every child has the right to grow up in a healthy environment. . . . The biggest threats to children's health lurk in the very places that should be safest—home, school, and community. . . . More than five million children die each year from environment-related diseases."[114] These words of perilous threat begin the section of the World Health Organization's (WHO) Web site devoted to healthy environments for children. Despite such grim reality, the same section of the Web site ends with words of hope: ". . . this suffering is not inevitable. There are solutions. Most of the environment-related diseases and deaths can be prevented using effective, low-cost and sustainable tools and strategies."[115] Director General of WHO in 1982, Dr. H. Mahler, poignantly observed:

> I fully realize that health is not the only thing, but that everything else, without health, is nothing, and I think that it is very important to realize this when we look at development at large. Whenever the health component is forgotten, you forget at the same time the vital factor in development, namely the human being, his creative energy, his physical energy.[116]

Rooted in insights like Mahler's, WHO professionals have long known that tackling environmental threats requires co-ordinated efforts of many different sectors such as health, education, housing, energy, water, and planning; thus WHO has established a global alliance to remedy environmental threats to public health. This alliance includes various partners such as the Healthy Environments for Children Alliance (HECA—launched at the 2002 World Summit on Sustainable Development, with the aim to mobilize support and intensify global action to make children's environments safe) and the Panel of Experts on Environmental Management for Vector Control (PEEM—established in 1981 to create an institutional framework for effective interagency collaboration of organizations involved in health, water, and land development as well as the protection of the environment). The Global Environmental Epidemiology Network (GEENET), established in 1987 as a part of WHO itself, works with professionals around the globe to increase national capacity of developing countries to improve environmental health.

Often credited to Mark Twain is the observation "Climate is what you expect. Weather is what you get." Both climate and weather impact the health of the environment and humans. Storms, hurricanes, and floods kill thousands each year, affect levels of pollution, and trigger epidemics of malaria and other illnesses. These torrents of water also affect the quantity and quality of food, drinking water, and shelter. In large measure—though this reality is changing—climate and weather are beyond our control.

But what of acts willfully initiated by humans? In 1989, while talking of worldwide deforestation that had occurred on a scale most had not envisioned even as recently as a decade earlier, Dr. H. Nakajima (a director general of WHO after Mahler) uttered emphatically:

When the motivation is export-driven, the cost burden in terms of human health and services is never included in the price of the exported commodity, such as rice, lumber, and other natural products. Natural resources are irretrievably lost, the health of populations is damaged, and the underbudgeted health services are left to bear the burden. These actions compound the effects of natural disasters, such as flood, storm, earthquake, and drought.[117]

Unfortunately, public-health specialists frequently are not invited to participate in discussion about new projects. Calls come after problems emerge and the public's health is already impacted negatively. I suspect this omission is not an intentional slight but one of ignorance—public health simply does not come to mind even when thinking of the environment. Usually development projects are "planned by economists, agricultural specialists, and engineers, debated by politicians, and contended by community groups."[118] This is one more manifestation of our slowness in comprehending the importance of preventive care for the health both of the environment and of persons. Although this lag in understanding exists particularly in the United States, it is also seen in other places. Thus, one of WHO's aims in its global and regional programs is education. Part of that education is emphasizing prevention rather than curative measures.

The largest disease category in the world is acute respiratory infections (ARI),[119] such as pneumonia and influenza. Note, however, that the most basic of risk factors for disease and death is not poor health but poverty itself.[120]

But what is poverty? Just lack of money at the household level is an insufficient criterion, because provision of money on its own is not effective in most cases in producing permanent and substantial improvements. If one assumes, however, that alleviation of poverty would bring along with it advantages of better education, nutrition, environment, access to medical care, and so on that has generally accompanied it in the currently developed countries, the attribution of disease in the third world to poverty is almost a tautology.

More tellingly, much of the history of public health can be viewed as success in pinpointing the specific subcategories of attributable risk in the form of better nutrition, environment, and medical care that can be effectively modified by education, technology, and management to achieve better health *before people become rich.* To propose poverty alleviation as the primary means to improve health is to ignore the huge potential improvements that can be achieved well before that far-off day when poverty is eliminated. It also fails to recognize that improved health is itself a prerequisite for achieving and maintaining viable sustainable economic development. The causality goes both ways.[121]

Frequently my writings on justice highlight children. While researching environmental and public health injustices, I again found children suffering disproportionately. Although children make up only 12 percent of the world's population, globally children under the age of five suffer about 43 percent of the total burden of disease due to environmental risks. Eighty percent of all ARIs (including upper and lower respiratory infections as well as otitis media) affect children under the age of five. And 86 percent of all diarrheal diseases affect young children. All these ills—such as ambient air pollution, housing conditions, crowding, poor sanitation, hygiene, access to clean water and safe food—are related to environmental risk factors, especially in children and pregnant women.[122]

Add to these toxic stressors those which do not exist in a chemical or physical sense but are very real nonetheless—verbal child abuse, racism, televised violence—and quickly one perceives the need for additional global initiatives aimed at establishing and sustaining justice in the environment and public health.

United Nations Children's Fund

Created by the United Nations in 1946 to help children in Europe after World War II, UNICEF was originally called the United Nations International Children's Emergency Fund. Seven years later its name was shortened but its well-known acronym was kept and is the term most often used even today to refer to the permanent part of the United Nations with the task of helping children living in poverty in developing countries.

Headquartered in New York City, UNICEF carries out its work in more than 160 countries. In this country we frequently forget that girls are not educated in all parts of the world. UNICEF encourages families to educate their daughters as well as their sons. Also here in the United States, we all too often forget how many countries are still developing policies and programs to protect children and their rights. Halloween has been the annual day when children, through the "Trick-or-Treat for UNICEF" program, become more aware of the global needs of other youngsters. Such awareness is an education that we dare not lose if we want to raise our children with a sense of justice.

Since the 1960s UNICEF has been involved in water, environment, and sanitation (WES) issues in more than 90 countries. Simply satisfying the need for water can mean walking several miles and keeps children out of school in attempts to keep entire families hydrated. Children who live in unsanitary conditions are ill more often and have higher death rates (before the age of five) than children who live in cleaner environs. And, of course, children who do not die from such water-related illnesses as diarrhea, cholera, and malaria all too often lag behind others their age in growth and development.

Historically UNICEF has advocated for the protection of children's rights; has strived to establish those rights as enduring ethical principles; has insisted that the survival, protection, and development of children are integral to human progress; has committed to ensuring special protection for the most disadvantaged children (including victims of war, disasters, poverty, and all forms of violence and exploitation) as well as those with disabilities; has promoted equal rights for women and girls; and has worked with partners, including children themselves, toward attaining sustainable human development, peace, and social progress.[123] With only four executive directors in 55 years, UNICEF has had uncommon consistency in its leadership and ability to respond to the needs of children around the world.

UNICEF was one of the first agencies to address concerns of the children in Iraq. Prior to the first bomb dropped on Iraq by the United States, UNICEF staff immunized half a million children under the age of five against measles and immunized four million children against polio. However, children make up half the population of Iraq and so not all were reached. Many of these children were already malnourished when they were displaced from their homes. One quarter of children under the age of five in Iraq are chronically malnourished and nearly 60 percent of the population depend on government food rations.[124]

As the hostilities in Iraq continue to drag on, concerns about the safety of water, the availability of food, and the potential of future outbreaks of disease continues to be just as real as concerns over unexploded munitions, outbreaks of diarrhea and cholera, and the stress of health centers and hospitals trying to cope with these ills. Carol Bellamy, Executive Director of UNICEF in 2003, pointed out that "putting children first in national recovery efforts rallies a population and leads to greater stability and political consensus. . . . Nothing will do more to immediately improve the well-being and protection of Iraq's children than getting them back in the classroom."[125] Because emphasis on getting children back to school previously galvanized persons in Afghanistan and Angola and gave children focus and structure in those countries, getting children back to school in Iraq has been an urgent priority of UNICEF staff.[126]

Inconsistency in humanitarian aid reaching areas where it was needed led to recurrent insecurity in Iraq during the years of economic sanctions (the embargo itself is often regarded as a deadly weapon) and to looting during the war. Of continued concern is the war's disturbance of the environment not only for humans but also for animals. For instance, disrupting the migration of storks from Eastern Europe to Africa will affect the environment of many countries even if the migration path is disturbed "only" in Iraq; polluting the air *is* more than a human respiratory problem. UNICEF's trucking into Iraq more than 2 million litres of clean water each day is more than a trickle, but not much more, in an arid land devastated by war. Ongoing malnutrition cannot be alleviated if food and water are kept from those in need. Almost half of Iraq's population is under the age of 18 and many of these children have lived in a state of war three times in less than 20 years. Surely these children in Iraq are "those in need."

Environmental Justice Initiative,
University of Michigan

Environmental justice differs from other environmental issues in that it combines concern for the earth with a consciousness of the rights of minority and low-income populations. Although persons of color and/or low income in the United States have long been disproportionately impacted by environmental injustice, only in the last quarter century have scholars, policy makers, and activists become aware of the depth of this injustice. Is a safe environment a civil right? Do local governments trying to move beyond economic devastation have a moral obligation not to sacrifice long-term public health for short-term economic gain? Can laborers assert their rights to a safe and healthy workplace without fear of retaliatory unemployment? In times of war, should persons committed to environmental justice oppose military occupation, repression, and exploitation of land?

These questions are among those tackled daily at the University of Michigan through its Environmental Justice Initiative. The concerns of the environmental justice movement are global, reaching from inner-city America to rural Third World. In attempting to bring about environmental justice at home, people contribute to sustaining the whole planet. That truth is the focus of bumper stickers that are proliferating more than one might have guessed a few years ago: "Think globally, act locally."

The Environmental Advocacy Program at the University of Michigan took roots in 1972 when the program was first instituted as a programmatic area in the School of Natural Resources and Environment.[127] Four years later a husband-and-wife team from the program took jobs at the United Automobile Workers and were key organizers of "Working for Economic and Environmental Justice and Jobs," a four-day conference that brought together hundreds of union workers, environmentalists, farmers, professors, and members of the local African-American community. Workers were intent on dealing with "environmental blackmail" because their jobs were threatened if they were not willing to fight proposed environmental regulations. Other local citizens were not inclined to listen to environmentalists until basic needs for food, shelter, and clothing were met. The strength of the conference was the significant dialogue that began among various persons who previously had not interacted.

In 1987, while attending a meeting in Alabama, Bunyan Bryant, professor at the University of Michigan and key architect of the Environmental Justice Initiative, was given a copy of the newly released United Church of Christ "Report on Race and Toxic Waste in the United States." The report indicated that race was the best predictor of the location of hazardous waste facilities in this country. This report further indicated that 40 percent of the nation's commercial hazardous-waste landfill capacity was in three predominately African-American and Hispanic communities. The largest hazardous waste landfill in the nation was found in Sumter County, Alabama, where nearly 70 percent of the 17,000 residents are African-American and 96 percent are poor.[128]

It is not difficult to ascertain the connection between racism, poverty, and environmental justice. In this country most big industries are still headed by white males. It is safe to assume that virtually all will say "Not in my backyard" (NIMBY) when it comes to deciding where hazardous wastes will be dumped. In a world still too segregated, these wastes become the problem of minorities and the poor. Consequently it should come as no surprise that the Congressional Black Caucus has "the best environmental record of any voting bloc in Congress."[129]

In 1991 the Environmental Justice Initiative was represented on the advisory committee to the First National People of Color Environmental Leadership Summit in Washington, D.C. The conference developed 17 principles of environmental justice that are still used for organizing local environmental projects. Three years later the University of Michigan group was instrumental in persuading President Bill Clinton to sign an environmental justice executive order, "Federal Actions To Address Environmental Justice in Minority Populations and Low-Income Populations: Executive Order 12898." This order mandated that every major federal agency make achieving environmental justice part of its mission.[130] Although the intent of this order was significant, follow-through was gravely lacking.

Today the Environmental Justice Initiative continues to explore significant questions: What are the forces responsible for the problems of environmental injustice? What is the interaction of race, class, and political power? What are the effects of specific environmental hazards on the health of local communities? Is global climate change the biggest environmental injustice to date?

In the last century, two theologians and a religious/political leader spoke succinctly to these points. Two of the men made their observations even before the link between racism and environmental injustice seemed obvious. Gandhi observed that "The earth is sufficient for everyone's need but not for everyone's greed."[131] James H. Cone commented that "The logic that led to slavery and segregation in the Americas, colonization and apartheid in Africa, and the rule of white supremacy throughout the world is the same one that leads to the exploitation of animals and the ravaging of nature. It is a mechanistic and instrumental logic that defines everything and everybody in terms of their contribution to the development and defense of white world supremacy."[132] Years earlier Reinhold Niebuhr reflected that "If the white man were to expiate his sins committed against the darker races, few would have the right to live."[133] Still there are people who reject any connection between racism and environmental injustice.

If we conclude that it is unjust to dump waste in Baltimore, Chicago, or Staten Island, we must also conclude that it is unjust to dump waste in Grenada, Vietnam, or Iraq. If we are concerned about smog in Los Angeles, we must also be concerned about SARS (Severe Acute Respiratory Syndrome) in Beijing. If we are concerned about polluted water in Milwaukee, we must also be concerned about malaria in Khartoum. Why? One answer lies in the Old Testament: "The earth is the Lord's and all it holds, the world and those who live there" (Ps 24:1).

Conclusions

Clearly we are in a period of transition with the plethora of communication media available to us. In 1995 Georgetown University realized the importance of this transition and established its "Communication, Culture, and Technology" (CCT) program, the first graduate program in the country to foster critical inquiry into social, cultural, economic, and political impacts of information technologies. This master's program focuses on convergence and complexity as the key words of the information age because every day our newly networked society changes how we learn, acculturate, develop policy, and create economic opportunities. "Technology and media are always embedded in culture and politics; communication is simultaneously a technical, social, economic, linguistic, and political event. Educational programs based on a single academic field, therefore, simply cannot meet the knowledge needs of this information age."[134] Georgetown's CCT program is now using the Internet as a forum for student projects and is serving as a model for other schools to review their approaches to curricula.

This country is currently embroiled in a quiet discussion that will color for ever the breadth of media content. The Federal Communications Commission (FCC) was established in 1934 to see that the nation's broadcasters served the public interest, that is, making sure that the airwaves were not used solely for commercial ventures. In the decades since then, media have grown beyond radio to include new technologies such as the Internet, cable, and satellite television. In more recent years consolidation has been the trend. In 1975 there were about 1,500 owners of television stations and newspapers. By 2000 that number had dropped to just over 600 owners. Radio ownership has dropped by a third. One conglomerate, Clear Channel, owns more than 1,200 stations and controls 11 percent of the market.[135] Most of these stations have music and chat piped in from a distant point and have no live person on site. This monopoly already proved to be a problem when a train derailed in Minot, North Dakota, and hazardous gases were released into the air. Police tried in vain to reach someone who could broadcast an emergency warning to advise people to stay indoors and close their windows. One company, Clear Channel, owns all six radio stations in Minot. Not one of those stations had a person in the building who could answer the phone and broadcast an announcement. As a result, 300 persons were hospitalized and others were blinded.

"Quiet discussion" is a term I chose intentionally. Although there was some public discussion concerning a vote about media consolidation that came before the FCC in June 2003, not much had been said about the vote in mainstream media. "Of the major broadcasters, only ABC reported the FCC's recent decision to review media ownership rules . . . and that report was at 4:40 in the morning."[136] After the FCC's vote to allow media giants to go beyond the 35-percent-penetration limit in any given market, the Senate surprisingly showed its disapproval with a 55-40 vote to disapprove the FCC's green light. Unfortunately, even though a House majority would agree with the Senate and a federal appeals court in Philadelphia put a hold on the FCC's ruling, it is generally conceded that big media will ultimately get their way.

Cable costs have been steadily increasing, and the country's seven largest cable companies control more than 75 percent of the market. If a community ends up with only one company owning the newspaper, the television station, the radio station, and the cable system, a plurality of voices seems unlikely. Given the amount of time people in this country spend in front of a TV or computer monitor and the amount of time they or others spend listening to radio, it is hard to believe that media consolidation is going to be an asset in achieving justice in the United States or globally. A concern about controlling the media brings to mind a prayerful petition sent to me by the Reverend Peter Craven Fribley, who penned these words in the early days of the 2003 war in Iraq:

> That in a time of war, we give thanks for the blessing of the Internet: empowering ordinary people to connect, to share what they trust and to challenge what they do not; to encourage one another; to pray; to take heart; to take to the streets if so moved; in the unkept and uncontrollable democracy of cyberspace, overthrowing fallen angels and rulers and powers of a kept media. For in the Gospel according to St. John, it is recorded, "You shall know the truth, and the truth will make you free" (Jn 8:31). And the truth cannot be controlled, kept, or spun. Not by ratings. Not by fear. Truth, like sun and rain, like youth and age, like seedtime and harvest, has a life all its own.

The vast array of communication available to us, especially the Internet with its amazing speed, brings the world to our fingertips. That proximity brings with it responsibility. It is increasingly difficult to say we are not aware of injustice on our block, in our state, in our country, around the globe. Greater access to information automatically brings greater responsibility to work for justice.

> This is what Yahweh asks of you, only this:
> to act justly,
> to love tenderly,
> and to walk humbly with your God.
> (Mic 6:8)

Notes

I. Justice Analyzed

1. Synod of Bishops, *Justice in the World* (Washington, D.C.: United States Catholic Conference, 1972) 34. One may argue whether the Latin *constitutiva* in the document means "integral" or "essential." Thus, the 1976 document of the International Theological Commission, "Human Development & Christian Salvation," *Origins* 7, no. 20 (Nov. 3, 1977) 311, states that "it seems more accurate to interpret [*ratio constitutiva*] as meaning an integral part, not an essential part"; a discussible affirmation. What is beyond argument is that the synod saw the search for justice as inseparable from the preaching of the gospel.

2. For texts see David Hollenbach, S.J., "Modern Catholic Teachings concerning Justice," in *The Faith That Does Justice: Examining the Christian Sources for Social Change*, ed. John C. Haughey, S.J. (New York: Paulist, 1977) 207-31, at 208. To Hollenbach's essay I am indebted for its clear presentation of the Catholic tradition from Leo XIII to Vatican II.

3. *Rerum novarum*, nos. 1-3.

4. Hollenbach, "Modern Catholic Teachings" 210.

5. *Quadragesimo anno*, no. 137 (tr. in Terrence P. McLaughlin, ed., *The Church and the Reconstruction of the Modern World* [Garden City, N.Y.: Doubleday Image, 1957]).

6. For details see the devastating critique by Richard A. McCormick, S.J., "Notes on Moral Theology: The Abortion Dossier," *Theological Studies* 35 (1974) 312-59.

7. See Pope John XXIII, *Mater et magistra*, no. 65.

8. C. H. Wu, "Law," *New Catholic Encyclopedia* (New York: McGraw-Hill, 1967) 8:545-46, at 545.

9. New York: Sheed and Ward, 1960.

10. Ibid. 7-8.

11. Hollenbach, "Modern Catholic Teachings" 219.

12. Ibid. 220.

13. Philip Land, S.J., "Justice," *The New Dictionary of Theology*, ed.

Joseph A. Komonchak, Mary Collins, and Dermot A. Lane (Wilmington, Del.: Michael Glazier, 1987) 548-53, at 549.

14. John R. Donahue, S.J., "Biblical Perspectives on Justice," in *The Faith That Does Justice* (n. 2 above) 68-112, at 69; italics in text. For details on the covenantal aspect, see Marc Ouellet, "Covenantal Justice," *Communio*, winter 2000, 619-33; in summary, "with covenantal justice, we are proposing a virtue that surpasses the ancient model of justice which renders to each his due in accordance with the common good; we intend more than the moral ideal of exercising justice in action according to a rational measure of the good willed for its own sake; we of course include the balance of merits and punishments in light of the biblical concept of saving justice within the context of the covenant. The justice of the new covenant proposes a balance of truth and love, of mercy and justice, which provides the foundation for an authentic participation in the witness of the Just Man *par excellence*" (633).

15. John R. Donahue, S.J., *What Does the Lord Require? A Bibliographical Essay on the Bible and Social Justice* (Studies in the Spirituality of Jesuits 25/2: March 1993; St. Louis: Seminar on Jesuit Spirituality, 1993) 21. For one significant aspect of the image tradition, see the chapter "From Genesis to Bonhoeffer: Free Like God" in my *Long Have I Loved You: A Theologian Reflects on His Church* (Maryknoll, N.Y.: Orbis Books, 2000) 209-33.

16. Dennis Olson, "God the Creator: Bible, Creation, Vocation," *Dialogue: A Journal of Theology* 36, no. 3 (summer 1997) 169-74, at 173-74.

17. Donahue, *What Does the Lord Require?* 12.

18. Ibid. 8.

19. See Lynn White Jr., "The Historical Roots of Our Ecologic Crisis," *Science* 155 (1967) 1203-7. This influential article focused the blame for the world's environmental crisis squarely on Christianity. As he saw it, a marriage between a human-centered Christian theology deriving from the Middle Ages and Western expansionist goals had produced a ruthless attitude toward nature.

20. Donahue, *What Does the Lord Require?* 8. See, however, Bruce Vawter, *On Genesis: A New Reading* (Garden City, N.Y.: Doubleday, 1977) 60: "'Subdue' (*kabas*) is part of the same uncompromising rhetoric within which 'have dominion' falls: literally it implies trampling under one's feet, and it connotes absolute subjugation. . . . Probably no distinction is intended between the two terms even though one is applied to the earth itself and the other to the animals. Man's dominance is declared absolute, subject always to the example of the supreme dominance of God after which it has been imaged." I suspect that the final phrase limits significantly the human application of the harsh expression "absolute subjugation" and brings Vawter quite close to Donahue.

21. Theodore Hiebert, *The Yahwist's Landscape: Nature and Religion in Early Israel* (New York: Oxford University Press, 1996) 158-59. I have borrowed this quotation from David Toolan, *At Home in the Cosmos* (Maryknoll, N.Y.: Orbis Books, 2001) 20.

22. Joseph A. Fitzmyer, S.J., *The Gospel according to Luke (X-XXIV)*, Anchor Bible 28A (Garden City, N.Y.: Doubleday, 1985) 884.

23. Ibid. 1127.

24. So Benedict T. Viviano, O.P., "The Gospel according to Matthew," *The New Jerome Biblical Commentary*, ed. Raymond E. Brown, S.S., Joseph A. Fitzmyer, S.J., and Roland E. Murphy, O.Carm. (Englewood Cliffs, N.J.: Prentice-Hall, 1990) 42:133, p. 666.

25. Ibid.

26. See the illuminating article by Raymond E. Brown, S.S., "Roles of Women in the Fourth Gospel," *Theological Studies* 36 (1975) 688-99.

27. Ibid. 691-92.

28. On this text see John R. Donahue, S.J., "The Parable of the Sheep and the Goats: A Challenge to Christian Ethics," *Theological Studies* 47 (1986) 3-13. The usual interpretation—Jesus identifying with his needy and suffering sisters and brothers, a summary of the gospel that serves as a mandate for universal charity—has been challenged. Some scholars argue that Matthew is depicting the punishment of pagans who reject Christian missionaries.

29. Here I have found helpful an illuminating address by David Hollenbach, S.J., "The Common Good in a Divided Society," Santa Clara Lecture 5, no. 3, April 18, 1999, published in pamphlet form by Santa Clara University, California. See also his recent book *The Common Good and Christian Ethics* published in 2002 by Cambridge University Press.

30. Ibid. 1. See Aristotle, *Nicomachean Ethics* 1094b; Thomas Aquinas, *Summa contra gentiles* 3.17. For John XXIII, the common good in broad terms was the sum total of those conditions of social living whereby men and women are enabled to achieve their own perfection more fully and more readily; see his encyclical *Mater et magistra*, no. 65. See also Wu, "Law" (n. 8 above).

31. John Rawls, *Political Liberalism* (New York: Columbia University Press, 1993) 201.

32. Alan Wolfe, *One Nation after All: What Middle-Class Americans Really Think about God, Country, Family, Racism, Welfare, Immigration, Homosexuality, Work, the Right, the Left, and Each Other* (New York: Viking, 1998).

33. Hollenbach, "The Common Good" (n. 29 above) 3; see Alan Wolfe, "Couch Potato Politics," *Sunday New York Times*, March 15, 1998, sec. 4, p. 17.

34. See Hollenbach, ibid., 6-9.

35. Ibid. 6.

36. Pope John Paul II, encyclical *On Social Concern*, no. 38 (Washington, D.C.: United States Catholic Conference, n.d.).

37. Rosemary Haughton, *The Passionate God* (New York/Mahwah, N.J.: Paulist, 1981) 301.

38. Donahue, *What Does the Lord Require? A Bibliographical Essay on the Bible and Social Justice* (revised and expanded; Saint Louis: Institute of Jesuit Sources, 2000) 28.

39. Ibid.
40. Ibid.
41. Ibid.
42. This section draws, often verbally, from my *Long Have I Loved You* (n. 15 above) 169-73. The late revered Philip S. Land, S.J., author of *Catholic Social Teaching: As I Have Lived, Loathed, and Loved It* (Chicago: Loyola University Press, 1995), used "teaching" rather than "thought" in his title because he was "persuaded that *thought* is too fixed, too determined, too eternal. It suggests 'fixed in cement.' It is already there, the Church's possession, its doctrine, firmly set and binding, only needing to be taught. . . . Catholic social teaching, I now believe, consists largely of truths for social action fabricated through reading signs of the times. Alternatively, Catholic social teaching may very well evolve from a people who, suffering some particular situation, work out their social and political truth by allowing their suffering to guide their analysis and their theologizing" (ibid. xvii).

43. Edward B. Arroyo, S.J., "Solidarity: A Moral Imperative for an Interdependent World," *Blueprint for Social Justice* 42, no. 1 (September 1988) 1-7, at 5.

44. See Joseph Sittler, "Ecological Commitment as Theological Responsibility," *Idoc*, Sept. 12, 1970, 75-85; also his remarks in *Vatican II: An Interfaith Appraisal*, ed. John H. Miller, C.S.C. (Notre Dame: University of Notre Dame Press, 1966) 426-27.

45. Rosemary Radford Ruether, *New Woman, New Earth: Sexist Ideologies and Human Liberation* (New York: Seabury, 1975) 204. See her more recent *Gaia and God: An Ecofeminist Theology of Earth Healing* (San Francisco: HarperCollins, 1992).

46. See, e.g., Thomas Berry, *The Dream of the Earth* (San Francisco: Sierra Club, 1988).

47. Anne Lonergan and Caroline Richards, eds., *Thomas Berry and the New Cosmology* (Mystic, Conn.: Twenty-third, 1990) 107, 108.

48. John F. Haught, *The Promise of Nature: Ecology and Cosmic Purpose* (New York/Mahwah, N.J.: Paulist, 1993) 38.

49. Ibid. 65.
50. Ibid. 87.
51. Ibid. 137.

II. Justice Applied

1. So Robert J. Karris, O.F.M., "The Gospel according to Luke," *The New Jerome Biblical Commentary*, ed. Raymond E. Brown, S.S., Joseph A. Fitzmyer, S.J., and Roland E. Murphy, O.Carm. (Englewood Cliffs, N.J.: Prentice-Hall, 1990) 43:126, p. 702.

2. The exact meaning of "poor" in the Prior Testament varies in different periods and with different types of literature; see, e.g., John L. McKenzie, S.J., "Poor, Poverty," in his *Dictionary of the Bible* (New York: Macmillan, 1965) 681-84. I am simplifying a highly complex word.

3. See Children's Defense Fund, *The State of America's Children Year-book*, 2000 (Washington, D.C.: Children's Defense Fund, 2001) ix-xvi.

4. Malachy McCourt, *A Monk Swimming: A Memoir* (New York: Hyperion, 1998) 2. I have retained the punctuation (or lack of it) in the text.

5. From a letter to *Commonweal* 124, no. 10 (May 23, 1997) 30.

6. Quoted by Asher Finkel, "Aging: The Jewish Perspective," in *Aging: Spiritual Perspectives*, ed. Francis V. Tiso (Lake Worth, Fla.: Sunday Publications, 1982) 133.

7. In this section I have profited from Angel Salvatierra, "The Immigrant and Stranger in the Bible," *Theology Digest* 42, no. 2 (summer 1995) 141-44, itself a digest of his article "El emigrante y el extranjero en la biblia," *Lumen: Revista de síntesis y orientación de ciencias eclesiásticas* 42, no. 2 (March-April 1993) 175-87. Useful, too, has been John L. McKenzie's article "Stranger" in his *Dictionary of the Bible* (n. 2 above) 847-49. I have also used material published in my *Preaching the Just Word* (New Haven: Yale University Press, 1996) 7, on relationships between citizen and stranger or resident alien, based on information provided by Scripture scholar Carolyn Osiek in a Preaching the Just Word retreat/workshop.

8. Salvatierra, "Immigrant and Stranger" 141.

9. See John L. McKenzie, "Hospitality," in his *Dictionary* (n. 2 above) 374.

10. McKenzie, "Samaritans," ibid. 765-66, at 766.

11. McKenzie, "Stranger," ibid. 849.

12. *Atlantic Monthly* 278, no. 5 (November 1996) 52-54, 56, 58, 61, 64, 66-68. What follows is a summary of that article.

13. Ibid. 52.

14. Ibid.

15. Ibid. 56.

16. Ibid. 56, 58.

17. Ibid. 58.

18. Ibid. 64.

19. Here I am indebted to George J. Borjas, "The New Economics of Immigration," ibid., 72-74, 76-78, 88.

20. Ibid. 76.

21. Ibid. 78.

22. Ibid. 88.

23. Moises Sandoval, "Huddled Masses: The History of Our Immigrant Church," *U.S. Catholic,* July 2001, at 28-29.

24. Here I have profited from Robert W. McChesney, S.J., "Immigration and Terrorism," *America* 185, no. 13 (Oct. 29, 2001) 8-11. McChesney was the director of the Jesuit Refugee Service Immigration Detention Program in Los Angeles and serves as Immigration Detention Coordinator for the Archdiocese of Los Angeles.

25. Ibid. 8-9. Pertinent here is a report by David Oliver Relin, "Who Will Stand Up for Them?" *Parade Magazine*, Aug. 4, 2000, 4-6, claiming, "Each year, thousands of foreign children—some as young as 18 months—are

incarcerated by U.S. immigration officials after arriving alone or being abandoned here." He quotes Sen. Dianne Feinstein (D., Calif.), who is aware that we need to tighten our borders to prevent terrorists from entering our country illegally, but insists that "We cannot continue to allow children who come to our country—often traumatized and guilty of no crime—to be held in jails and treated like criminals." In January 2001, Feinstein introduced the Unaccompanied Alien Child Protection Act, which would wrest custody of these children away from the U.S. Immigration and Naturalization Service and create an Office of Children's Services to provide for their care. In December 2001, the Homeland Security Act transferred responsibility for care and placement of newcomer children from immigration authorities to the Office of Refugee Resettlement.

26. "The U.S. Penal System: Restorative and/or Retributive Justice?" A panel discussion co-ordinated by Raymond B. Kemp, *Woodstock Report,* no. 61 (March 2000) 3-10, at 4; see also 5.

27. Ibid. 6. Recently the United States surpassed Russia to become the world leader in incarceration. The U.S. rate is 690 prisoners per 100,000 population; the Russian rate, 675 per 100,000. Source: Roy Walmsley, *World Prison Population List* (2nd ed.; United Kingdom Home Office Research, Development and Statistics Directorate, July 2000).

28. Jim Dwyer, "Ex-Officer off Tough Beat Seeks To Free the Innocent," *New York Times,* June 10, 2001, 1 and 34.

29. Paragraphs quoted are from the first part of a three-part article, electronic version, http://www.theatlantic.com/issues/98dec/prisons.htm

30. For the information that follows I am indebted to Carol Ann Morrow, "Dana Blank: Making Prison a Safe Place," *St. Anthony Messenger* 108, no. 10 (March 2001) 16-21. For additional statistics, see graph "Highest Rates of Women in Prison," *USA Today,* Sept. 5-7, 2003, 1A.

31. Washington, D.C.: United States Catholic Conference, 2000. See electronic version, http://www.usccb.org/sdwp/criminal.htm (page references in my text are to the printed version).

32. John Paul II, *On Social Concern,* no. 38 (Washington, D.C.: United States Catholic Conference, 1987) 74.

33. Robert M. Morgenthau, "What Prosecutors Won't Tell You," *New York Times,* Feb. 7, 1995, OpEd page.

34. Ibid.

35. For information on executions in the United States, see http://www.policyalmanac.org/crime/archive/bjs_capital_punishment.shtml. For the names of the 152 men and women executed during Bush's governorship, see http://www.wf.net/~connally/apdxAbush.html

36. See Bob Herbert, "Criminal Justice," *New York Times,* June 24, 1999, A31.

37. Quoted ibid.

38. See ibid.

39. Ibid. A more recent pertinent OpEd piece by Bob Herbert, "Countdown to Execution No. 300," *New York Times,* March 10, 2003, tells the

story of Delma Banks Jr., a 43-year-old black man (the victim was white) scheduled in about 48 hours to become the 300th person executed in Texas since the resumption of capital punishment in 1982. The significant evidence for the murder charge was the testimony of two hard-core drug addicts, one a paid informant, the other a career felon facing a long prison term who was told that a pending prison term would be dismissed if he performed "well" in testifying against Mr. Banks. In addition, prosecutorial misconduct and racial bias. About ten minutes before he was to receive a lethal injection, the Supreme Court halted the execution (his sixteenth stay) to determine if the issues raised in the new appeal deserved appellate review. Banks's attorneys were expected to ask the high court to hear issues of ineffective counsel and racial discrimination in jury selection.

40. Margaret Carlson, "Why This Test Helps Bush," *Time* 155, no. 24 (June 12, 2000) 34.

41. Jim Yardley, "Texas Said To Shift in Wake of Furor on Death Penalty," *New York Times,* June 1, 2002, 1 and 14, at 1.

42. See http://news.bbc.co.uk/2/hi/americas/1393887.stm

43. See n. 41 above.

44. See the *Washington Post,* Jan. 6, 2003, A1, 8, 18. On Jan. 30, 2003, Maryland Attorney General J. Joseph Curran Jr. urged state leaders to abolish the death penalty, saying that mistakes are inevitable in the capital murder system and that the prospect of executing an innocent person is an "intolerable risk."

45. Bob Herbert, "Criminal Justice Breakdown," *New York Times*, Feb. 14, 2000, A27.

46. Jodi Wilgoren, "Panel in Illinois Seeks To Reform Death Sentence," *New York Times*, April 15, 2002, A1.

47. Terry McCarthy, "Dead Men Walking Free," *Time* 160, no. 18 (Oct. 28, 2002) 64.

48. George M. Anderson, S.J., "Fourteen Years on Death Row: An Interview with Joseph Green Brown," *America*, March 29, 1997, 17-20, at 18. Another striking example: In February 2001 Earl Washington Jr., a Virginian with an IQ of 69, was freed, through DNA testing, after serving 17 years in prison, much of it on death row, for a rape and murder he did not commit. Notes columnist Richard Cohen: "[Washington's] investigators and prosecutors are hardly the first to casually dismiss exculpatory evidence or to be so convinced of their man's guilt that they ignored facts that did not conform to their beliefs. This happens all the time. This will continue to happen all the time" ("One Fatal Mistake Not Made," *Washington Post*, Feb. 15, 2001, A23).

49. U.S. Department of Justice, *Survey of the Death Penalty System: 1988-2000* (Washington, D.C., 2000).

50. Raymond Bonner, "Veteran U.S. Envoys Seek End to Execution of Retarded," *New York Times,* June 10, 2001, 3. These views were set forth in a supporting brief filed with the Supreme Court June 8 in the case of Eugene P. McCarver, on death row in North Carolina.

51. For the details see Bob Herbert, "The Confession," *New York Times,* June 21, 2001, A27.

52. For the details see Charles Lane, "O'Connor Expresses Death Penalty Doubt," *Washington Post,* July 4, 2001, A1 and A12; also an editorial of the same day in the *Post,* "Second Thoughts," A18. The quotations in the article are based on an Associated Press account. Pertinent here is the fact that, in a solitary dissent from the court's refusal to stay an execution in Texas, Justice Harry A. Blackmun, 85 years old and near the end of his tenure, wrote in February 1994: "The problem is that the inevitability of factual, legal and moral error gives us a system that we know must wrongfully kill some defendants, a system that fails to deliver the fair, consistent and reliable sentences of death required by the Constitution." After more than 20 years of unsuccessful efforts by Blackmun and a majority of his colleagues to bring an acceptable level of fairness to the system of capital punishment, he had to declare: "I feel morally and intellectually obligated simply to concede that the death penalty experiment has failed" (see Bob Herbert, "Death-Penalty Dissenters," *New York Times,* July 9, 2001, A19). Pertinent here is the conviction of Supreme Court Justice Antonin Scalia, reiterated in an address at Georgetown University on February 4, 2002, that he is justified in defending capital punishment on the basis of St. Paul's Letter to the Romans (13:4) and the long history of the Church's support for the death penalty. He could disagree with John Paul II on this matter, he said, because the pope had not spoken *ex cathedra* (see *Catholic Standard* [Washington, D.C.], Feb. 14, 2002, 3). He also claimed that a jurist who does not think the government has a right to execute criminals has no right to be on the bench in a society where the death penalty is constitutional. In an OpEd piece in the *Washington Post,* "Scalia: Stuck in the Past" (Feb. 26, 2002, A21), Anne Thompson, a Georgetown University undergraduate who had raised questions after the address, wrote: "His claim rests on the assumption that what was acceptable in the past must continue to be acceptable. Following this kind of logic, progress and reform are impossible, and the church should still tolerate witch hunts and holy wars." Not to mention slavery.

53. John Paul II, *The Gospel of Life* 56 (tr. *Origins* 24, no. 42 [April 6, 1995] 709). For an uncommonly striking presentation of the background of, rationale for, and response to capital punishment, public execution, claims of deterrence and closure, and all in the context of Timothy McVeigh's execution for the deadly Oklahoma City bombing, see Garry Wills, "The Dramaturgy of Death," *New York Review of Books* 48, no. 10 (June 21, 2001) 6, 8, 10. I find his argumentation in each area persuasive. Splendidly useful for the history of capital punishment and the underlying theologies is James J. Megivern, *The Death Penalty: An Historical and Theological Survey* (New York/Mahwah, N.J.: Paulist, 1997). Megivern takes us from early Christianity to the medieval Church; through the Renaissance and Reformation dilemmas; the post-Tridentine troubles and tribulations; the Enlightenment; from Vatican I to Vatican II; the American context; the U.S. Catholic bishops' "turnaround"; down to the tensions, setbacks, and advances of the late-twentieth century. He concludes that "the real issue, the central issue, the deciding issue, is the assess-

ment of the human person. If the 'mad dog' or the 'putrid limb' analogies are acceptable, the debate is over and it is time to get on with the execution of such monsters. But if 'made in the image of God' is taken as having any serious content, then the debate is also over, and it is time to get on with the work of finding higher ways of dealing with human failure than willful destruction of divine handiwork" (p. 453). Also worth reading is the more recent work by John Kavanagh, S.J., *Who Count as Persons? Human Identity and the Ethics of Killing* (Washington, D.C.: Georgetown University Press, 2002), a radical position that claims we may not kill intentionally in war or in self-defense, through abortion or euthanasia or the death penalty; only thus can we live as ethical animals and value one another as persons.

54. Here, and in quoting Justice Scalia, I am using not the excerpts in the *New York Times* (June 21, 2002, A14) but the complete texts from electronic version *Atkins* v. *Virginia* (00-8452); see http://supct.law.cornell.edu/supct/html/00-8452.ZO.html

55. *New York Times*, June 21, 2002, A24.

56. Antoinette Bosco, *Choosing Mercy: A Mother of Murder Victims Pleads To End the Death Penalty* (Maryknoll, N.Y.: Orbis Books, 2001).

57. Ibid. 13-14.

58. See ibid. 14.

59. Ibid. 50.

60. Ibid. 62-63.

61. Ibid. 73.

62. See ibid. 77-81.

63. Ibid. 82-83. MVFR was founded by Marie Deans of Richmond, Virginia, a quarter century ago. In June 2001, 400 members of MVFR met at Boston College for a "victims' summit" called "Healing the Wounds of Murder." See the informative article by Page McKean Zyromski, "Healing the Wounds of Murder," *St. Anthony Messenger* 109, no. 8 (January 2002) 34-39. The author is a member of the Secular Franciscan Order. A Florida prison inmate is responsible for the death of one of her family members. She has worked for 22 years toward the commutation of his sentence to life imprisonment. The two have "made peace," and she has visited him and corresponds with him. As of February 2002, he remained on death row.

64. Lynn White Jr., "The Historical Roots of the Ecologic Crisis," *Science* 155 (1967) 1203-7.

65. For the text see my booklet *Towards Reconciliation* (Washington, D.C.: United States Catholic Conference, 1974). For the address on reconciliation with nature, including the quotations from Erich Fromm, see pp. 25-30. For easier reference to these texts, see my *Preaching the Just Word* (New Haven: Yale University Press, 1996) 13-14.

66. See Charles A. McCain, manager for development of alternative products, DuPont Corporation, *New York Times*, March 7, 1989; Robert Watson, chief of NASA's atmospheric program, *Washington Post*, Oct. 6, 1989.

67. See, e.g., Pastoral Constitution on the Church in the Modern World (*Gaudium et spes*), nos. 57 and 60. The English text of the pope's address may

be found in *Origins* 19 (1989) 465-68. Still, the Columban missionary Sean McDonagh took John Paul II to task because the encyclical *Veritatis splendor*, on the foundations of morality, did not devote a single sentence to "the morality of disfiguring the image of God in creation" ("Care for the Earth Is a Moral Duty," *Month* 248, no. 8021 [April 30, 1994] 514).

68. See Joseph Sittler, "Ecological Commitment as Theological Responsibility," *Idoc*, Sept. 12, 1970, 75-85; also his remarks in *Vatican II: An Interfaith Appraisal*, ed. John H. Miller, C.S.C. (Notre Dame, Ind.: University of Notre Dame Press, 1966) 426-27.

69. H. Paul Santmire, "In God's Ecology: A Revisionist Theology of Nature," *Christian Century* 117, no. 35 (Dec. 13, 2000) 1300-1305. My summary is indebted to this splendid article.

70. Ibid. 1300.

71. Ibid.

72. Ibid. 1301.

73. Ibid. 1305.

74. David Toolan, *At Home in the Cosmos* (Maryknoll, N.Y.: Orbis Books, 2001) 14. This is a remarkably evenhanded study of all the significant aspects of the environmental crisis. "We dwell within a promising universe, I will argue, and our function, our great work, is to make something beautiful of it, to pour soul and spirit into it" (5).

75. Pastoral Constitution on the Church in the Modern World, no. 57. The same document has a section (39) on a new earth God is preparing "where justice will have its home," when "all that creation which God fashioned for humanity's sake will be delivered from vanity's bondage."

76. For English text, see *Origins* 19, no. 28 (Dec. 7, 1989) 465-68, at 466; emphasis mine.

77. Ibid. 467-68.

78. Twelve U.S. and Canadian Bishops, "The Columbia River Watershed: Caring for Creation and the Common Good," *Origins* 30, no. 38 (March 8, 2001) 609-19, at 609.

79. Ibid. 610.

80. John Paul II, encyclical *On Social Concern*, no. 28 (Washington, D.C.: United States Catholic Conference, n.d.) 48-49.

81. For frequently updated information on issues concerning the stewardship of creation, see "Brethren Witness: Care for Creation," electronic version, http://www.brethren.org/genbd/witness/CareforCreation.htm

82. Anup Shah, "Behind Consumption and Consumerism," electronic version, http://www.globalissues.org/TradeRelated/Consumption.asp

83. New York/Mahwah, N.J.: Paulist, 1999.

84. Ibid. 93-94. Another work worth consulting is *Environmental Stewardship in the Judeo-Christian Tradition: Jewish, Catholic, and Protestant Wisdom on the Environment*, ed. Michael B. Barkey (Grand Rapids, Mich.: Acton Institute for the Study of Religion and Liberty, 2000).

85. See Gregg Easterbrook, *A Moment on Earth: The Coming Age of*

Environmental Optimism (New York: Penguin, 1995). For a detailed critique of this work, see Toolan, *At Home in the Cosmos* (n. 74 above), to which I am indebted for my own summary observations.

86. Toolan, *At Home in the Cosmos* 84; quotations from Easterbrook, *A Moment on Earth* 316.

87. For the full text, see my *To Be Just Is To Love: Homilies for a Church Renewing* (New York/Mahwah, N.J.: Paulist, 2001) 108-12.

88. These two paragraphs are borrowed, almost verbatim, from Roger Rosenblatt, "Reaching the Top by Doing the Right Thing," *Time* 154, no. 16 (Oct. 18, 1999) 89-91, at 90.

89. Ibid.

90. The factual material in this section on ASPI is borrowed from Carol Ann Morrow, "Renewing the Face of the Earth: Jesuit Al Fritsch," *St. Anthony Messenger* 110, no. 1 (June 2002) 22-26.

91. Ibid. 25. For Fritsch's books and videos, see ibid. 26.

92. Ibid. 26.

93. The data, given here as preached in my homily "That They May All Be One," are borrowed gratefully from the National Coalition for Homeless Veterans, "Most Often Asked Questions Concerning Homeless Veterans," electronic version, http://www.nchv.org/background.cfm#questions

94. Data from the Center for Applied Research in the Apostolate (CARA), see http://cara.georgetown.edu/bulletin/index.htm

95. John Courtney Murray, S.J., "Remarks on the Moral Problem of War," *Theological Studies* 20 (1959) 40-61, at 57. Although written more than four decades ago, Murray's article continues to speak powerfully to the present generation; my presentation is deeply indebted to it.

96. R. A. McCormick, S.J., "War, Morality of," *New Catholic Encyclopedia* (New York: McGraw-Hill, 1967) 14:802-7, at 803.

97. See ibid.

98. *Acta apostolicae sedis* 37 (1945) 18.

99. McCormick, "War, Morality of" 803.

100. Murray, "Remarks on the Moral Problem of War" 53. I should note that today the Catholic position overwhelmingly favors the legitimacy of conscientious objection.

101. McCormick, "War, Morality of" 804.

102. Ibid. 805.

103. Still among the finest articles assailing obliteration bombing was written during World War II by John C. Ford, S.J., "The Morality of Obliteration Bombing," *Theological Studies* 5 (1944) 261-309.

104. McCormick, "War, Morality of" 806.

105. See "Remarks on the Moral Problem of War," esp. 54ff.

106. Ibid. 56-57.

107. Ibid. 55.

108. Ibid. 59.

109. John Langan, S.J., "The Just-War Theory after the Gulf War," *Theological Studies* 53 (1992) 95-112.

110. Editorial, "Coscienza cristiana e guerra moderna," *La civiltà cattolica* 142 (1991) 3-16; English translation by William Shannon in *Origins* 21 (1991) 450-55.

111. Langan, "The Just-War Theory" 103.

112. *30 Days* 4 (1991) 3.

113. Langan, "The Just-War Theory" 103-4. Langan lists a number of such inconsistencies.

114. Ibid. 105.

115. Ibid. 106.

116. Well worth reading are the questions raised by Langan on the actual conduct of the fighting during the Gulf War: e.g., noncombatant immunity, damage to the Iraqi infrastructure, coalition decision to end the war with Saddam Hussein still in power, failure to eliminate all Iraqi weapons of mass destruction.

117. Michael Elliott, "The 'Axis of Evil' in Action," *Time* 160, no. 26 (Dec. 23, 2002) 41. Writing almost 11 months after Bush's address, Elliott felt that in the light of certain events and realities in the three nations, "the phrase sounds a lot better now than it did a year ago."

118. See the informative article by Romesh Ratnesar, "How Dangerous Is North Korea?" *Time* 161, no. 2 (Jan. 13, 2003) 22-29; quotation at 24-25.

119. Michael Duffy, "Does Might Make It Right?" *Time* 160, no. 14 (Sept. 30, 2002) 39.

120. Ibid.

121. See electronic version, http://www.usccb.org/sdwp/international/bush 902.htm

122. For the details of this U.N. resolution on Iraq, see electronic version, http://www.cnn.com/2002/US/11/08/resolution.text

123. See electronic version of bishops' statement, http://www.usccb.org/ bishops/iraq.htm. It will be clear that in large measure the bishops are reinforcing their September 13th letter to President Bush, while "taking in account developments since then, especially the unanimous action of the U.N. Security Council on November 8th."

124. "Just war teaching has evolved . . . as an effort to prevent war; only if war cannot be rationally avoided, does the teaching then seek to restrict and reduce its horrors. It does this by establishing a set of rigorous conditions which must be met if the decision to go to war is to be morally permissible. Such a decision, especially today, requires extraordinarily strong reasons for overriding the presumption in favor of peace and against war. This is one significant reason why valid just-war teaching makes provision for conscientious dissent" (from *The Challenge of Peace: God's Promise and Our Response* [1983] and included in this episcopal statement on Iraq [n. 123]).

125. J. Bryan Hehir, "The Hawkish Doctrine of Mr. Bush," London *Tablet*, Jan. 4, 2003, 4-5, at 5.

126. *Sunday New York Times*, March 9, 2003, Section 4, p. 12.

127. Ibid., p. 13.

128. Ibid.

129. Ibid.

130. From lengthy article "Desert Caution: Once 'Stormin' Norman,' Gen. Schwarzkopf Is Skeptical about U.S. Action in Iraq," by Thomas E. Ricks, *Washington Post*, Jan. 28, 2003, C1. See also the OpEd column by Bob Herbert, "With Ears and Eyes Closed," *New York Times*, March 17, 2003, A25.

131. William Safire, "Getting On with It," *New York Times*, March 17, 2003, A25.

III. Justice Sacramentalized

1. Here I am dependent on the splendid treatment by Keith F. Pecklers, S.J., *The Unread Vision. The Liturgical Movement in the United States of America: 1926-1955* (Collegeville, Minn.: Liturgical Press, 1998) 1-23.

2. Ibid. 6.

3. Letter to Paul Marx, Sept. 27, 1952; quoted in Marx, *Virgil Michel and the Liturgical Movement* (Collegeville, Minn.: Liturgical Press, 1957) 28.

4. Pecklers, *The Unread Vision* 21.

5. The text is from *National Liturgical Week: Proceedings* (Liturgical Conference, 1947) 11; reproduced by Pecklers, *The Unread Vision* 22-23. See also the fine sketch of Michel's vision by Anne Y. Koester, "Just Live the Liturgy," in *Assembly* (Notre Dame Center for Pastoral Liturgy) 27, no. 1 (January 2001) 2-3: "He saw in the liturgy the promise for bringing unity to a divided world, healing to the broken human spirit, and order to the chaos. . . . He saw the world's need for right relationships, which is why he directed so much of his energy to pointing out the injustices that shattered people's lives and tarnished society."

6. Virgil Michel, O.S.B., "The Liturgy the Basis of Social Regeneration," *Orate fratres* 9 (1935) 545.

7. For details see Pecklers, *The Unread Vision* 97-124. It is this section I am summarizing in the paragraphs that follow.

8. Margaret M. Kelleher, "Liturgy and Social Transformation: Exploring the Relationship," *U.S. Catholic Historian* 16, no. 4 (fall 1998) 58-70, at 59.

9. Virgil Michel, O.S.B., "Natural and Supernatural Society," *Orate fratres* 10 (1936) 244-45.

10. J. Bryan Hehir, "Foreword" to Mark Searle, ed., *Liturgy and Social Justice* (Collegeville, Minn.: Liturgical Press, 1980) 9.

11. Interview with Pecklers, Dec. 14, 1994, De Paul University, Chicago, as reported by Pecklers, *The Unread Vision* 149, n. 184. Hillenbrand merits far more than this passing mention. His eight years (1936-44) as rector of St. Mary of the Lake Seminary brought the principles of the liturgical movement to seminarians and priests of Chicago. He brought to the seminary Dorothy Day, labor priests like Francis Haas of Milwaukee, interracial Jesuit activist John

LaFarge, Hispanic activist Bishop Robert Lucey of Amarillo. He helped to establish a series of labor schools in the industrialized areas of the archdiocese, taught labor school classes to steel workers, with strong doses of papal social teaching. His commitment to social transformation was a seamless garment that included the celebration of corporate liturgy and the creation of a social order that reflected the organic principles of the Mystical Body. His strong sympathies for the working class, his solidarity with organized labor shown at times by participation in strike demonstrations and picket lines, led to his forced resignation as rector. As pastor he transformed Sacred Heart parish into a showplace for many of the new developments in liturgical life. For details see Steven M. Avella, "Chicago's Sons: George G. Higgins and Reynold Hillenbrand," *U.S. Catholic Historian* 19, no. 4 (fall 2001) 25-32; more fully, the 1989 doctoral dissertation at the University of Notre Dame by Robert Tuzik, "The Contribution of Msgr. Reynold Hillenbrand (1905-1979) to the Liturgical Movement in the United States: Influences and Development."

12. Hehir, "Foreword" (n. 10 above) 10.

13. Kelleher, "Liturgy and Social Transformation" (n. 8 above) 64.

14. Ibid. The quotation from John J. Egan is taken from his *Liturgy and Justice: An Unfinished Agenda* (Collegeville, Minn.: Liturgical Press, 1983) 5.

15. Michel, "The Liturgy the Basis of Social Regeneration" (n. 6 above) 545.

16. Hehir, "Foreword" (n. 10 above) 10.

17. Here I am borrowing liberally from my 1999 Gregory Diekmann Lecture at St. John's University, Collegeville, Minnesota, "Just Word and Just Worship: Biblical Justice and Christian Liturgy," published in *Worship* 73 (1999) 386-98.

18. Mark Searle, "Serving the Lord with Justice," in *Liturgy and Social Justice*, ed. Searle (n. 10 above) 13-35, at 15-16.

19. Constitution on the Sacred Liturgy (*Sacrosanctum concilium*), no. 35; see also no. 52: "part of the liturgy itself."

20. Mary Collins, *Contemplative Participation:* Sacrosanctum concilium *Twenty-five Years Later* (Collegeville, Minn.: Liturgical Press, 1990) 54-57.

21. Searle, "Serving the Lord with Justice" (n. 10 above) 23-24.

22. I have this quotation as a whole from Robert W. Hovda's funeral card; part of it from his "The Vesting of Liturgical Ministers," *Worship* 54 (1980) 105.

23. See Searle, "Serving the Lord with Justice" (n. 10 above) 25-26.

24. See Patrick Marrin, "Diekmann Says Hold Fast to Hope," *National Catholic Reporter*, Feb. 26, 1999, 11-12.

25. John Paul II, encyclical *On Social Concern*, Dec. 30, 1987 (Washington, D.C.: United States Catholic Conference, n.d.) 48-49.

26. See the fine articles by Stephen Happel, both entitled "Symbol," in *The New Dictionary of Theology*, ed. Joseph A. Komonchak, Mary Collins, and Dermot A. Lane (Wilmington, Del.: Michael Glazier, 1987) 996-1002, and in *The New Dictionary of Sacramental Worship*, ed. Peter E. Fink, S.J. (Collegeville, Minn.: Liturgical Press, 1990) 1237-45.

27. Elizabeth A. Johnson, "Community on Earth as in Heaven: A Holy People and a Sacred Earth Together" (Santa Clara Lectures 5, no. 1; Santa Clara, Calif.: Santa Clara University, 1998) 13.

28. See John A. Coleman, S.J., "How the Eucharist Proclaims Social Justice," *Church* 16, no. 4 (winter 2000) 5-9; 17, no. 1 (spring 2001) 11-15.

29. Constitution on the Sacred Liturgy, no. 10.

30. See the splendid biography by liturgical scholar Kathleen Hughes, R.S.C.J., *The Monk's Tale: A Biography of Godfrey Diekmann, O.S.B.* (Collegeville, Minn.: Liturgical Press, 1991), specifically 277-82.

31. Ibid. 282; italics in text; Greeley material from a taped interview dated Nov. 24, 1987.

32. "Liturgies with the Power To Change Your Life," interview with J-Glenn Murray, S.J., *John Carroll University Magazine* 3, no. 1 (spring 1999) 10-11, at 10.

33. Vatican II, Constitution on the Sacred Liturgy, no. 10 (tr. mostly from *The Documents of Vatican II,* ed. Walter M. Abbott, S.J. [New York: Herder and Herder/Association, 1966] 142-43).

34. This type of reflection on "took, blessed, broke, gave" I first heard from biblical scholar David Stanley, S.J., who had an enviable gift for shaping contemporary spirituality from the New Testament. I am reproducing here what I first presented in "Characteristics of a Social Justice Spirituality," *Origins* 24, no. 9 (July 21, 1994) 157, 159-64.

35. Rembert Weakland, O.S.B., "The Right Road for the Liturgy," London *Tablet,* Feb. 2, 2002, 10-13, at 10. The article first appeared in *Commonweal* Jan. 11, 2002, under the title "The Liturgy as Battlefield: What do 'Restorationists' want?"

36. Ibid. 13.

37. Bernard J. F. Lonergan, S.J., *Method in Theology* (New York: Herder & Herder, 1972) 14.

38. Ibid.

39. Ibid. 14-15; emphasis mine.

40. Ibid. 238.

41. Ibid. 238-40.

42. Ibid. 240-41.

43. Ibid. 241-42.

44. Ibid. 240-41; emphasis mine.

45. Ibid. 242.

46. Ibid. 241.

47. David W. Fagerberg, "Cosmological Liturgy and a Sensible Priesthood," *New Blackfriars* 82 (February 2001) 76-87.

48. From *A Maréchal Reader,* ed. and tr. Joseph Donceel, S.J. (New York: Herder & Herder, 1970) 116.

49. Etienne Gilson, *The Elements of Christian Philosophy* (New York: Mentor-Omega Books, 1960) 114.

50. Fagerberg, "Cosmological Liturgy" (n. 47 above) 79-80. The quotation beginning with "Alongside" is taken from Paul Evdokimov, *The Art of the*

Icon: A Theology of Beauty (Redondo Beach, Calif.: Oakwood, 1990) 26. I recall that, for some theologians of the early Church, the Greek *logikēn latreian* of Romans 12:1, usually translated as a worship or service that is "rational" or "reasonable" or "spiritual," was interpreted as a worship of the Logos (God the Son) by our logos (mind or spiritual nature).

51. Fagerberg, "Cosmological Liturgy" (n. 47 above) 82.

52. Ibid. 85.

53. Subhash Anand, "The Inculturation of the Eucharistic Liturgy," *Vidyajyoti: Journal of Theological Reflection* 57 (1993) 269-93.

54. Constitution on the Sacred Liturgy, no. 37.

55. Michael Amaladoss, "Inculturation and Evangelization," in *Church in India: Institution or Movement? A Commemorative Volume in Honor of Fr. D. S. Amalorpavadass,* ed. Paul Puthanangady (Bangalore: NBCLC, 1991) 152.

56. Peter Schineller, S.J., *A Handbook on Inculturation* (New York/Mahwah, N.J.: Paulist, 1990) 6.

57. Ibid.

58. Ibid. 7.

59. Karl Rahner, "Towards a Fundamental Theological Interpretation of Vatican II," *Theological Studies* 40 (1979) 716-27, at 718, 721.

60. Ibid. 725.

61. For statistics and information on organized hate groups throughout the United States, see the Web site of the Intelligence Project, an initiative that monitors hate crimes and militia-like patriot groups, http://www.splcenter.org/intelligenceproject/ip-index.html

62. http://www.vidahumana.org/english/hispanics/hispanics-us.html

63. Ibid.

IV. Justice Globalized

1. Romesh Ratnesar, "Chaos Incorporated," *Time* 158, no. 3 (July 23, 2001) 33-36, at 33.

2. *New York Times,* July 22, 2001, 8.

3. My description of globalization in the next several paragraphs borrows, often verbally, from an unpublished paper of the Woodstock Theological Center, "Global Economy and Culture," the work of Jesuits Drew Christiansen and Gasper F. Lo Biondo.

4. Thomas L. Friedman, *The Lexus and the Olive Tree* (newly updated and expanded edition; New York: Anchor Books [Random House], 2000) xvi. All my citations from and references to *Lexus* are from this first Anchor Books edition, not the original edition published by Farrar, Straus and Giroux in 1999. The subtitle, "Understanding Globalization," appears only on the front cover, not on the title page. Friedman notes that "the Merrill Lynch ad would have been a little more correct to say that *this* era of globalization is ten years old. Because from the mid-1800s to the late 1920s the world experienced a

similar era of globalization" (ibid.). Putting together the floods of immigration and the inventions of the steamship, telegraph, railroad, and telephone, Friedman finds it "safe to say that this first era of globalization before World War I shrank the world from a size 'large' to a size 'medium'" (ibid. xvii). To explain his title, Friedman says that olive trees "represent everything that roots us, anchors us, identifies us and locates us in this world—whether it be belonging to a family, a community, a tribe, a nation, a religion or, most of all, a place called home" (ibid. 31). Lexus, the luxury car, "represents an equally fundamental, age-old human drive—the drive for sustenance, improvement, prosperity and modernization—as it is played out in today's globalization system. The Lexus represents all the burgeoning global markets, financial institutions and computer technologies with which we pursue higher living standards today" (ibid. 32-33).

    5. See ibid. 7-15.

    6. I am working from a manuscript text kindly supplied to me by the author; hence the absence of the usual references to pages.

    7. Robert J. Schreiter, *The New Catholicity: Theology between the Global and the Local* (Maryknoll, N.Y.: Orbis Books, 1997).

    8. David Held, Anthony McGrew, David Goldblatt, and Jonathon Perraton, *Global Transformations: Politics, Economics, and Culture* (Stanford: Stanford University Press, 1999) 16 (emphasis mine).

    9. L. Kroeber and Clyde Kluckhohn, *Culture: A Critical Review of Concepts and Definitions* (New York: Vintage, 1963).

    10. Michael Paul Gallagher, S.J., *Clashing Symbols: An Introduction to Faith and Culture* (New York/Mahwah, N.J.: Paulist, 1998) 15. As will become clear in the following pages, I have profited much from this informative work.

    11. Clifford Geertz, *The Interpretation of Cultures* (New York: Basic Books, 1973) 89.

    12. Clifford Geertz, *Local Knowledge: Further Essays in Interpretive Anthropology* (New York: Basic Books, 1983) 85.

    13. Ibid. 75.

    14. Bernard Lonergan, S.J., *Insight: A Study of Human Understanding* (London: Longman Green, 1958) 179, 419, 237.

    15. Bernard Lonergan, S.J., *Method in Theology* (London: Darton, Longman & Todd, 1972) 301.

    16. Gallagher, *Clashing Symbols* (n. 10 above) 17. The quotation from Lonergan stems from *Bernard Lonergan, A Second Collection*, ed. W. Ryan and B. Tyrrell (London: Darton, Longman & Todd, 1974) 101.

    17. Quoted by Gallagher (*Clashing Symbols* 21) from Hervé Carrier, *The Church and Culture since Vatican II*, ed. Joseph Gremillion (Notre Dame: University of Notre Dame Press, 1985) 19.

    18. Gallagher, *Clashing Symbols* 33, based on Walter J. Ong, S.J., *Orality and Literacy: The Technologizing of the Word* (London: Routledge, 1982) 78, 178-79. In the several passages that follow in the text above, I continue to avail myself of Gallagher's summary (33-35) of Ong.

19. Walter J. Ong, S.J., *The Presence of the Word: Some Prolegomena for Culture and Religious History* (New York: Simon & Schuster, 1970) 111, 117.

20. Ibid. 125. See also Ong's *Ramus, Method, and the Decay of Dialogue* (Cambridge, Mass.: Harvard University Press, 1958).

21. Walter J. Ong, S.J., *Interfaces of the Word: Studies in the Evolution of Consciousness and Culture* (Ithaca, N.Y.: Cornell University Press, 1977) 222.

22. Gallagher, *Clashing Symbols* 34-35; the quotations are taken from Ong's *Faith and Contexts* (*Collected Essays 1952-1991*), ed. Thomas Farrell, 2 vols. (Atlanta: Scholars Press, 1992) 2:162.

23. Ibid. 37.

24. Pastoral Constitution on the Church in the Modern World no. 53. My translation, here and below, has profited from the versions provided by Gallagher, *Clashing Symbols*; by *Vatican Council II: The Conciliar and Post Conciliar Documents*, ed. Austin Flannery, O.P. (Northport, N.Y.: Costello, 1975); and by *The Documents of Vatican II*, ed. Walter M. Abbott, S.J. (New York: America, 1966).

25. Gallagher, *Clashing Symbols* 39.

26. Ibid. 42.

27. For more detailed information, see Gallagher, *Clashing Symbols* 44-55.

28. Ibid. 43.

29. Ibid. 45.

30. Avery Dulles, S.J., "The Prophetic Humanism of John Paul II," *America*, Oct. 23, 1993, 9.

31. Gallagher, *Clashing Symbols* 48.

32. Ibid. 50.

33. I borrow the translation from Gallagher, ibid. 53. The final quotation is taken from an address of John Paul II on March 20, 1982.

34. Translation from Gallagher, ibid. 55.

35. See Kenneth Himes, O.F.M., "Globalization and Inequality: Perspectives from Catholic Social Teaching," *Origins* 32, no. 2 (May 23, 2002) 17, 19-22. The title given by the journal is "Globalization's Next Phase." I have simply summarized some segments of this important address. All quotations are from this text.

36. Vatican II, The Church in the Modern World, no. 42.

37. *The Lexus and the Olive Tree* (n. 4 above) 251.

38. Ibid. 250-51.

39. What is the Golden Straitjacket? "To fit into the Golden Straitjacket a country must either adapt, or be seen as moving toward, the following golden rules: making the private sector the primary engine of its economic growth, maintaining a low rate of inflation and price stability, shrinking the size of its state bureaucracy, maintaining as close to a balanced budget as possible, if not a surplus, eliminating and lowering tariffs on imported goods, removing restrictions on foreign investment, getting rid of quotas and domestic monopolies, increasing exports, privatizing state-owned industries and utilities, dereg-

ulating capital markets, making its currency convertible, opening its industries, stock, and bond markets to direct foreign ownership and investment, deregulating its economy to promote as much domestic competition as possible, eliminating government corruption, subsidies and kickbacks as much as possible, opening its banking and telecommunications systems to private ownership and competition, and allowing its citizens to choose from an array of competing pension options and foreign-run pension and mutual funds. When you stitch all of these pieces together you have the Golden Straitjacket.

"Unfortunately, this Golden Straitjacket is pretty much 'one size fits all.' So it pinches certain groups, squeezes others and keeps a society under pressure to constantly streamline its economic institutions and upgrade its performance. It leaves people behind quicker than ever if they shuck it off, and it helps them catch up quicker than ever if they wear it right. It is not always pretty or gentle or comfortable. But it's here and it's the only model on the rack this historical season" (ibid. 105).

40. Ibid. 329.
41. Ibid.
42. Ibid. 330-31.
43. Ibid. 331. "In 20 years General Motors cut 297,000 hourly jobs . . . the bulk of the people were replaced by machines. . . . So not only do you need more skills than ever if you want to get a job in manufacturing today, but you need multiple skills to keep your job from going to a robot" (333).
44. Ibid. 334.
45. Ibid. 337.
46. Ibid. 342.
47. Ibid. 343.
48. Ibid. 345.
49. Ibid. 346.
50. Ibid. 349.
51. Ibid. 350.
52. Ibid. 355-64.
53. Ibid. 373.
54. Ibid. 380.
55. Ibid. 381.
56. Ibid. 385.
57. Ibid. 386.
58. Ibid. 407.
59. See ibid. 406-33, at 418, 425, 429, and 431.
60. Ibid. 405.
61. Ibid. 444-45.
62. New York: Farrar, Straus and Giroux, 2002.
63. Geoffrey Wheatcroft, review of Thomas Friedman, *Longitudes and Attitudes, New York Times Book Review*, Sept. 8, 2002, 5.
64. Tina Rosenberg, "The Free-Trade Fix," *New York Times Magazine*, Aug. 18, 2002, 28-33, 50, 74-75.

65. Ibid. 30.

66. Ibid. 31.

67. Ibid. 32.

68. Ibid.

69. Ibid. 33.

70. Ibid. 50.

71. Ibid.

72. Ibid. 69.

73. Ibid. 75.

74. The words are quoted from the author and article I shall now summarize: Andrew Hartman, "The Globalization of a Movement," *Humanist* 1, no. 6 (November-December 2001) 15-18.

75. Ibid. 15.

76. Ibid.

77. Ibid.

78. Ibid. 16.

79. Ibid.

80. Ibid. 16-17.

81. Ibid. 17.

82. Ibid.

83. Ibid. 18.

84. Ibid.

85. I shall be making use once again of Schreiter's address "Pursuing Social Justice in an Age of Globalization" (see n. 6 above) and his book *The New Catholicity: Theology between the Global and the Local* (see n. 7 above), as well as his more recent article "Globalization, Modernity, Religion, and Violence," *Doctrine and Life* 51, no. 8 (October 2001) 454-68.

86. See the informative treatment of this issue by Francis A. Sullivan, S.J., "The Teaching Authority of Episcopal Conferences," *Theological Studies* 63 (2002) 472-93.

87. Editorial, "The Failure of Capitalism," London *Tablet*, July 6, 2002, 3.

88. http://www.un.org/esa/ffd/themes/introducton.htm

89. Ibid., no. 1.

90. Ibid., no. 3.

91. Aldo Caliari, "A Disappointing Document: Financing for Development," *Center Focus* (News from the Center of Concern) no. 156 (May/June 2002) 9-11.

92. From "Home News: Christian Greens Prepare for Summit," London *Tablet*, Aug. 17, 2002, 24.

93. John Gummer, "How Europe Showed America the Way," London *Tablet*, Sept. 14, 2002, 4-5, at 4.

94. Ibid.

95. Ibid. 5.

96. Jim Hug, S.J., "Evaluating the World Summit on Sustainable Devel-

opment," *Center Focus,* no. 157 (September 2002) 12. All material and quotations here are from this single page.

97. See "Our Mission Today: The Service of Faith and the Promotion of Justice," Decrees of the 32nd General Congregation I, no. 4, in *Documents of the 31st and 32nd General Congregations of the Society of Jesus* (Saint Louis: Institute of Jesuit Sources, 1977) 411.

98. See Robert Blair Kaiser, "A Jesuit at the Summit," London *Tablet,* Sept. 14, 2002, 6-7.

99. Ibid. 6.

100. Ibid. 7.

101. See "A tale of many Summits," electronic version, *News from the Jesuit Social Apostolate,* Sept. 5, 2002, http://www.Jesuit.ie/ijnd/WSSD13.pdf

102. Emphasis mine in printed text. Electronic version (including graph "Comparing Aid Volume" with data taken from the OECD DAC Report 2001 and World Bank Database GDP figures concerning official aid from the United States, the European Union, the United Kingdom, and the combined volume of aid of Germany, France, and Italy) may be found at www.nccbuscc.org/sdwp/international/faud.htm

103. I am using a copy of his manuscript graciously supplied me by John Carr, long-time director of the Secretariat for Social Development and World Peace at the U.S. Bishops' Conference in Washington, D.C.

104. John Paul II, encyclical *On Social Concern,* no. 39 (Washington, D.C.: United States Catholic Conference, n.d.) 76.

105. Ibid., nos. 39-40 (USCC 77-78).

106. www.un.org/events/wssd/statements/openingsaE.htm

107. See http://www.globalissues.org/TradeRelated/FreeTrade/Criticisms.asp

108. Responses to the criticisms, to the "antiglobalists," largely from the *Economist,* for example, "Globalization and Its Critics," Sept. 23, 2001, are often valid, some completely, others only if looked at from a narrow perspective. For details, for example, the claim that fair wages to the poor will eventually be bad for everyone, see ibid.

109. So, e.g., by Georgetown University professor of theology Thomas N. King, S.J., "Globalization and the Soul—according to Teilhard, Friedman, and Others," *Zygon: Journal of Science and Religion* 37, no. 1 (March 2002) 25-33. Extensive excerpts from that article are contained in King's "Globalization and the Soul," *Teilhard Perspective* 35, no. 1 (spring 2002) 1-5. The section on Teilhard in the *Zygon* article has been "digested" under the title "Teilhard and Globalization" in *Theology Digest* 49 (2002) 211-15. I am deeply indebted to King, who has found in Teilhard an inspiration and masterly guide for his theology and spirituality. My presentation makes particular use of the electronic version of the *Teilhard Perspective* article and also the *Theology Digest* summation.

110. King, "Globalization and the Soul," electronic version, p. 2, www.orgs.bucknell.edu/teilhard/spring2002.PDF

111. Ibid. See also Teilhard's "Hymn to Matter" (1919) with his powerful recognition that "If we are ever to reach you, matter, we must, having first established contact with the totality of all that lives and moves here below, come little by little to feel that the individual shapes of all we have laid hold on are melting away in our hands, until finally we are at grips with the *single essence* of all subsistencies and all unions. . . ." This hymn has appeared in several books including *Hymn of the Universe* (Harper Torchbooks; New York: Harper & Row, 1960) 68-71, at 70. This same edition begins with "The Mass on the World" (1923), in which Teilhard revealed another of his insights about the interconnectedness of all creation: "The deeper the level at which one encounters you, Master, the more one realizes the universality of your influence. This is the criterion by which I can judge at each moment how far I have progressed within you. When all the things around me, while preserving their own individual contours, their own special savours, nevertheless appear to me as animated by a single secret spirit and therefore as diffused and intermingled within a single element, infinitely close, infinitely remote; and when, locked within the jealous intimacy of a divine sanctuary, I yet feel myself to be wandering at large in the empyrean of all created beings: then I shall know that I am approaching that central point where the heart of the world is caught in the descending radiance of the heart of God . . ." (32-37, at 35-36).

112. King, "Globalization and the Soul," electronic version, 2-3.

113. Ibid. 3.

114. Ibid.

115. Ibid.

116. Ibid. 3-4.

117. Ibid. 4.

V. Justice Communicated

1. See Ben Segal, "A Short History of Internet Protocols at CERN," http://www.info.cern.ch/pdp/ns/ben/TCPHIST.html

2. See the online encyclopedia entry, "The Difference between the Internet and the World Wide Web," http://www.webopedia.com/DidYouKnow/Internet/2002/Web_vs_Internet.asp

3. John R. Levine, Margaret Levine Young, and Arnold Reinhold, *The Internet for Dummies*, 2nd ed. (Foster City, Calif.: IDG, 1995) 6-7.

4. Matthew Gray of the Massachusetts Institute of Technology, graph of "Web Growth Summary," http://www.mit.edu/people/mkgray/net/web-growth-summary.html

5. John Paczkowski, "Excite@HomeBack from the Grave and Ready To Party!" at http://www.siliconvalley.com/mld/siliconvalley/business/columnists/gmsv/4182587.htm?template=contentModules/printstory.jsp

6. See http://ci.columbia.edu/ci/

7. See http://scpd.stanford.edu/scpd/default.htm

8. See http://www.barnesandnobleuniversity.com/index.asp?nhid=bn& userid=2VDO6QI782

9. See http://www.bbc.co.uk/learning/courses/

10. Robert Kuttner, "Beyond Regime Change Dissent: Antiwar and Post-war, Too? You Bet," electronic version, *Washington Post*, March 23, 2003, http://www.washingtonpost.com/wp-dyn/articles/A8220-2003Mar21.html

11. http://moveon.org/about.html

12. *National Catholic Reporter*, March 28, 2003, 28, electronic version, http://www.natcath.org/NCR_Online/archives/032803/032803p.htm

13. See http://www.earthfuture.com/stopthewar/email.asp

14. See http://www.votetoimpeach.org/

15. See "Women United for Peace," http://www.petitiononline.com/waw 2002/petition.html

16. Pierre Teilhard de Chardin, *Building the Earth* (Wilkes-Barre, Pa.: Dimensions, 1965) 19.

17. Pierre Teilhard de Chardin, *The Phenomenon of Man* (New York: Harper, 1959) 264-65.

18. http://www.bpfna.org/aboutbpfna.html

19. See "What Does Restorative Justice Look Like in Practice?" electronic version, http://www.bpfna.org/rjbrochure.html#practice

20. http://default.asp?bFlash

21. "Peace Programs: Global Development Initiative," electronic version, http://www.cartercenter.org/peaceprograms/showdoc.asp?programID=14&sub menu=peaceprograms

22. See http://www.mpfweb.org/200204_detroit.html

23. http://bpf.org/html/about_us/mission/mission.html

24. Ibid. (see photo).

25. Ibid.

26. See http://www.bpf.org/html/resources_and_links/links/links.php

27. http://www.catholicpeacefellowship.org

28. See "Catholic Peace Fellowship Makes Timely Revival," electronic version, http://salt.claretianpubs.org/sjnews/2002/04/sjn0204f.html

29. http://www.paxchristiusa.org/whoweare.html

30. See http://www.paxchristiusa.org/links.html

31. http://www.homelandministries.org/DPF/

32. See ibid.

33. William Davidson, "EPF History: Summary," see http://www.urgent call.org/php/epf.php

34. Ibid.

35. Ibid.

36. http://www.episcopalpeacefellowship.org/home.htm

37. See http://www.jewishpeacefellowship.org

38. Ibid.

39. See the section on "Prophet and Preacher" in my *Long Have I Loved You: A Theologian Reflects on His Church* (Maryknoll, N.Y.: Orbis Books, 2000) 129-33, at 130.

40. http://www.jewishpeacefellowship.org/Resources.htm#Links

41. See "Profiles of Injustice," http://justice.policy.net/cjreform/profiles/

42. In 1967 Yale sociologist Stanley Milgram described "the small world phenomenon" now referred to as "six degrees of separation." His hypothesis was based on the notion that every person *in America* is connected to every other person by a chain of no more than six individuals. The 1993 movie *Six Degrees of Separation*, based on the 1990 John Guare play of the same name, popularized this theory and revised the concept to indicate that there are no more than six individuals separating any two persons *on earth*. Since that time both Columbia's Small World Research Project and Ohio State's Electronic Small World Project have attempted to map e-mail and "test assumptions about online communication, such as the idea that the Internet transcends barriers of race, sex and economics." See Kendra Mayfield, "Kevin Bacon: You've Got Mail," electronic version, http://www.wired.com/news/print/0, 1294,49343,00.html

43. http://members.tripod.com/~lutheran_peace/board_stmnt2002.html

44. Among the links is one to Michael Moore's *Bowling for Columbine*, a film written about the "violent soul of America"; see www.lutheranpeace.org

45. See www.mpfweb.org/200110_5ways.html

46. See http://www.combase.com/~westilson/koran/koran.htm. This site is an electronic version of The Holy Qur'an, translated by M. H. Shakir and published by Tahrike Tarsile Qur'an, Inc., in 1983.

47. http://www.incommunion.org/misc/webdoc1.asp

48. Ibid.

49. "A Plea for Peace," electronic version, emphasis mine, http://ortodox.webconnect.no/undersider/a_plea_for_peace.htm

50. See http://www.redcross.ca/article.asp?id=001738&tid=006

51. Vicki Kemper, "Study Finds More in U.S. Lack Health Insurance," *Los Angeles Times*, March 5, 2003, A18.

52. *Gaudium et spes*, no. 90, quoted in the "Pontifical Council for Justice and Peace" section of the Vatican Web site, http://www.vatican.va/roman_curia/pontifical_councils/justpeace/documents/rc_pc_justpeace_pro_20011004_en.html

53. See Web page of Pontifical Council for Justice and Peace (n. 52 above).

54. Ibid.

55. Ibid.

56. http://www.vatican.va/holy_father/john_paul_ii/messages/peace/documents/hf_jp-ii_mes_20021217_xxxvi-world-day-for-peace_en.html

57. See http://www.vatican.va/roman_curia/pontifical_councils/hlthwork/index.htm

58. See http://www.vatican.va/roman_curia/pontifical_councils/migrants/

59. For text of the bishops' statements and letters, see http://www.usccb.org

60. http://www.jesuit.ie/ijnd/

61. Ibid.

62. Quotation initially in Pope John Paul II's address to the diplomatic corps, Jan. 13, 2003; it was later cited in the opening line of a letter dated Feb. 7, 2003, from Fernando Franco, S.J., to the Provincial Co-ordinators of the Social Apostolate, electronic version, http://www.Jesuit.org/images/docs/8F5aVg.pdf

63. Ibid.

64. See http://www.wcc-coe.org/wcc/who/index-e.html

65. See http://www.wcc-coe.org/wcc/who/histor-e.html

66. See http://www2.wcc-coe.org/dov.nsf/f2b3c6f6c91ade2ec1256bea002bc786/302b92c5772c8f57 c1256c1a0025f986?OpenDocument

67. Ibid.

68. See http://www.churchworldservice.org/aboutcws.htm

69. See http://www.jesuitaids.net/

70. See http://www.churchworldservice.org/news/Iraq/carter-statement.html

71. See http://churchworldservice.org/news/archives/2003/03/80.html

72. See http://www.catholicworker.org/index.cfm

73. Patrick McColloster, M.D., "Who Gets Organ Transplants? Undocumented Give More Than They Receive," electronic version, *Houston Catholic Worker* 23, no. 1 (January-February 2003), http://www.cjd.org/paper/organs.html

74. Ibid.

75. Tom Cornell, "From the Cradle of Civilization—to the Grave?" electronic version, http://www.catholicworker.org/roundtable/essaytext.cfm?Number=195

76. See www.senate.gov

77. See www.house.gov

78. See www.whitehouse.gov

79. See www.un.org/Overview/rights.html

80. See http://docs.lib.duke.edu/igo/guides/ngo/define.htm

81. See http://www.un.org

82. See http://www.un.org/apps/news/infocusRel.asp?infocusID=50&Body=Iraq&Body1=inspect

83. See http://www.cyberschoolbus.un.org/infonation/index.asp

84. See http://web.amnesty.org/web/aboutai.nsf

85. See http://web.amnesty.org/web/aboutai.nsf/22dc9af0e16ca83380256a54005f43f7/84224b0377ce27df8025677f004bb799!OpenDocument

86. For annual reports, see http://web.amnesty.org/ailib/aireport/index.html

87. See http://web.amnesty.org/library/Index/engACT790032003

88. Ibid.

89. Ibid.

90. See http://www.restorativejustice.org/rj3/about_default.htm

91. See http://www.restorativejustice.org/rj3/intro_default.htm

92. See http://www.restorativejustice.org/rj3/web_tour/r&r.html

93. To read more about the complexity of issues surrounding mandatory minimum sentencing explored in the documentary *Prisoners of Love*, see

CourtTV's Web site http://www.courttv.com/onair/shows/thesystem/g_p _episodes/prisoners_of_love.html

94. Statistic cited in documentary *Prisoners of Love.*

95. See http://famm.org/nr_sentencing_news_guilt_release_february_ 2002.htm

96. See http://www.famm.org/rs_mission_strategy.htm

97. See ibid.

98. See http://famm.org/nr_sentencing_news_advocacy_institute_award_ 10_02.htm

99. See ibid.

100. See http://famm.org/si_sp_features_main.htm and also http://www .drugpolicy.org/race

101. http://www.hrw.org/reports98/vote/usvot98o.htm (emphasis mine).

102. See http://electronicIraq.net/news/1.shtml

103. See http://www.wri.org/wr-98-99/irrigate.htm

104. See http://www.anglicancommunion.org/networks/iafn/newsletters/ 1999/advent/waterforfood.html

105. See "Report [on the] Workshop on Environmental Justice," electronic version, http://www.panos.org.np/resources/reports/ej_workshop

106. http://www.chej.org/Lovecanal.html

107. Ibid.

108. Ibid.

109. See http://chej.org/about.html

110. See http://www.panos.org.np/programmes/environment_justice.htm

111. http://www.panos.org.np/activity_reports/ej_workshop/workshop _bg.htm

112. See http://www.biodiv.org/doc/publications/guide.asp

113. "Report [on the] Workshop on Environmental Justice," (n. 105 above).

114. http://www.who.int/features/2003/04/en

115. Ibid.

116. Preface of "PEEM Guidelines 2—Guidelines for Forecasting the Vector-borne Disease Implications of Water Resources Development," electronic version, www.who.int/docstore/water_sanitation_health/Documents/ PEEM2/english/peem2pref.htm

117. Ibid.

118. Ibid.

119. Kirk R. Smith, Carlos F. Corvalán, and Tord Kjellström, "How Much Global Ill Health Is Attributable to Environmental Factors?" electronic version, p. 577, http://www.who.int/environmental_information/Disburden/ Articles/smith.pdf

120. Ibid., p. 578.

121. Ibid.

122. See ibid., pp. 579-80.

123. See www.unicef.org/emerg/emergencies_HAR_missionstatement.pdf

124. See http://www.unicef.org/newsline/2003/03pr17iraq.htm

125. http://www.unicef.org/newsline/2003/03pr31iraq_printer.htm
126. See ibid.
127. See http://www.umich.edu/~snre492/history.html
128. This United Church of Christ "Report" was summarized by James H. Cone, professor at Union Theological Seminary, in his essay "Whose Earth Is It Anyway?" See electronic version, http://www.crosscurrents.org/cone.htm
129. John Lewis' observation is quoted by Deeohn and David Hahn-Baker in their article "Environmentalists and Environmental Justice Policy," in *Environmental Justice: Issues, Policies, and Solutions*, ed. Bunyan Bryant (Washington, D.C.: Island, 1995) 68.
130. For full text of Order 12898, see http://www.epa.gov/civilrights/eo12898.htm
131. Gandhi's observation, quoted by Leonardo Boff, *Cry of the Earth, Cry of the Poor* (Maryknoll, N.Y.: Orbis, 1997) 2, and cited in Cone (n. 128 above).
132. Cone (n. 128 above).
133. Reinhold Niebuhr, "The Assurance of Grace," in *The Essential Reinhold Niebuhr: Selected Essays and Addresses*, ed. Robert McAfee Brown (New Haven, Conn.: Yale University Press, 1986) 65.
134. http://cct.georgetown.edu/cctphil.cfm
135. For "Transcript: Bill Moyers Journal," Oct. 25, 2002 edition of PBS weekly program "NOW with Bill Moyers," see electronic version, www.pbs.org/now/transcript/transcript_bmjfcc.html
136. Ibid.

Index

About the Author

Walter J. Burghardt, S.J., is the founder and past codirector of Preaching the Just Word, the pioneering program at Woodstock Theological Center, Georgetown University. The program encourages and assists ministers throughout the United States and abroad to become effective preachers of biblical justice. He is professor emeritus of patristic theology, the Catholic University of America; coeditor of *The Living Pulpit;* former editor-in-chief of *Theological Studies;* and a past president of the Catholic Theological Society of America, the American Theological Society, and the North American Academy of Ecumenists. Twenty-three colleges and universities have awarded him honorary degrees. Father Burghardt has published more than 300 articles and written 22 books, including his award-winning memoir *Long Have I Loved You: A Theologian Reflects on His Church*, also published by Orbis Books. In 1996 a worldwide survey conducted by Baylor University in Texas named him one of the 12 most effective preachers in the English-speaking world.